Author's Note

Dear Reader:

    This book, <u>Seeking Self Validation</u>, is the story of my life from age six to sixty-two when in 1999, I retired from my last employment. All of the experiences described and the characters are real; however, the names of most characters have been changed or only the position title is used. Also, quotes are contrived based on my feelings, memories, and the circumstances being discussed.

    In writing my memoir in the form of a novel, I have described in great detail processes used in some of the jobs in which I participated, for example, methods in farming. I have done so because some titles and words used in my youth are not part of the vocabulary used today in describing processes that produce the same results. Thanks to modern technology, some of the work on farms and in other industries can be accomplished with machines today.

    I'm sharing my experiences in society and my lack of self-esteem due partly to those experiences because I hope to demonstrate the effects environment, family, community, and government can have upon life in general and one's self-concept in particular.

    Thank you for your interest in my first book. I hope it will be an enjoyable and, perhaps, an enlightening read for you.

    Sincerely,
    Anece F. McCloud

SEEKING PERSONAL VALIDATION

THE LIFE AND TIMES OF A BLACK, FEMALE ACADEMIC

ANECE F. MCCLOUD

Copyright © Anece F. McCloud. All rights reserved.

No part of this publication may be reproduced, distributed, or transmitted in any form or by any means, including photocopying, recording, or other electronic or mechanical methods, without the prior written permission of the publisher, except in the case of brief quotations embodied in reviews and certain other non-commercial uses permitted by copyright law.

Because of the dynamic nature of the Internet, any web addresses or links contained in this book may have changed since publication and may no longer be valid. The views expressed in this work are solely those of the author and do not necessarily reflect the views of the publisher, and the publisher hereby disclaims any responsibility for them.

Any people depicted in stock imagery provided by Getty Images are models, and such images are being used for illustrative purposes only.

ISBN: 978-1-958895-12-2 (Paperback Edition)

ISBN: 978-1-958895-13-9 (E-book Edition)

Printed in the United States.

Contents

Section	Pages

Author's Note i
Seeking Personal Iii
Validation. iii
Introduction ix
Chapter 1 1
Chapter 2 10
Chapter 3 14
Chapter 4 21
Chapter 5 31
Chapter 6 36
Chapter 7 43
Chapter 8 46
Chapter 9 56
Chapter 10 66
Chapter 11 70
Chapter 12 81
Chapter 13 84
Chapter 14 87
Chapter 15 92

Chapter 16 102
Chapter 17 104
Chapter 18 111
Chapter 19 117
Chapter 20 149
Chapter 21 154
Chapter 22 165
Chapter 23 169
Chapter 24 176
Chapter 25 181
Chapter 26 189
Chapter 27 200
Chapter 28 213
Chapter 29 222
Chapter 30 227
Chapter 31 232
Chapter 32 236
Chapter 33 238
Chapter 34 244
Chapter 35 249
Chapter 36 252
Acknowledgments 256

Introduction

"What the superior man seeks is in himself; what the small man seeks is in others."

—Confucius

For most of my life, I sought what was in others, what they possessed, some of which I could never have, much of which I could earn given the motivation to study and work for life's rewards. But how could I, a child, who loathed myself so much and felt excluded from all but the dregs of society believe that there was any quality in me worth seeking and developing? This is my story.

Chapter 1

"Your mother's going to be mad at you for getting your dress dirty," Maggie said. She and her sister, Carolyn, were walking, one on each side of me, as we strolled home from the school bus stop. The dust from the unpaved road rose up to greet us with every step. These teenage girls were my third cousins and my next-door neighbors. However, our houses were some distance apart. What was once a field of corn lay between their house and ours. The field was bare then because the corn had been harvested. It was September in our community. Maggie and Carolyn looked out for me while we were being transported to and from school. It was 1943 in Dudley, a small, rural piedmont district of North Carolina. I was six years old and a first-grader.

The dress in question was blue and white checkered with box pleats and a large white collar trimmed with lace. It was new and I had a small smudge on the front of the skirt from playing outside at recess. That morning while I was dressing for school, my mother mentioned how cute the dress looked on me. I was a petite, round-faced girl with a coffee and cream complexion and soft, black crinkled hair.

My hair, which barely touched my shoulders, was too unruly to be worn loose, so Mother usually parted it on the side and braided it, one plait on top and one on each side of my head. In contrast to me, Maggie and Carolyn were very light. Their complexion was a soft mellow color, like that of a ripe peeled, banana. And they had shiny, black, wavy hair that fell just below their shoulders. It was *naturally* "good" —no hot combs were used on them. Their hair texture was the norm in our community. Some of my neighbors were slightly darker in color than they were, but most had wavy or curly black hair, with a few whose locks were light brown or nearly blond. Regardless of the color, most of the women's hair reached to their waist or below. Obviously, I did not fit the norm.

And even at my young age, I was beginning to feel like an outsider because my physical appearance differed from others in the community. However, my mother always saw to it that I was very clean and dressed neatly. My cousins knew this.

I wrinkled my forehead and poked out my lips. "No, she won't!" I said angrily. My mother was a single parent, with two children—my older brother and me. I thought to myself, she has more to worry about than my getting a dress dirty. Maggie and Carolyn must have noticed the expression on my face because they started laughing. I realized they were teasing me. I laughed, too, and began hitting and chasing them. All three of us giggled harder.

These cousins and I lived in a section of Dudley called Simmons Town. Nearly all the families settled along the two roads, which met at a corner forming an **L**, were the descendants of 9 siblings whose surname was Simmons. The four sons settled on the land their father had left them. My mother's father, James Simmons, was one of the four. He and his three brothers died before I was born. There were five sisters, two of whom were still living at the time Maggie, Carolyn, and I were walking home from the bus stop. One had married a man from Dudley, but he was not a resident of Simmons Town; rather, he was from an area nearby. The other sister's family built a home and lived in our community. The land in Simmons Town had been passed to succeeding generations.

In about ten minutes, I arrived home. I ran up the four steps to the front porch and heard the old clock that hung in the front bedroom striking four. Our house was an early American, single story, wooden structure, badly in need of paint. It sat on red brick pillars. The porch was a little ragged along the front edge, but this was home, and I was glad to be there.

From the porch, I went into the living room, letting the front screen door bang shut. It had been a beautiful, warm, sunny day so the windows and doors were open to let in the refreshing breezes. I glanced in the bedroom to my left. As usual, Aunt Clara, my mother's sister, was sitting in her rocking chair next to a cold, potbellied stove. She was crippled from "rheumatism," the doctors said back then. She had walked with a crutch under her right arm since her teen years when she first became ill. This caused her left hip to protrude out of line with the rest of her body. She once told me that she used two crutches at first but that hindered her in doing minor tasks. She got around very well in the house using only one crutch and often cooked the family meals. She was able to work outside the home at the end of the tobacco season when a farmer hired her to assist his wife in tying cured, that is dried, tobacco. This job was done sitting down. When she was seated, her lopsided body was not evident, not that the slant of her body would make any difference in tying tobacco.

In addition to my aunt's rheumatism, she had another health problem that caused her to endure excruciating pain in all parts of her body. This occurred every six months or so. When she had these painful episodes, she screamed in agony—calling upon the Lord to please help her! Sometimes, when she was screaming and calling out to God, I believed in my young mind that she was faking her illness and her pretense was mainly to punish me. I felt so shaken and uncomfortable when she was sick and carrying on like that. I always knew there would be three or more days of listening to her, day and night, before the spell she was going through ended and home life was back to normal. Years later, doctors diagnosed her condition as sickle cell anemia.

Intermittent with her physical suffering, Aunt Clara had outbursts of anger. She would get angry with my mother or grandmother over something minor and accost them verbally—spewing curse words and vulgarity at them. They never responded to her tantrums. She stayed mad for two or three days, slamming things around. Then she would say something pleasant to her most recent target. Her comment was not an apology. But she resumed an amicable relationship with that person as if her anger at the victim had never occurred. She was never disgruntled with my brother or me, but her times of rage were nonetheless disconcerting to me.

Aunt Clara was small in stature with a slim, oval face and she was one of those people whose complexion reminded me of a ripe, peeled banana. She had thick, straight, black hair that fell to her hips when it was loose. She usually wore it in two big buns, one on each side of her small head. She was very prejudiced toward dark Negroes. However, it didn't seem to matter to her that my brother, Jim, and I were brown with nappy hair. My mother's first husband, Jim's, and my father, whom I had never met, was from Mt. Olive, N.C. His folk were from a purer African heritage than the Simmons family. His mother was half white, his father, who was deceased, was a "full-blooded" African, so Mother told us. My brother was a bit darker than I, but Aunt Clara was very accepting and affectionate toward both of us, maybe because she depended on us so often to fetch things and to help her in other ways. Our parents were divorced.

"Hi, baby. How was school today?" Aunt Clara asked as I looked in on her from the living room. "It was fine," I said. I stepped into the bedroom and proceeded to tell her about my day. After talking with her for a few minutes, I walked through her room to the back bedroom. I dropped my books and lunch box on the bed. I heard someone on the back porch. It was either Mother or my grandmother, whom we called Momma.

The house had four rooms situated around a central chimney: the living room with the dining room located behind it, the front bedroom where Aunt Clara was sitting and the adjoining back bedroom. All interior walls were whitewashed plaster. Aunt Clara and my grandmother shared the bed in the front bedroom. My mother and I shared one bed in the second bedroom and my 14-year-old brother, James, slept in the other bed. A door led from the second bedroom to the back porch and the water pump. Sure enough, Mother was the one I heard on the porch.

She was busy emptying water from two large tin tubs in which she had washed clothes earlier that day. They were the same tubs we used for our Saturday night baths. On other nights of the week, we used a foot tub (a smaller version of the other tub) for taking sponge baths. I noticed the big iron pot that sat in the backyard appeared cold, so I guessed she had not boiled the white clothes that day. Silky black curls framed Mother's light tan, sweaty face as she struggled into the backyard and a distance from the house to empty pails of water. She was 33 years old, a five-foot-three, very petite woman. Already, the strains of life were beginning to cause small lines on her face. I asked if she wanted me to help. She said, "Not now, but you can help me bring the clothes in from the line later. Go change your clothes. I'll call you when I'm ready for you." She didn't say anything about the dirty spot on my new dress. I knew she wouldn't be mad.

Mother had completed only the seventh grade. However, she, like others in Simmons Town, spoke mostly correct English. Perhaps, we had a slight southern cadence to our speech, but it was not as distinctive as the drawl of white folks in the south, and it was not the usual Negro dialect of the time. The one thing that nearly all the residents of Dudley had in common was using the word "ain't." In sixth grade, our teacher required his class to go through the ritual of burying "ain't." That broke me from the habit of using that word.

I left Mother and reentered the back room where I took my play clothes from an old chest of drawers. I placed my school dress on a wire hanger and put it on a nail behind the door. I redressed, picked up my lunch box, and went to the kitchen to put the box on a table.

The kitchen was adjacent to the back porch and shared a common wall with the dining room. There were two rectangular tables along one wall in the kitchen: one, white enamel on metal, and the other, wood, covered with a faded floral oilcloth. A ladder back chair was between the two tables. That was Aunt Clara's seat where she rested while cooking and where she sat to eat at the end of the white table. The rest of us sat around the remaining three sides during meals. The other table was used for preparing food and washing dishes. Washing dishes was usually my chore.

The kitchen was small and rectangular in shape. On the wall across from the two tables were a metal cabinet and two additional chairs. A black, flat top, iron cook stove was along the end wall, where there was a chimney. The one window in the room was beside the stove, providing a view of the side yard and a plot of land where my grandmother planted a vegetable garden every year.

I glanced out the window and saw my grandmother. She was leaving the chicken house with a few eggs in each hand. She was a tall woman with angular features and a rosy-tan complexion. Her silky, black hair was mixed with some gray and hung in a long braid down her back. Aunt Clara once told me that my grandmother was of mixed heritage. Her father was part Indian and Negro and her mother was half white. She said my great-grandmother's four children were fathered by the master on the plantation where she lived. Aunt Clara emphasized the point that my grandmother and her siblings were "free-born." That was important. In some instances, it meant the "master thought enough of a slave or a slave's children to free them before the Emancipation Proclamation was signed," she explained.

Looking out the window, I saw the wooden outdoor toilet that sat several yards behind the chickens' wire enclosure. Although the pigpen couldn't be seen from the window, I know it was in the back at the very end of the property. My grandmother owned six acres, one on which the house and outbuildings sat and an additional five acres east of the house. When she could find someone who wanted to grow an extra crop—like peas, corn, or cotton—she rented the five acres.

Momma's property was not a farm in the true sense of the word. We didn't have horses, cows, or many chickens like the farmers around us. There wasn't a tobacco allotment (governmental approval) on the five acres, so no one could grow the greatest money-making crop in the area on that land. We usually had only one or two hogs in the pen. Momma "went in with" another farm family during hog killing time—they killed and dressed her animal. In exchange, she assisted them in cutting up and preparing her pork and theirs for storage. In later years, when times became tougher, we didn't have any pigs.

Momma's husband, my grandfather, had worked as a fireman on the Atlantic Coastline Railroad. Train engines during his time ran on steam. The steam was produced by men constantly stoking the train's furnace with coal. Those men were called firemen. My grandfather's occupation had provided a better living for his family than farming. So, he owned less real estate than his brothers. His savings were maintained in other holdings. And he used his money in ways to make his family happy. For example, he bought a Model-T Ford for his daughters. They were the envy of their cousins and others when they drove around Dudley. The car was sold after his death, many years before I was born.

Grandfather was only in his forties when he died of a ruptured appendix. His family could have remained well-off after his death. However, my grandmother was illiterate—not able to read or write. She did not know how to manage the money she inherited. She held on to the house and land but the savings were not invested and were soon gone.

Momma entered the house from the back porch. She stopped in the kitchen where I was and took a bowl from the cabinet for the few eggs she was carrying. "Hey, Hon," she said. "I didn't know it was late enough for you to be home. I have to start dinner." She went into the dining room and put the bowl of eggs in the icebox. I followed her and saw a large block of ice in the top compartment of the box.

"The iceman came today?" I asked.

"Yeah," Momma replied. She checked the container under the box to make sure it was placed correctly to catch drips from the ice as they drained out of the bottom of the box.

I glanced around and noticed the large round table and chairs where we eat only when we had company, and the curved glass-front china cabinet which contained Momma's pretty white china with pink flowers and scalloped edges. The plates were so thin you could see a shadow of your hand through them. I was not allowed to handle them when I helped with the dishwashing after we'd had guests. Those were the only treasures remaining from the first house the family had lived in before my grandfather died and afterward, before it burned down—all before I was born. In our dining room, there were two French doors between the corner where the cabinet sat and the opposite corner where there was a wood-burning heater. The doors opened into the living room, but no one was there at the time.

Seeking Personal Validation

I went out through the kitchen and ran down the porch steps to the backyard. Mother was ready for me to help her. As she took clothes off the line and folded the larger pieces, she handed them to me. I held a few pieces to my nose and sniffed them before putting them in the basket—the clothes smelled so sweet and fresh. I folded the smaller items as Mother handed them to me.

I was so happy to be with my mother that I felt like skipping in circles around her. She was away from home much too often. In fact, she would leave in a few weeks. During the late fall and winter, she was a maid for a white family in Raleigh, North Carolina. When her employers left at the beginning of the summer to go to their cottage on the coast, Mother returned home and became a day laborer for neighborhood farmers.

This wasn't a steady job, she only worked days when farmers required assistance beyond what a family could provide. The jobs available to her were chopping weeds from the rows of different crops, "suckling tobacco" (that is breaking off the flowering tops of tobacco stalks), and later in the season, handing tobacco. In the latter instance, she and others stood around a tobacco sleigh (truck) to which opened burlap bags formed sides. The truck had been pulled by a horse into the shade of the tobacco barn. The horse was unhooked from the sleigh. Six people, usually women, stood around the sleigh, picking up four or five sticky tobacco leaves at a time, holding them by the stems, and giving each handful to the woman on her side of the truck. Those women took the leaves handed to them and, using a special technique, tied each bunch to a stick laying horizontally on a man-made rack. Their job was called looping tobacco. At the end of the day, the sticks of tobacco were put on rafters in a tobacco barn where the leaves were "cured" for about a week. Curing involved the farmer feeding a fire in the furnace of the barn and keeping the heat going 24 hours a day for several days, during which the tobacco turned a golden yellow. When I was older, I, too, worked in tobacco for six to seven weeks each summer. I used my money for school clothes.

While Mother and I took the clothes down, Boss, my brother's mixed breed, reddish-brown dog romped around us with his tail switching from side to side like windshield wipers. He wanted our attention and probably sensed it was time for Jimmy to come home.

My brother, James, we called him Jimmy or Jim, was in his first year of high school, the ninth grade. In the mornings, he rode the bus with Maggie, Carolyn, and me to the all-Negro Dudley Elementary School. Then he transferred to another bus that took him and other high school students to the all-colored Carver High School in Mt. Olive, North Carolina. Mt. Olive was five miles south of Dudley. When Jimmy returned from school, he'd get off the school bus at the Smith Brothers grocery store. It was on the corner of Highway 117 and another paved road that ran east to west in Dudley. He worked in the grocery store until it closed for the night. Afterward, he usually "caught" a ride home. Our family didn't have a car and no public transportation ran in Dudley.

By the time Jimmy arrived home on that particular day, Mother and I had taken the clean clothes inside and were talking in our room. She was reminding me again of how important getting an education was if I wanted to get ahead in life. She managed to bring that topic up with me every day. Momma and Aunt Clara were in the kitchen talking about heaven only knows what. The aroma of collards with salt pork cooking escaped from the kitchen into the night air. Momma was also fixing baked sweet potatoes and biscuits. Boss was on the back porch walking back and forth in front of the screen door to the kitchen. The smell of food and his desire to get in were clearly frustrating him. He should have remembered that he was never allowed in the house.

Boss's agitation ceased momentarily when we all heard a car door close. That sound was followed by footsteps on the back steps. Boss started barking excitedly. "Hey, boy. How ya' doing?" Jim said as he scratched the dog behind his ears.

"Jimmy, you're home," I said, rushing out of the house. I was as happy to see him as Boss. He was eight years my senior and the only male in my life. I adored him. He was everything to me: my protector, the person who most often soothed my feelings when something had gone wrong in my life, and the one who made me laugh frequently over his crazy stories and imitations.

Years later, when we were both adults and I would tease him about something, he'd say, "Remember, Sis, I use to change your diapers." He was referring to his taking care of me at times when I was a baby. I would usually say something equally smart in response to his embarrassing comment.

"Who brought you home, Son?" Mother asked.

"Chip gave me a ride," he answered. Chip was one of the Smith brothers. They were white but the younger ones were chummy with my brother. "There wasn't anyone coming out this way," Jimmy added.

Boss settled down. We humans washed our hands at the pump and retreated to the kitchen where we gathered around the white table to eat. It was dark outside. The flame of a kerosene lamp flickered, giving a soft glow to the room. We all bowed our heads while Momma said the blessing: "Thank you,

God, for the food we are about to receive. May it nourish our bodies and keep us strong. Thank you, too, for all the other blessings bestowed on this family. Please continue to be with us. In Christ's name we pray. Amen."

My grandmother was a very religious woman. I often overheard her through the wall whispering prayers before getting in bed at night, and frequently during the days when Aunt Clara was sick. She practiced her religion quietly in that she lived what she believed rather than just talking about Jesus, God, and what the Bible said. She treated everyone kindly and never used a "bad" or curse word no matter what she was experiencing at the time.

As we began eating, we exchanged accounts of the day's activities. I looked around the table at each person. Mother was sitting next to me. Momma and Aunt Clara were seated at opposite ends of the table. The table was pulled out from the wall and a chair was added to that side. My brother sat there, across from me. His brown face and close-cropped, woolly, black hair were obscured somewhat in the shadows. But his small, dark eyes shone as the flickering flame reflected off them. I thought to myself, *he is always so kind to me. I'm very lucky to have him as my brother.*

That was my family in 1943—three women and one young man. Those were the people that I loved most in the world. Those were the people whom I knew loved and accepted me for who I was, no matter that I didn't have long silky hair or light skin. I knew this! They showed me their love every day. I felt secure and appreciated when I was in this family setting. I knew I belonged. I was a legitimate part of the family unit. But that was the only place where I had such warm feelings. My not having physical characteristics that were considered desirable in our community and, therefore, I thought in all of society, made me feel that I didn't belong in any group outside the family. Furthermore, I didn't have a father at home, and that also made me different from other youths in the community. Eventually, I became haunted and torn by my irreconcilable ideas of blackness, beauty, and myself. I became suspended between self-hate and the desire to be admired, liked, and accepted unconditionally by other people—all people, blacks and whites. Well into adulthood, I would continue to feel disconnected, that I had no firm foundation in any group or society to which life's circumstances introduced me. To a great extent, those feelings would dictate the type of person I would be in the future

Chapter 2

My feelings of not being a valid member of the Simmons' legacy and the belief that my color and hair texture precluded my belonging to the group were rooted in the history and sociology of the Dudley community— something I realized many years later. Not just my aunt, but many of the light-colored Negroes in Dudley were prejudiced against dark-skinned people with nappy hair. All of Simmons' descendants were of mixed heritage—this was more obvious with some than others. Those people called themselves Indians. But I didn't think they were real Indians, in my childhood reasoning. They just didn't want to be called Negroes. I blamed *them* for my self-hate and the discomfort that bubbled within. I didn't realize those feelings had no substance in reality. Everyone treated me kindly, but I was sure that they were nice to me out of respect for my mother, grandmother, and aunt.

As an adult, I talked with my mother's first cousin, Hilda, who was also my godmother. She was a teacher by profession. I explained to her my childhood suspicions about the people, our relatives in Simmons Town. She told me that our ancestors were believed to be descendants of the Lost English Colony and a friendly Indian tribe. I searched for confirmation of her statement and found some historical sources that described "The Lost Colony." It was a group of 100 men, women, and children from England who arrived on Roanoke Island on the North Carolina coast in 1587.

Within three years, the English colonists had disappeared. My godmother reasoned that they were taken in by an Indian tribe and mixed marriages resulted. She talked about her paternal grandmother who lived in Clinton,

North Carolina, which was not far from the coast and only a few miles from Dudley. "I remember my grandmother's coloring," she said, "her skin was the color of a new copper penny. And she had long straight black hair that looked like strands of silk." That was the coloring and hair texture of many of the Simmons' descendants in our community. Plus, some members of the Dudley group had straight blond or brown hair and light eyes. They could have been mistaken for whites. Some of those who looked like Indians as well as some who looked white moved to Clinton, North Carolina when their children became teenagers. Others who could pass for white went north and claimed to be Caucasian. There was the possibility that my godmother's reasoning was true. So, I went back to the internet to search more thoroughly for The Lost Colony and North Carolina Native American history. I found a plethora of information. The following quote from Wikipedia related most directly to the evidence I sought:

"Croatian" was the name of an island to the south of Roanoke Island, modern-day Hatteras Island, where a friendly native tribe was known to live. In the 1880s, a man living in North Carolina wrote about what the Natives there looked like. He wrote that he had noticed that some of them had 'fair skin and light eyes and hair, with Anglo bone structure.' Some people today persist in believing that survivors of the Roanoke colonists were assimilated into the Croatian Indian Tribe. This is a legend for which there is no confirmation. Also, there were other opportunities for European-Native American contact."

Clinton, North Carolina is in Sampson County. Indians moved there between 1729 and 1746. They were descendants of the Neusioks. Those who called Clinton home in more recent times, many of whom are of mixed heritage, are called the Coharie Tribe, a designation they gave their organization in 1967 and the group received recognition by the Federal Government as an Indian tribe some years later. Family surnames in their group are the same as those of some of our relatives in Dudley when I was growing up. These included Carter, Jacobs, Brewington, Bryant, and Simmons—to name just a few.

Another source I found reported a settlement of Pembroke Indians who settled in Robeson County during the 18th century. Many claimed their ancestors came from Roanoke [Island?]. The Pembrokes spoke pure English and some bore the last names of many of the lost colonists. Some of the Pembrokes were said to have European features: light eyes, fair hair, and Anglo bone structure.

The information I came upon during my research gave credence to my godmother's theory. So, I was wrong as a child. The relatives in Simmons Town and those scattered throughout other parts of Dudley were not full Indians but could claim some Indian, as well as white ancestry. Their African heritage was also present in them. However, none claimed or talked about their African heritage, yet they were classified as Negroes by the white people and the darker colored folk. Furthermore, they seemed to accept the Negro Classification but thought they were superior to others who were considered blacks.

I developed my own theories about this conundrum. It goes like this: My relatives in Dudley were, as I said before, of mixed ancestry— African, Indian, and Caucasian. The Indian and white fore-parents may be explained by the circumstances described above or with similar co-mingling of these two groups. Indians and whites could be lawfully married at that time. It was unlawful for blacks and whites to marry back then. African ancestry was probably introduced into the mix by slaves (contrabands) who were living on the fringe of the Union camp on Roanoke Island around 1863. Or there could have been slaves or freed blacks in the region by other circumstances. Finally, some Africans joined the Indians in marriage or, certainly, in procreation. This racial mixture was indigenous to many parts of southeastern North Carolina.

Assuming the explanation I gave above was the case, the mixed descents of African people with the other two races were classified as Negroes because the laws of that time mandated individuals with even a small percentage of "African blood" be considered Negroes. As some African Americans have commented in recent times, "that African blood was mighty powerful stuff."

It is evident my relatives were trying to avoid or ignore their African heritage. It seems that they believed being Caucasian was the desirable human classification. Very black Americans were considered the dredges of society— certainly thought to be lower in status than Indians. My relatives in Dudley had one thing in common: they all had varying degrees of white and/or Indian Blood. So, they strove to exhibit lifestyles and behavior they thought to be consistent with the values of the white middle-class population. These included marrying within one's own color caste, not speaking broken English, not being excessively loud, keeping one's home clean and in repair to the extent their incomes allowed, going to church, and ensuring a good education for their children. They, like whites in that time and place, thought dark Negroes were inferior and treated them accordingly.

Once the light-skinned blacks had observed and emulated what they thought was appropriate white behavior, they became aware that some of the white people in Dudley did not fit their white model. They saw the lower class, uneducated whites as not being legitimate members of the white race. Thus, this group was called "crackers" and they were shunned in much the same way as the dark-skinned blacks. That was the environment in which I spent my formative years. However, my research, theorizing, and speculations presented here, didn't occur until I was an adult.

Chapter 3

Back during my formative years, Highway 117 ran north to south through Dudley. It served as a dividing line during my childhood, separating the Simmons' relatives who lived in the west and owned their land, from the Negro sharecroppers and other types of laborers who lived mostly in the east. White people in Dudley lived on both sides of the highway but were closer to it than most black residents. Those areas near the highway as well as other small, nearby communities, including Simmons Town, were all a part of Wayne County.

Negro children from different sections of Wayne County were bused to Dudley Elementary School. There were people—students, faculty, and administrators—of every hue in the African American rainbow. The hair colors and textures varied. Some had silky brown or black straight, curly, or wavy hair, but most had a dark wooly head of hair. All of us were called "colored" or Negro. Local whites lumped all colored people into the same racial group, but the Negroes practiced a caste system based on shades of skin color and hair textures. Children often chanted: "If you're white, you're right. If you're brown, stick around. If you're black, step back." It was an insult to refer to anyone as being "black."

All Negroes were the victims of legalized segregation at the time. But my childhood knowledge did not include that fact. I knew there were certain doors in buildings through which we could not enter. I knew that when I rode the bus to Goldsboro with Mother, we always had to go to the back to sit or if there were only vacant seats in the front, we had to stand in the aisle. I observed that even adult Negroes always said "sir" and "ma'am" when addressing whites. I knew that only Negroes went to our church and school. What I didn't know, yet, was that a "separate but equal" law ruled the south. And I didn't realize that facilities and situations for black citizens were not nearly equal to those of whites. Knowledge of all these facts slowly entered my thoughts and understanding as I advanced in my awareness and formal education.

The school I attended, Dudley Elementary School, consisted of two buildings. The smaller one had three rooms which housed grades first through third. We sat around low tables that had six small chairs. We used textbooks for reading and arithmetic. The "Dick and Jane Reader" was the first book we learned to read. Our books were never new. (I learned later that they were "hand-downs" from the local white school.) There was a wood-burning heater in each classroom. Sometimes, on really cold days, our teacher allowed us to sit in a circle around the stove while having lessons. Our games at recess were similar to those of other children at that time. We played hopscotch, ball, jump rope, swinging, and on the see-saw. Older children also played jump-board. It was a game that involved stacking three or more boards and placing a single board across the stack. A person stood on each end of the crossboard and took turns jumping up and coming down on the board. Being suspended in the air, even for a little while, looked like great fun—as if the two people were going to ascend to the sky.

I enjoyed school and worked hard on my studies. It was important for my family to be proud of me. My hard work paid off each term when I received above-average grades in everything, including grooming. Each morning, after standing and pledging allegiance to the flag, students in the first three grades remained standing to be inspected. The grades were in separate rooms, but each teacher practiced the same ritual. That is, the teacher checked to see if each student's ears, neck, teeth, and nails were clean. She also commented on whether our clothes were clean and if our hair was combed and neat. Our appearance was graded and a summary grade for the term was recorded on our report cards along with grades for the subjects we took. The good grooming grade I always received was due to my mother's care and home teachings.

I lived in my grandmother's home in Dudley but once while in second grade, I traveled by train to Raleigh to visit my mother and her new husband, Mr. Winters. It was her second marriage. Mr. Winters was from Mississippi. He was a tall, dark chocolate-colored man with jet black hair that seemed to be a combination of kinky and curly. He wore an army uniform. World War II was in its fourth year and Mr. Winters, an enlisted soldier, was stationed at Fort Bragg, North Carolina. Commuting back and forth to Raleigh, he met Mother when she worked as a maid and they were both having a day off. When I visited them, they were married and Mother was no longer working.

They lived in an apartment on the second floor of a private home. The house was owned by an older Negro couple who fawned over me. While in Raleigh, Mother and I went shopping one day and I get my first professional hairdo. Usually, Mother washed my hair, greased it with Vaseline, and combed out the tangles before braiding it. On that day, the colored beautician shampooed my hair, combed it out, straightened it with a hot comb, and finally curled it with a curling iron. When she finished, it was styled like Shirley Temple's, and I felt pretty for the first time in my life. I thought, *I finally look like many of the other girls in Simmons Town*. Of course, my "good" hair would last only until it came in contact with water.

The war was very much a part of everyone's life. One night, when Mr. Winters was away on base, Mother and I sat in a dark living room with the landlady and her husband. The adults had received word to extinguish all lights. "We're having a "blackout." Mother said to me, "You weren't here, but this has happened before. This exercise is to prepare people for enemy attacks." She continued to explain. "Dousing all lights will prevent the enemies from knowing where American cities are located in case they want to bomb us." The landlady nodded in agreement and her husband mumbled something that I couldn't understand.

A fire was burning in the fireplace, producing a glow bright enough to be seen through the light-colored window shades. A man knocked on the window and said in a low yet stern voice, "Put that light out!" The landlady quickly put a solid metal screen in front of the fireplace. The stranger's unexpected voice frightened me even more. I cuddle closer to my mother on the sofa. She enfolded me tightly in her arms and whispered "Don't be afraid, baby, this will all be over soon. Everything is alright." We did make it through the night without anything happening.

A few months after my visit and return to Dudley, Mother left Raleigh and moved back to Momma's house. Mr. Winters visited us when he was on leave from the base. Aunt Clara didn't like him because of his dark skin. When she couldn't avoid speaking to Mr. Winters, she addressed him rudely. She often spoke to Mother in an angry voice when Mr. Winters was there; "For," in her words, "bringing that black man into my Momma's house."

I was in fourth grade when Mother gave birth to the first of two children fathered by Mr. Winters. The new baby was born in the back bedroom of

Momma's house, just as I had been. A white doctor from Mt. Olive came to our house to deliver the baby—there weren't any doctors in Dudley. It was a sunny and somewhat warm day for January. So, Mamma said to me, "Go outside and play while the doctor takes care of your mother." I did as I was told. I didn't have any idea what was going on in the house. I wasn't privy to information about women having babies at my age. In fact, I would learn those secrets from girl-talk as I advanced in grade school.

My first awareness of sex came when a classmate told a couple of us that a boy we knew had stuck his "thing" into the "pussy" of a girl we knew. I never learn if this actually happened between those two people. But, hearing that gossip about such an act was very hard for me to understand or believe at first. I couldn't imagine a boy and girl doing something that dirty when we were not even supposed to see each other's "things." Once I did glimpse a boy who was showing off to some of his friends. They didn't know I was watching.

I thought about the difference in the way girls and boys looked down there and I realized it was possible for the boy to be in the girl. Why would anyone want to do that? The thought was utterly disgusting to me. Later, another classmate shared the startling information that the act our friend described, "is what gives a woman a baby." The blanks in my knowledge on this topic were filled later in biology classes.

Momma stood on the back porch and called to me, "Anece, come in and see the new baby." I ran up the steps, across the unpainted porch, and crept quietly into the bedroom. Mother was lying on the bed with this blanket-wrapped little bundle in the curve of her arm. I looked with surprise at his small face and then at Mother. She seemed tired but managed to smile at me and said, "This is your new brother. When he's older, you can hold him if you want." A baby! I was so excited. I didn't know then where he came from, but the doctor must have had something to do with his being there. George, as Mother named him later, was not a cute baby. I thought he was too small and wrinkled. One thing he had that I envied right away was his black, curly hair. He had inherited our mother's beautiful locks. As a young boy, after he understood the significance of his inheritance, he reminded me of his "good" hair and teased me for not being as lucky as he. However, George was doomed to have a very dark complexion like his father. I overheard one of the women who stopped by to see my mother and the new baby say the color an infant was going to be when it was older could be determined by the color of the newborn's ears and around its fingernails. I was curious and inspected these on George as soon as I had a chance. His true color was indeed going to be dark, dark brown. As a result of his rich dark chocolate-colored complexion, Aunt Clara was never affectionate toward him, but the rest of us welcomed the little fellow into the family. I could hardly wait until the next day to tell my schoolmates about my new brother.

Our class advanced to the larger building for fourth grade. This, the main building, sat at the front of the campus facing a wide dirt road. The building had lots of windows on all sides. Classes four through eight met in that building and each class had its own room. Our classroom was in the right-wing of the school—to the right of the entrance and the center hall. The sixth and eighth-grade classes were behind the hallway, extending into the left-wing of the building, with the seventh-grade classroom and principal's office adjacent to them but on the front side of the building. Each room was large enough to hold approximately 30 desks with attached chairs—the kind of desk we slid into from one side. There was a portioned area in the back corner of each room for hanging outerwear. It was called the "coatroom." Our bathrooms were outdoor toilets, just as we had at home.

The eighth-grade classroom had a stage with curtains across it. These remained closed during classes. A piano was in one corner of the room. A wall, separating this and the sixth-grade classroom behind it, slid open and the two rooms together created an auditorium. Sometimes, movies, such as <u>A Cabin in the Sky</u> and Negro comedies, were shown in the big area. The movies were infrequent treats that were shown late on a school day. They were announced days in advance and the student body was admitted free. Parents and others not enrolled in our school were not invited. I didn't like the comedies because they always showed Negro men, and sometimes women, acting crazy, rolling their eyes and such. The auditorium was used mainly for weekly all-school assemblies, monthly PTA meetings, play rehearsals and presentations, and, of course, the annual eighth-grade graduation ceremony every spring.

There was a kitchen toward the front of the school building on one side of the wide entrance hall across from the principal's office. A couple of women from the community were hired to prepare lunches for the students. Those who were getting lunches lined up by class in the hallway and went to a pass-through window where they picked up their trays of food. These were complete meals consisting of a main dish, like macaroni and cheese, a vegetable, a salad, fresh or canned fruit or some other dessert, and milk. The school didn't have a cafeteria. All students returned to their classrooms to eat. Free lunches were available to needy children and some students brought lunch from home—

which I did most of the time. Students whose families had money paid for their meals.

A few years later, my stepfather, Mr. Winters, was discharged from the army. Our little family: he, mother, my younger brother, and I, moved into a house they rented in Dudley. Mother was expecting her second child by Mr. Winters. He let us know that he hated Dudley. He drank and argued a lot. To make matters worse, he couldn't find work. He didn't want to be a day laborer. So, he left Mother, went to New York, and never provided support even for his own children. The family had less money than when Mother was working as a maid before she married him. We moved back to my grandmother's house and Mother soon had the new baby, John. She couldn't work full-time then because she had to care for my two younger brothers. I was their sitter when I had a day off from school and Mother could manage to get "day work" as a maid. This was especially true on holidays and during the summer. My grandmother's health was becoming frail as she got older. She continued to care for her daughter, Clara, when one of my aunt's sick spells struck. The family had no alternative but to go on welfare. As a result, I was classified as a "needy" child and began getting free lunches at school.

Times were hard for our family. The Aid to Dependent Children acts made it possible for Mother to receive approximately eighteen dollars per month for each of her children under sixteen—three of us. My oldest brother was excluded from ADC because he was 16. (He would finish high school at 18 and leave home to go to Brooklyn, New York, where he would stay with Dad and his wife.) It was difficult for Mother and Momma to provide enough food for four adults—including my older brother, Jimmy– and three younger children. Many of our meals consisted of biscuits and homemade gravy—gravy made by browning flour in drippings from fried pork saved during better times and adding salt and pepper as the mixture thickened. This was eaten with biscuits. We also ate a lot of dried beans and bread. There were not enough table scraps to make slops for hogs, so the pigpen stood empty.

When the winter came, a major problem was purchasing coal, to heat the one bedroom where we gathered during the day, and wood for cooking meals. There was a corn mill in Dudley across the road from the Smith Brother's store. Large stacks of corn cobs were always available at the mill waiting to be hauled away. Anyone who wanted them could take a load for personal use. Momma often asked a neighbor to deliver a large load to our house. The cobs were dumped in the backyard a distance from the house. It was my job to carry buckets of cobs into the house where we used them to prolong the use of coal and wood. A neighborhood boy, who was also a distant cousin, openly made fun of me at school because our family used corn cobs for fuel. Some of the children nearby heard him and snickered. I was embarrassed but tried to ignore all of them. At night, when the fire was out at home, everyone snuggled in bed under layers of quilts. In the mornings, it took the room a while to warm up. We shivered with cold as we got ready for school.

Chapter 4

I recall a very happy day when the sun shone brightly in an almost cloudless sky and balmy, gentle breezes caressed our faces as Mother and I walked along a dirt road. Birds in trees clustered along some parts of the road sent cheerful calls to each other. It was September, a new school year had begun, and I was in fifth grade. Mother and I were walking the mile and a half to highway 117 and the Smith Brothers' store where we would catch a bus to Goldsboro. Being just nine miles north of Dudley, it was the closest large city to shop for clothes and things. We were going that day to buy school shoes for me and a few other things if there was enough money. We talked about the new school year as we walked along and we greeted neighbors who were in the yards of the few scattered homes that we passed.

When we reached the railroad tracks, I could see Highway 117 ahead of us. The highway was some distance from the railroad but ran parallel to it. Just before we crossed the tracks, I looked at our church, the First Congregational Christian Church, a medium-sized brick building with a bell tower that rose from its roof. It was to my right. There seemed to be a glow around the large, arch-shaped, stained-glass window that faced the road. Of course, I saw that church every Sunday and sometimes during the week when my cousin, Evelyn, and her husband, Mr. Powell, took me to various church activities. Nearly all of us attending this church were from Simmons Town or were relatives of those living there. A few years later, I would hear it rumored that our church had had a color code, meaning only tan Negroes or of a lighter color were welcomed there.

After Mother and I crossed the railroad, we passed homes that were a little closer together along each side of the road. With the exception of one family—whose last name was Simmons—white people lived along this stretch of road. A large white frame house to our right had the post office attached to one side. That section of the building was closed off from the rest, where the post-mistress, Mrs. Jones, and her family lived. Mother cleaned house for this Jones woman frequently.

A few minutes later, we were at the Smith Brothers' Store. We didn't have to wait long before the bus arrived. The big, long vehicle with a racing greyhound pictured on the side came to a screeching stop in front of us. We mounted the high steps. Mother paid the driver and we went to the back past some empty seats that were available upfront. Mother had explained to me before that we must always go to the back of any bus. She let me sit next to the window. I looked at the scenes as we passed them: a few houses, some scattered trees, the side rails of the Nouse River Bridge, a camp of small brick huts in which Gypsies lived, gas stations, and other types of buildings. Before I realized it, we were getting off the bus at the terminal in Goldsboro.

The first store we went to was Sears Roebuck. I couldn't wait to see what kind of shoes they had, so I was anxious to get to the children's shoe department. But we didn't go directly there. As she held my hand, Mother led me through the store to an area outback. There was a wide opening that led to an extremely large porch. I learned later that this was called a loading dock. The structure extended into a dark area—an alley—where there were two big trucks, one that was open and backed up to the dock. Several Negro men were moving heavy crates from the truck to the dock. They looked at us. One of them, a rather tall man with skin the color of caramel candy, and reddish-brown wooly hair thick as a bear's coat, walked over to Mother and me.

They smiled at each as he said, "Good mon'ing, ladies. What brings y'all out to the big city today?"

Mother replied, "We are going to buy shoes for my daughter," then glanced at me and said, "Honey, this is Andrew Bowden, an old friend of mine." I moved closer to her side as the man reached out and took my hand in his.

He exclaimed, "What a cute little girl. The las' time I saw you, you waz hardly walking."

"Yeah, since we hadn't seen you in such a long time, I thought we'd stop by and holler at ya'," Mother said.

"What grade ar'ya in, sweetheart?" he asked. "Fifth grade," I answered in a low, timid voice.

"She's doing real well in school, too," Mother added.

"I'll bet she is," he said as he released my hand. "She looks like she's smart."

He then turned his attention to Mother as they continued talking, asking each other how they'd been and making other exchanges. I moved a few steps away from them and watched the other men struggle with their heavy loads. However, every few seconds, I'd glance up at Mr. Bowden and would find him looking down at me. I had an uneasy feeling about him and I wondered who he was—really!

I was often suspicious of the words and actions of people whom I knew. I hadn't been around very many strangers so I was doubly distrusting of them. It seemed that all the characteristics people had observed in me coalesced to make me extra sensitive at that moment. For example, some adults had told my mother I was mature for my age. That was easy enough to believe because I was growing up with three adults—women—and when I wasn't in school, I spent most of my time around them. People said I was smart. This was true because I was very curious and studied hard in school. In a way I had hoped being smart would help me make up for not having lighter skin and "good" hair. Although I had heard some say "she sure is a pretty child," I believed they were saying that to be polite. They didn't want me to know what they really thought about me. I was very imaginative, and at the moment, my imagination was creating all types of reasons for our being with that man and for his seeming to be interested in me. I finally settled on the idea that he was a relative I hadn't met before. I moved closer to Mother's side again and took hold of her hand. We soon said goodbye to the man and left. But my curiosity about him was still nagging at me, worrying my mind like prickly thorns might worry my skin. After we left him, I asked Mother, "Who was that man?"

Like a parrot, she repeated what she had said earlier: "He's just an old friend. Come on, let's go buy your shoes."

My mood never returned to the happy state I had known earlier. Meeting that man, Andrew, had left me feeling confused and sad. However, I kept those feelings to myself. We didn't talk about Andrew again—at least not on that day.

One Sunday afternoon in early November, I was in our front yard. The sun was out but weak. Grey clouds wandered across the sky, so it was cold out. My two younger brothers, George four years old and John nearly two, were playing in the house. Children from the neighborhood, mostly cousins, came over to play with me sometimes, but I was most happy when I was by myself. The front yard was my favorite place to play. It was bare of grass and looked like a sea of white sand. Two evergreen shrubs stood guard in the center at the very front of the yard. They had a space between them that allowed entrance to the yard from the dirt road. It looked like a gate should have been there. A big mulberry tree with long branches that provided a roof for my playhouse in the summer was on the left side of the house. The single layer of red bricks I had placed end to end to outline the rooms of my playhouse were still in place. I thought about my pretend friend, Ella, and the times we had spent there with my dolls—children—during the hot days of the past summer. We worked at chores I had watched the three women of our family perform in the real house. But that Sunday afternoon, I was playing hopscotch.

I heard a car coming from a distance down the road. I didn't pay much attention to it until it stopped on the road near the two bushes in front of our house. I stopped with the small rock in my hand that I was ready to throw into the next square. I was puzzled as I stared at the car. It was a dusty, light blue car, not in very good shape. There were three Negro men in it, two in the front and one on the back seat. I could tell that all three were looking at me. I dropped the stone and backed up to the steps that led to the front porch. The man in the back had his window down and his face was framed by the opening. He was wearing a big grin. I recognized him as Andrew Bowden, the man Mother had met with and introduced me to on the Sear's dock some two months earlier.

He said, "Hi. Remember me?" I didn't answer but stared wide-eyed at him. He continued, "I brought some of my friends by to see you. Come over to the car and meet them." There was no way I was going near that car. Without saying anything, I turned and dashed into the house.

Mother was coming through the dining room and saw me as I enter the living room. "What's wrong?" she said.

I responded breathlessly, "That man we saw at Sears when we went shopping is out there in a car with some of his friends. He wants me to go up to the car and meet them. I don't want to. I'm scared!"

She quickly looked out the front window, then turned to me and said, "There's no car out there." I said, "Maybe they drove off when I ran inside, but they were there. I'm not telling a story!" (Not telling a story was the way I'd been taught to convey I wasn't lying.)

"I believe you," she said. "I'm sorry they came up here and frightened you—you were very wise not to go up to the car. If I ever see him again, I'm going to give him a piece of my mind for doing this. I'll make sure he and his friends don't come here again. You don't have to mention his visit to Momma or Clara. It'll only upset them." She hugged me. "Come on and wash up for dinner. I was just about to call you when I heard you came in." She put her hand on my shoulder as we walked to the kitchen together.

Thoughts of my two encounters with Andrew Bowden remained with me for the rest of that day and caused shadows of curiosity and doubt to hang over me like a dark cloud. I was concerned about who he was, if and how he was related to me. I was afraid that he would turn out to be my father since I had not had any contact with the person who was supposed to be father to Jim and me. Anything that made me different from other children in the neighborhood concerned me immensely. I was already self-conscious about my skin color, hair length, and texture not being like others around me. I didn't know the man who was said to be Jim's and my father. Jim knew him well and spent some weeks in Brooklyn visiting him and his second wife. Mother had, of course, been his first wife. Somewhere, not so well hidden in the crevices of my mind, I *knew* this guy from the store in Goldsboro was my father. If he were, I'd be even more of an outsider in our community. Furthermore, I would be only half-sister to the older brother I loved and admired so much. The possibility made me feel very ill. I returned to school the next day which was Monday. I tried to carry on as usual but my thoughts kept returning to the "mystery" man who had come unwelcomed into my life.

Time seemed to pass very fast and before I realized it, the Christmas season was upon us. Christmas was always a joyous time in our household. During the weeks leading up to Christmas Day, Mother was hired by several white families for day work to do house cleaning and help with the pre-holiday cooking. Therefore, she earned money to supplement the December welfare check. She used some of the extra money to buy presents for me and my brothers and most of the rest to buy special foods for the holidays. That was the only time of the year when we had store-bought apples, grapes, oranges, nuts, and candy. At night after Mother came in from work, she and Momma would make cakes, pies, and cookies. As Christmas Day approached, they would stuff and bake a large chicken.

On Christmas Eve, we lit sparklers. We were always very excited upon hearing the pop-pop-pop as the long magical sticks were lit and to see sparkles shooting from them like miniature stars. Afterward, festively giddy, George, John, and I would snuggle under the heavy covers on our cold beds. The heater in the back bedroom where we slept wasn't used during the day. Our older brother, Jimmy, was out with his friends. While we younger children were warming up and drifting off to sleep, we could hear the three women as they sat around the heater in the front bedroom listing to carols on the small radio, talking and snacking on Christmas goodies. Before she went to bed, I knew Mother would sneak our gifts under the Christmas tree we had decorated a week or so earlier. We were all pleased with the way the bright multi-colored glass bulbs seemed to glow in the dim light of two kerosene lamps, each placed on a table in opposite corners of the living room. On that Christmas Eve, I imagined Mother blew out the flame of each lamp and closed the door to the living room. She probably smiled as she thought about the beaming faces and excited voices of her children as we would rush into that room early the next morning.

My younger brothers and I were awake at dawn Christmas morning. Aunt Clara always slept in late, but Mother and Momma were up and making a fire in the slim stove in the living room. The room was just beginning to feel toasty warm when we ran in to see what had been left under the tree for us. We stopped briefly to kiss Mother and Momma and to wish each a happy Christmas before we pulled our gifts from under the tree.

Mother and Mamma stood by in their thick, old bathrobes watching as we tore into the packages. At that moment, our older brother entered the room carrying an arm full of cut wood and dumped it behind the heater. "Good morning," he said cheerfully, then quickly added, "and merry Christmas!"

Mother and Momma responded in unison, "Same to you, son." Without looking up, George and I mumbled our responses, "Yeah. Same to ya'."

Mother said, "It's a sunny day out there, how's the temperature?" "Pretty cold right now," Jim replied, "it'll probably warm up later in the day."

He joined the two women and watched us open our gifts—they laughed and made comments to each other as we oohed and ahhed over what we had received. There were three gifts for each of us younger kids and one for Jim. Two of our three contained toys we had asked for and the third had a few articles of clothing. Jim's gift was something to wear, also. As usual, there was nothing under the tree for the adults.

Mother dressed and left for work. Every year on Christmas, she would spend the day helping a white family prepare their meals, serve them, and clean up afterward. I resented her having to leave on such an important day. And I hated the plates of prepared food that she would bring home, left-overs sent by Mrs. So and So "for you and yo' family to enjoy." Mother would mimic the white woman's southern drawl. Mothers of other children I knew in our neighborhood were able to stay at home with their families on Christmas day. Why did we have to be so different?

After all gifts were opened, the rest of the family left the living room. I stayed behind thinking about how nice it would be to have a normal family life, with both a mother and father, no concerns over money, always having fruit and other snacks even on days other than just through the holidays.

My thoughts were diverted when I noticed a small, wrapped box that we had overlooked. I took it off a branch in the middle of the tree and saw it had my name on it. I anxiously tore the wrapping away and opened the approximately two-inch square, white box. In it was a small, beautiful dress pin resting on a square of white cotton. I moved the pin to the palm of my hand to examine it in detail. It was the golden outline of a small clown in which a pearl was its head and face. The pearl was too small for facial features to be added.

It had a round, clear ruby-red stone for its body, small opaque, purple stones for its arms, and opaque pink ones for its legs. The pin had a back of what looked like gold with a clasp attached, a golden pointed cap resting on its pearl head. I held it up to my robe and imagined how nice it would look on one of my Sunday dresses. Who could have given this to me? I wondered. If it were a member of the family, they would have realized that it wasn't opened earlier when the other gifts were. Mother must be the one who put it on the tree. Why hadn't she mentioned it to me?

Then an awful thought blasted its way to the forefront of my mind. Suddenly, I felt like I had been struck by a bolt of lightning. I became hot, sticky, and weak. Could this pin be a gift from that man, the one we saw at Sears, who then came to our house to see me? Why is he so interested in me? He didn't look like he had the money to buy something like this, but I was sure it was from him, and I felt sick. I had tried to put him out of my mind during the happy holiday season, but the thought of him was always there and now with the sight of this gift, thinking about him and the horror of him possibly being my father over-shadowed everything else. I closed the box and left it under the tree. I turned away—angry, frustrated, and hurt. It was going to be hard for me to be cheerful during the rest of the day.

When I joined the others in the kitchen, Momma looked at me and said, "You look pale, honey, are you feeling ok?"

I quietly replied, "Yes, ma'ma," and cast my eyes down toward the table.

We ate the breakfast of flat-jacks with syrup, fried eggs, and ham Momma had prepared. Afterward, I cleaned up the kitchen and later played with the new, blond-haired doll and the sewing set I had received that morning. Time dragged by like a turtle I saw once creeping across the back yard. I could hardly wait for Mother to come home. I had a question to ask her and while I almost trembled at the thought of what I was going to ask, I wanted to get it over with.

When she came in that afternoon, I ran to her and said excitedly, "Mother, I found a small gift on one of the branches of the Christmas tree, way back near its trunk. It had my name on it, so I opened it. It contained a pretty dress pin. Do you know who gave it to me?"

"Lordy," she said and laughed, "I'd forgotten that thing. Mrs. Jones' youngest daughter, Lou Anne, gave that to me a few weeks ago to give you. She received it on her birthday and didn't like it. She thought it would be a nice Christmas gift for you. I tried to hide it on the tree so you wouldn't see it until today. I'd planned to tell you about it this morning. I forgot. So you like it, do you? You'll have to write Lou Anne a thank-you note."

As I listened to her, I could feel the weight of depression leaving me. The gift was not from "him"! I had been wrong and I was never so happy to be wrong about something. Thank God! No, I didn't ask her who my father was. I was afraid I would not like the answer she'd give. I enjoyed the rest of the day. And again, I pushed my concern about who my father was to the back of my mind. I had no way of knowing that some months later, this troubling question would creep to the forefront of my thoughts again like a snake slithering through the grass.

It was the middle of April nearing the end of my fifth year in school. The days were warm and balmy. Students could hardly wait to get outside to play at recess. On that particular day, I tagged along with two other girls, Sarah and Nadine. They were very good friends with each other and were the exact opposite in physical appearance. Sarah was a rather short, fat girl with a chocolate brown complexion and short nappy hair braided in small plaits that stood out around her head. Nadine was small in size and shorter than Sarah or me. She had a rather weird color I thought, light but more like the yellow of a banana peel than the creamy color of a banana. Her hair was wooly, too, about four inches long, plaited in five braids. They were not close friends of mine. I just followed them to the swings because the three of us had exited the building together.

We played on the swings for a long while. Breezes brushed past our faces like soft feathers. Swinging high, seemingly meeting the blue, cloudless sky, made me feel like I was flying. Finally, we had to give up the swings and leave our fanciful journey because four other girls came up and wanted to swing. The teachers had taught us to share the playground equipment since there was not a lot of it. After getting off the swings, we walked over to a tree under which a carpet of wild green grass invited us to sit. We dropped to the ground and sat cross-legged in a small circle facing each other. We were silent for a while, just watching various antics of our fellow school mates playing nearby.

Finally, Nadine said in her quiet, timid voice, "I ain't done well on that math quiz this morning." "Me n'ither," Sarah responded. "How 'bout you, Anece? How'd you do?"

I said, "OK. I think." Most of my classmates seemed to think I was very smart in school. Both girls looked at me with sly, devilish smiles.

Without any warning, Sarah said, "We know you and Nadine is sisters."

"What?" I exclaimed. "What makes you say that?"

Sarah stopped smiling and said very sternly, "Her daddy," she pointed to Nadine, "told her he's yo' daddy, too."

My thoughts raced. It couldn't be! Nadine and I didn't look at all alike. I had heard her say once that she lived with her mother and step-dad. And I remembered then that her last name was Bowden, the same as that man who had shown so much interest in me. In spite of knowing these things, I responded very angrily, "He's wrong! My father lives in New York! I don't even know *her* daddy!" The bell rang summoning us back to class. I jumped up to leave those hateful girls and stopped only long enough to yell to them "Don't ever say that to me again!"

I felt dazed the rest of the afternoon. On the school bus going home and walking along the dirt road, I talked with Maggie and Carolyn as little as possible. I was not only shocked and angry, but also very, very hurt. My head was down when I walked in the house, and I didn't greet Aunt Clara with my usual smile. She was sitting in the front bedroom in her rocker.

When she noted my downcast mood, she asked, "What's wrong?" I answered in a subdued voice, "I have a bad stomachache."

"What did you have for lunch?" she asked. Without giving me a chance to answer, she added, "Go take your clothes off and lay down." I did as I was told.

Soon, Mother came in the back bedroom where I was. "Clara told me you have a bad stomachache. Here," she said as she handed me a small glass of water. "I fixed you some water with baking soda in it. If your pains are due to gas, this should help. Let me know if you don't feel better soon. Okay?"

I mumbled, "Okay." I took the soda water and drank it, then handed the glass back to Mother. I looked at her. I couldn't tell my mother what those girls had said. I couldn't tell her that I had figured out they were probably telling the truth. And I couldn't tell her how this revelation had hurt me deep down inside. I wanted to die. Instead, as she left the room, I turned over and cried into my pillow.

The girls never said anything else to me about my being Nadine's sister. And I never mentioned to them the little talk we had at recess that day. In my view, I was nobody. I didn't fit in or really belong anywhere. I was unlike the girls in my community because I wasn't light-skinned with long silky hair. I was from a very poor family. Finally, I was the only one in my own family who did not have a father—or at least not one acknowledged to me by the family I loved. I was no longer my older brother's real sister. What would he say or think of me when he knew this deep secret? Every day, I tried to avoid thinking about any of this. I buried myself in self-pity and my schoolwork as I became quieter than normal and withdrawn.

Chapter 5

Momma, my grandmother, began to grow frail when I was eleven and in the sixth grade. She never complained about anything. She could not keep her food down but kept this information from all of us until she lost so much weight that it was apparent something was wrong. She was questioned by her daughters and she finally revealed her condition to the family. We were alarmed and very worried. Mother asked one of our neighbors to take her with Momma to a doctor in Goldsboro. After doing numerous tests, the doctors determined that Momma had cancer of the esophagus. The growth was blocking the passage of the food she ate. Some weeks later, she was admitted to the colored ward of Goldsboro Hospital. A surgeon there inserted a tube in her stomach so that a special formula could be pumped into her body three times a day. This procedure provided nutrients to her, but she missed being able to taste food. Upon returning home when she smelled a meal cooking, she would say, "Oh that smells so-o-o good!

This woman, whom I had adored so much, passed away on a cold, dreary day in January of my seventh year in school. Just before lunch that day, Charlie, who was an older, distant cousin, who looked like a heavy-set white man, went to the school to take me home. My teacher told me that my mother had sent him to get me. But neither she nor Charlie told me why I was being excused to go home in the middle of the day. My cousin who hardly said a word looked very sad as he drove to our house. I thought I knew why I had been summoned home, but all the while, I hoped I was wrong.

As soon as he stopped the car, I grabbed my tan school bag, jumped out, and ran up the steps into the house and to the front bedroom. Charlie followed me. Mother, Aunt Clara, and my two younger brothers, who were still pre-school age, were gathered around the double bed that sat kitty-corner across from the door. All but Aunt Clara glanced at us as we entered the room. Everyone had watery, red-rimmed eyes. Aunt Clara was sobbing and repeating over again, "My momma is gone. My momma is *gone!* Oh Lord, my Momma is gone, why did you take her!" I gently nudged George to move over so that I could get closer to the bed. Momma was lying there with a white sheet pulled up to her chin. Her eyes were closed as if she were sleeping. Her face looked pale, even pasty. But she wore a pleasant expression as if she were happy and at peace. I could feel tears as they made wet tracks down my cheeks and saw some drop on the edge of the bed when I leaned over and pressed my lips to her cold forehead. I, too, started crying loudly. Mother pulled me to her and held me tightly allowing the sounds of my grief to be absorbed into her thick sweater.

Cuddled there in the warmth and comfort of my mother's arms, I had fleeting thoughts about some of the things Momma and I had done together but would do no more: making "hardtacks" (cookies), picking fresh vegetables from her little garden, walking the dusty roads from our house to the church and back on Sundays when her duties allowed her to go, her teaching me to do hand sewing, giving me a rag doll, and teaching me how to braid her long hair of white twine so that I could one day braid my own. She had never raised her voice to scold me. Furthermore, she always treated me like I was very special, although I knew I wasn't. She was gentle but strong and I know that as long as she was there, all of us would be alright. My reverie of things past was interrupted when the undertaker from Mt. Olive arrived in his hearse to take Momma away. Charlie had called him from the Smith Brothers' store before he picked me up at school. As I looked at her body being rolled out on a gurney, new tears obscured my vision.

At the time I was growing up in the rural south, the death of a loved one, especially in Negro families, caused great lamenting, but also a feeling that the deceased had gone on to a better place. In God's kingdom, there would be no more hardships and troubles. Therefore, dressing the dead suitably and planning a funeral service that reflected love and respect for the departed were of utmost importance. Although the people in Simmons Town did not identify with others of African heritage, they nevertheless shared this belief in doing meticulous planning.

On a cold, overcast day after Momma's death, Mother, Aunt Clara, and my older brother, Jim, who had come home from New York, went to the colored funeral home in Mount Olive "to make the funeral arrangements." This included, among other things, selecting the shroud, casket, and a floral spray from the family. All the adults in our family had a small life insurance policy to help defray funeral expenses. The policies were kept in force by paying the monthly premiums regardless of our limited income. I stayed home that day with my two younger brothers. As the gray afternoon began to slide into the night, the three adults returned home. Their cheeks and noses were pink from the cold. But they were smiling and enthusiastic as they told us what they had selected for Mamma's funeral. The casket was a soft gray, and the shroud was light pink with tucks in the bodice front. They were most pleased that they had been able to stay within the budget the life insurance provided. We enjoyed the most cheerful evening we had known since Mamma's death. By the next morning, the numbing sadness had crept back into our household.

The afternoon before the day of the funeral, Momma was delivered home by the undertaker. Her body would lie in state in the living room overnight. When I viewed her for the first time, she didn't seem as pale as she had when they took her body away. The pink she wore seemed to reflect the color on her cold cheeks. Her long gray hair was coiled into a bun to the right side of her head. Her hair was a little too puffy near the side part so I smoothed it down and used a bobby pin to hold it in place.

Just before nightfall, various relatives and friends stopped by to view the body and to console members of the immediate family. There was a lot of crying, hugging, praying, cheek kissing, and back-slapping. Some of the people stayed all night to sit up with the body and the family. Our little house was full. People were sitting everywhere—on chairs, the sofa, and the sides of beds. George and I took catnaps whenever we could find a vacant space to lie down. John slept mostly on Mother's lap.

The next day dawned sunny and by noon, it was fairly warm for January in piedmont North Carolina. Around midday, we got dressed to go to the church. It was important for all of us to wear our Sunday best but in dark colors. Jim wore a dark blue suit with a crisp white shirt and a dark blue, white, and gray striped tie. My two younger brothers wore gray pants, navy blue jackets, white shirts, and light blue bow ties. Each of the three males had a black band affixed to one of their jacket sleeves. Mother and Aunt Clara dressed entirely in black, including their shoes, stockings, dresses, and hats. I wore a navy-blue skirt with box pleats, a white blouse with ruffles down the front, and my usual full-length, black and white herringbone coat, with a black velveteen collar. A limousine arrived at our house at the same time as the hearse. Once Momma's casket was placed and secured in the larger black vehicle, we climbed into the limousine. All of us were very somber, lost in our own individual thoughts about the loving matriarch to whom we were saying goodbye. Some relatives in their cars followed the hearse and limousine forming a slowly moving procession.

When we arrived at the church, we saw additional family members and friends gathered on the lawn waiting for us. Some started moving into the building to be seated before the funeral party entered. The undertaker, Mr. Barnes, a tall, portly, light-skinned Negro man, dressed in a black suit, white shirt, dark tie, and black shoes, began organizing the participants right away. There was an array of wreaths on stands, baskets of flowers, and small plants that had been ordered earlier and delivered to the funeral home. Flower girls, mostly my grandmother's nieces and cousin, gathered around while the undertaker handed each an arrangement to take into the church. Six Negro men dressed in dark attire, all related in some way to our family and following the undertaker's directions, lifted Momma's casket and took it inside to the very front of the church. They placed it on a sliver bier that the undertaker's men had set up earlier. Flower girls put the flower containers around the bier. There were flowers of many different types and colors. The family's spray on top of the casket consisted of white carnations and white roses with green foliage and a large satin ribbon with gold letters that said, "the Family."

Funeral services for members of our church were much quieter than those in most other Negro churches. There were soft sobbing and mummers of responses to what the minister was saying, like "Yes," "Thank you, Jesus," and "She's gone on to a better place." However, there was no excessive screaming or shouting in the aisles. Aunt Clara was the most vocal of anyone in expressing grief that day. She had to be comforted several times by the undertaker's nurse, a black woman dressed totally in white who was available to assist the bereaved with quiet words and smelling salts when needed.

Once the funeral service began officially, bible scriptures were read, prayers were said, and messages of condolence addressed to the family were noted. Our regular church minister, Reverend Greene, delivered the eulogy. He knew our family quite well. The church choir sang several hymns during the service. Their last one was "Leaning on His Everlasting Arms," which had been Momma's favorite.

When the funeral service ended, the flower girls were again given the floral arrangements and they lined up in twos. Pallbearers lifted the casket and moved in position behind the women with flowers. Immediate family members lined up behind the casket. Aunt Clara with her single crutch, assisted by Jim and the nurse, was the first person in line. Mother was second with John, my baby brother. George and I were next. All of us were teary-eyed. The rest of the attendees joined the procession as we moved slowly down the aisle and outside to the vehicles waiting near the church. Then the slow-moving procession of automobiles proceeded to the cemetery where Mamma was "laid to rest." After the last words were said over the casket by Reverend Green, it was lowered into the ground and two men began shoveling dirt into the grave. Once they finished, the beautiful floral arrangements were placed on and around the grave. Momma would have loved the flowers, I thought as we rode away.

Life for our little family continued as normal as possible without Mamma. Jim returned to New York. I returned to school. Mother cared for Aunt Clara during her sick spells and did day work on weekends and holidays whenever she could get it. Winter turned into spring with beautiful sunny days, the vegetation of various kinds breaking free of the soil, and trees dressing again in their new, green foliage. Before very long, it was Easter. I had no way of knowing what a day of mixed emotions it would bring to me.

Chapter 6

Early Easter Sunday morning, I wore my bathrobe out on the back porch to get water for washing up. I stopped for a moment to inspect the beginning of the glorious day. The sky was a soft blue with only a few clouds visible. The sun, just awaking, brightened the peaceful scene and enhanced my already cheerful mood. I stood for a few moments drinking in the beauty surrounding me. Then I hurriedly soaped and washed my hands, splashed water on my face, and dried off with a fresh towel. I had bathed the night before. All finished with cleaning up, I went inside to have breakfast. Mother was fixing scrambled eggs and fresh biscuits, which smelled delicious.

After eating, George and I dressed to go to Sunday school and church. Our cousin, Evelyn, and her husband, Mr. Powell, would, as usual, take us to the Congregational Christian Church. John was three and went to church only with Mother.

Following church that day, our activities varied only slightly from those of most Sundays: We had our family dinner at home in the early afternoon, after which I washed the dishes, swept the kitchen floor, and then sat in a chair on the front porch reading. Around three o'clock, our cousin and Mr. Powell took George and me back to the church for the annual Easter egg hunt. True, I was twelve years old and in the seventh grade but we older children in the church attended to help the adults with the younger kids and, perhaps, to find an egg or two for ourselves. Except for church activities, there was little else for us to do in Dudley. Upon arriving home from the egg hunt, we saw a large, light gray car with silver trim parked in our yard. Cousin Evelyn said, "It looks like your mother and Clara have company." I didn't recognize the car as belonging to someone we knew, and I wasn't in the mood to meet any people with whom I was not familiar. So, while George hurried out of our cousin's car and ran up the front steps into the house, I sauntered along. I overheard George exclaim, "Mother, look how many eggs I found!" There were six in a small basket we—the teenage assistants–had helped the little children make the previous week. I lingered on the front porch beside the open door to get some idea of who was visiting.

Mother responded to George saying, "Oh, how colorful and pretty they are. Did you find all of those yourself?"

He said, "Yes ma'ma. Well, Anece did point me to a few hiding places, though." John wanted George's eggs.

Mother said, "No, John, let's leave them in the basket and admire them for a while. George, put your basket on the dining room table if you're willing to share them with the rest of the family…and George, before you go, I want you to shake hands with Mr. Faison. He's from New York and came down to visit his mother."

Mr. Faison, I thought, *is he related to Jimmy—he also has **my** last name!* While I puzzled over this, the man and my brother exchanged greetings. Mother gave the two young boys further instructions. I was too involved in thought to hear any of this. As the boys left to go through the dining room to the back bedroom to play, I opened the screen door and stepped into the living room.

"Oh, there she is," Mother said.

I stood silently and stared at the man who sat on the opposite end of the drab purple sofa from her. He was a Negro man of a coffee and cream color similar to my own complexion. This man was about six feet tall and of a somewhat stocky build. His dark hair was cut short and looked like it was beginning to recede. He wore eyeglasses over dark brown eyes that were set in a round face. He was dressed neatly in gray slacks and a white short-sleeved cotton shirt opened at the collar.

He was standing, smiling at me, and I mumbled, "Hi."

He said in a moderately deep, gravelly voice, as if he had rocks rattling deep inside, "Hello, young lady. It's so good to meet you."

Mother injected excitedly, "Come on over and sit here between us." She patted the sofa. "We have something to discuss with you." I walked over slowly and sat down. He joined us. She continued rather haltingly, "Anece, this is your father."

My mouth popped open and hung that way as I drew in a deep breath. My eyes widened. I turned to look at him. He took my left hand, which was next to him, in his. I managed to say, "I don't understand—why am I just meeting you now? Why haven't I known you like Jimmy? Why haven't I been invited to New York to visit you?" My voice was shaking and I was on the verge of tears.

"I'm so sorry," he said and put his arm around my shoulders. "Those are some of the things we want to talk about with you."

What my mother and father told me on that Easter Sunday evening, and bits of personal information I gained as I grew older and became more aware of the nuances of love, marriage, birth, separation, and divorce, led me to the following understanding: My parents met when they were in their teens, fell in love, and married when they were young. Afterward, they lived in his hometown, Mt. Olive, N.C., only five miles from her family whom they visited several times a week. Mother's sister, Clara, and my grandmother were very fond and approving of James David Faison. His color was okay, especially in my aunt's thinking. The young couple had a son, my brother, Jim.

A few years into their marriage, they began to have problems. James David wanted to move to New York, where he thought he could make a better living. My mother was adamant about not being that far away from her mother and invalid sister. Thus, they experienced some periods of living apart, with him going to New York to investigate what that city could offer him and her staying at her mother's house. When Jim was seven years old, the couple made one final attempt to reconcile. I was conceived during that period. Mother did not learn that I was on my way until a month or so after she and James David separated for the last time. It was never made clear to me whether she told him she was expecting his second child. I guess not, because on that Sunday, he said he had thought someone else was my father. No one ever said but I guessed that Mother and Andrew Bowden probably dated after my parents' split. Their final separation was not an amicable one and led to divorce a few months later. Within that first year, James David married a woman from South Carolina he had met in New York, and they began a family. Years later, I learned that their oldest son was only eleven months younger than I.

Apparently, Mother and Dad had discussed me and the circumstances of my birth when my brother and I were at the Easter egg hunt. They explained portions of the story to me while we were sitting on the couch. The sad and serious expressions on their faces and the sincere tone of their voices convinced me that they were being truthful. Perhaps, they were also feeling guilty over my reaching twelve years of age without knowing my father—in essence, not knowing for certain who I was. I smiled and nodded my head to acknowledge what the adults were saying. I was shocked but happy. A warm feeling rippled through my body like gentle waves rolling toward the shore on a hot, sunny day. I had a father about whom I could speak openly to kids at school or anyone else. I didn't have to worry anymore about whether Jim and I were "whole" brother and sister. My last name was truly the same as his: Faison.

I never learned why Andrew Bowden had intruded in my life a couple of years earlier. Perhaps, he did wish or hope I was his child. The shadow of his existence and the relationship I thought he had to me infected my self-esteem like a sore or disease can infect the body or parts of it. The rest of my life, I would wonder about his interest in me. Why had he brought his friends to Dudley to see me that Sunday? Why did he tell my classmate, Nadine, that she and I were sisters, that he was my father? Maybe that's what he truly believed or wanted. I never asked and no one ever explained his relationship to me. I guess I was afraid to know. I had heard adults when facing a puzzling situation say, "Sometimes, it's better to let sleeping dogs lie." I knew that sage expression when applied to my dilemma meant it would be better for me not to worry over or try to gain answers about Bowden. Therefore, I became content in not knowing the full story about him and thinking of the Andrew Bowden episode as a "sleeping dog."

On that Easter Sunday afternoon, my parents began making plans for the two weeks Dad–it would take me some time to get used to using that word— planned to stay in North Carolina. He expressed interest in visiting my school. Mother, who was excited but practical as always, suggested that the three of us go to Goldsboro to do some shopping for me. Dad wanted to take me to Mt. Olive to meet his mother and sister.

We did all three things and more. It was fun having him around during his two-week stay. I saw him nearly every day. He liked my school and the principal, Mr. Brown. They talked for over an hour one day while I was in class. He told me as he drove away from the school that the principal had said many complimentary things about me. Then he added, "I am very proud of you." I thought, *your sentiments are very late, but better late than never, I guess.*

When we went shopping, I selected underwear, shoes, socks, and some outerwear. The thing we bought that I liked most was a soft, sky-blue dress. It was to be worn on special occasions, which for me meant to church. The dress was made of a fabric that had a dull sheen. It felt very smooth when I ran my hands along the lines of the skirt and bodice, both of which had tiny pleats all around. It had cap sleeves, a small Peter Pan collar, and a fitted waist with a self-belt that tied in front. The style emphasized my slim body. I felt like a princess when I tried it on and my parents said I looked beautiful. What a happy day I was experiencing: *This is what it's like to have a carrying father!* I thought.

The most uneasy time for me during Dad's visit was the day he took me to meet his mother and sister, Sylvia, who lived with her. I was very nervous as the two of us drove to Mt. Olive. Myriad questions bombarded my mind: *What would they think of me? How should I act toward them? What should I call them? Will they really accept me in their family?*

When Dad and I arrived at the house, I was mildly surprised. It was similar in style to what has become known as southern plantation architecture. It reminded me of some of the white folk's homes in Wayne County—just smaller and not as grand as theirs. It was a two-story, white frame house. Three steps led up to a large, gray porch that was across the front of the building. I could tell the place was old, but well-maintained.

We exited the car and proceeded up the steps, across the porch to the front door that opened directly into the living room. A plump, milk chocolate-colored woman with a big, toothy smile on her round face met us at the door.

"This is my baby sister, your Aunt Sylvia," Dad said. Then with a big grin, he added, "Sylvia, this is my daughter, Anece."

I started to reach my hand to her, but she ignored it and quickly folded me in her arms and squeezed me gently. As she released me, she said, "Welcome! Come on in here and see yo grandma."

I looked to my left where rose-colored wingback chairs were placed on each side of a floral sofa. An elderly, heavyset, very, very light-skinned woman sat in the one to the left of the sofa. She looked like some of my relatives in Simmons Town—those with that pale, creamy, peeled banana color. Her hair, twisted in a frizzy bun on the top of her head, was (in Negro jargon) not as "good "as the Dudley relatives." Her skin, except for a deep vertical wrinkle down each of her once full, but now deflated cheeks, looked like light smooth leather. She had thin lips, a hoarse voice, and spoke so fast it was hard to understand what she was saying.

"Come on in, child," she said while still seated and lifting her sleeved arms out to me, "And give your grandma a hug."

I did as I was told. Much to my surprise and relief, I was receiving a very warm welcome from my newfound relatives. No one mentioned that I was just now being acknowledged as part of their family, but I certainly thought about it *and* the hole in my life their absence had made. I sat on the end of the sofa next to Grandma's chair. Dad and Aunt Sylvia joined us, Dad on the sofa next to me, and Aunt Sylvia sat in the second wing back chair. She pulled it a little more in front of the sofa so that we could all have a better view of each other. As the four of us talked, they asked me questions about school and other activities and interests in my life. I answered politely and found myself becoming more conversant as I warmed up to them. Before long, Aunt Sylvia left us so she could finish preparing supper.

Later in the evening when we went to the back to eat, I was able to see more of the house. It was much more spacious than our home in Dudley. On the right side of the living room, a door opened into a bedroom where Grandma said she slept. There were two other bedrooms, one behind hers and a smaller one behind the living room. A hallway running parallel to the small room led to the back. I had noticed stairs on the other side of the house near Grand Momma's room. When I mentioned how impressed I was with the size of the house, Grandma told me there were four additional bedrooms upstairs. She added, "We raised five chil'ren in this old place. We wuz farmers and had land fu'her out in the county. Two of my chil'un built and live there now. Today, we mostly grow gardens, small crops of corn, and so fo'th for family use. We worked hard but managed to keep a ruf ov'r our heads 'n food in our bellies."

I thought, this is so different from our home and lifestyle. Why hadn't Dad seen to it that Jim and I were growing up with comforts like those he knew when he was young?

We finally entered the kitchen which was in the back of the house. A large, enclosed porch behind the kitchen had a table set for supper. From the porch windows, I could see the backyard with random clumps of grass interspersed in plain soil. At the far edge of the property sat an old shed with loose and missing boards. I could barely detect a large piece of rusting farm equipment peeking out from it. A small bathroom that had been added at some point during the 20th century was across the *hallway from the porch.*

Mealtime was pleasant. Aunt Sylvia explained that her husband, Uncle Joe, had gone over to help his sister who was sick and that was why he wasn't joining us. While we ate a meal of sliced country ham, candied sweet potatoes, home-canned greens beans, corn, and biscuits, we talked about "olden times" when Dad, Aunt Sylvia, and their three siblings were growing up—I mainly listened, smiled, and asked questions every once in a while.

Just as the dusk of night began to appear, Dad and I prepared to leave for him to take me back home. I thanked my relatives for a very enjoyable afternoon and said how happy I was to have met them. Both Grandma and

Aunt Sylvia invited me to come back to see them and spend the night. They especially encouraged me to stay with them some when I entered high school. Carver High School, to which Wayne County Negro students were bussed, was only a few blocks from their house.

A few days later, Dad left and returned to his family in New York. He had two sons by his second wife. He owned a grocery store not far from their home in Brooklyn and an apartment building. My brother Jim went to live with him after finishing high school. Jim's understanding was that his father would help finance him in college. That plan never reached fruition; instead, my brother worked in Dad's store full-time. Later, he was employed by the city but returned to the store to help on weekends and some evenings. This served as a warning that I would have to find my *own* financial means for attending college when the time came.

After Easter, I returned to school a bit more accepting of myself than I had been before. Dad's acknowledging me as his daughter brought a new dimension to my existence—a degree of credence. It was the first step toward my becoming the model of human being I most desired to emulate—middle-class whites. After all, isn't knowing from where one came an important step on the road to personal validation? Still at that point in my life, I would do anything to be more like the other youth in Simmons Town in appearance. It pains me now to think that was ever my primary goal in life—to be light-skinned with long, straight, hair so that I would fit in. It was a shallow, misguided objective. Could I, *would I*, ever get over that desire? Little did I know then that in my twenties, I would encounter a problem that would overshadow my concerns about looking like and being like whites. The problem would appear slowly and darken my life, like the moon eclipsing the sun.

Chapter 7

I completed the remaining six weeks of the seventh grade. "*School is over*" or similar expressions were shouted by the rowdier students at the end of the day when we rushed out of the building like a herd of cattle. Many feet, big, small, and in between, were shuffling and running, eager to have three months of fun—and for some, three months of work. During the summer, I helped at home while Mother worked at odd jobs. There were only the two of us to take care of the family since Momma had died, and Jim, now a high school graduate, was in New York with our dad.

Fall arrived with its chilly temperatures and feeble rays of sun coalescing to dress the trees and bushes in beautiful brown, gold, and orange colors. We returned to school as eighth-graders. It was our last year at Dudley Elementary. We were so excited that the first seven months of the year sped by much like a car speeding down a dirt road and as graduation approached, we retained only dusty memories of the last several months.

The Commencement ceremony was planned for an evening during the last week of May 1955. Approximately a month before that, our teacher told us in a class meeting that everyone's grade point average had been tabulated and he had the pleasure of announcing the two highest-ranking students. The second highest was Margaret Winston. Then he said, "The person who has the highest grade point average is Anece Faison." I was number one—the valedictorian of the class! I sat there with wide eyes and an open mouth. The news did not seem to surprise my classmates. Everyone applauded. I *would, of course, have to give the valedictorian address during commencement.*

When I told Mother about the honor, she cried, gave me a wet kiss on my cheek, and said how proud she was of me. Aunt Clara, my most vocal supporter, announced loudly, *"I Knew* you would be it! Come on over here and let me hug you." The elated feelings were catching: my two younger brothers ran into

Aunt Clara's room and wanted to know what we were all so happy about. We explained the meaning of the title I had earned. They joined in the chorus of praise and congratulations. That night, I wrote Jim with the good news. He had assured me that when I graduated, he would come home to attend the ceremony. I didn't bother telling our dad. Jim would share the news with him, but I knew he wouldn't come for my graduation. As it turned out, he didn't attend, nor did he send me a gift, card, or any message. The personal credence I had gained when he visited during Easter was beginning to slip away as I realized that I really didn't have a *caring* father.

On the night of graduation, I stood behind the podium in a new, white, knee-length, pique dress. It was simple in style—short-sleeved, white lace encircling the neck, small tucks on the front bodice, and a gathered skirt. A corsage of pink carnations adorned my left shoulder, a surprise gift from my family. My hair, due to the skill of a local, black beautician, formed a cap of shiny black curls. Mother, Aunt Clara, and my three brothers, including Jim, looked up at me from the sea of dark, splendiferous faces. They were beaming with pride and I was elated to be the incentive for their feelings of joy and excitement.

Earlier in the evening, I had thought about Ray Dagger, a boy who had been a member of our class until the sixth grade when his sister, Celestine, became a high school student and of dating age. They were Negroes who looked white. Celestine even had blond hair. Ray and Celestine's parents took them out of Dudley Elementary and Carver High School and moved their family to Clinton, North Carolina where there were others who looked like them or who thought they were Indian. Thinking about Ray reminded me of the division among black people and segregation in general. I thought about the school from which we were graduating being considered inferior to Brogden Elementary School, the one for white students located just down the road. Their used textbooks had been handed down to us. But in the warm glow of the evening, I quickly pushed that negative thinking out of my mind and concentrated on my speech. I was just happy to know most of my classmates were seated on stage with their parents and other relatives beaming in the audience just as mine were. Only two out of thirty in our class had not met the requirements to graduate.

In my valedictorian address, I briefly reviewed the good times and *not* so pleasant times of our eight years in Dudley Elementary School. Some of the students behind me chuckled over remarks when they remembered incidents to which I referred. I offered a challenge to my classmates for us to continue our education, no matter how "rough the road ahead." I told them that our people (the Negroes) our communities, state, nation, and the world needed the contributions we could make by becoming caring, productive citizens. Finally, on behalf of the class, I thanked our parents, teachers, and all others who had supported us during the past eight years. I then turned sideways to speak directly to the students sitting behind me. I wished them continued success in school and told them with emphasis to *study hard*. The audience gave enthusiastic applause as I returned to my seat. The loudest and most prolonged probably came from my family.

Chapter 8

High school! A jubilant group of new ninth graders gathered at Dudley Elementary School where we joined upperclassmen boarding a school bus that would take us to Carver High School in Mount Olive, North Carolina. There, we would join approximately seventy other freshmen who had finished *Carver* Elementary School the previous spring.

That fall day had arrived cool and sunny, sweater weather. We sat two to a seat in rows on each side of the bus. Our driver, Bob, was a dark, muscular high school senior who was quite friendly and seemed capable of controlling his noisy brood. The rising sun shone through the windows in much weaker rays than summer sun. I sat next to one of my classmates, Mildred. After a cheery good morning and "How was your summer?" exchange, we spent much of the five-mile trip looking out the window. Scenes of farms, vacant fields, alternating with clusters of bushes and trees seemed to float by like those in a colorful movie. Mildred and I would call each other's attention to points of interest outside and sometimes talked quietly about other students on the bus, like who was sitting with whom and, if they were boy and girl, we wondered if they were going together.

Finally, the bus was passing in front of the high school on its way to the back parking lot where we would disembark. I looked at the three buildings standing in a semi-circle. The middle one was the largest, a red brick building that served as a gymnasium and as an auditorium for large meetings and special occasions. I had attended my brother, Jim's, graduation there. I had also toured all of the campus during an eighth-grade visitation. The building to the right of the gym was one-story and light-colored. It consisted of classrooms along the sides of a hallway that ran from front to back. There were large windows in each room that framed views of the campus. I was to become very familiar with that building because, for four years, my homeroom would be there, located across the hall from the school library. Also, my classes in English, French, first-year math, algebra, geometry, and social studies were taught in various rooms in that building. Sciences were taught in the older, two-story red brick building to the left of the gym. That was where at various times during high school, I would enjoy general science and biology, struggle through chemistry, love home economics, try to participate as little as possible in physical education, and learn to type at a snail's pace in a typing class. Concrete walks connected the buildings. A well-manicured green lawn filled the front of the campus where a sign proudly announced, "Carver High, Home of the Tigers." I felt good about this being my stomping ground for the next four years. But I also worried about fitting in—would I succeed in gaining new friends and making a favorable impression on the teachers or would my timidity, self-consciousness, and discomfort with other people impede my social and academic success?

There were five school busses discharging students when we reached the parking lot. Immediately after stepping out of the busses, many friends from previous years greeted each other and fell into talkative groups as we walked to the gym. I thought, *They sound like a gaggle of geese.* I walked alone and my thoughts turned to our family—how our economic situation had fluctuated and our family dynamics had changed over the last few years, with Momma gone and my brother, Jim, living in New York. My main goal *had to be* helping my family, especially Mother. I determined then and there that I would be a success in high school and by some means get money to pay for college—but how? These thoughts were interrupted by a bell ringing.

It was eight o'clock. The local students and those of us bused in from other locations shuffled into the gym where folding chairs had turned the gym into an auditorium. Five faculty members, including the principal, sat on the stage. They were dressed impeccably in suits, presenting themselves as models of how professionals should look. The remaining teachers sat in the front row. The principal, Mr. Rodgers, stood and moved to the podium. Everyone became quiet. He was a nice-looking man: brown skin with a trim mustache under his rather pug nose. He was shorter than average and had closely cropped dark hair. When he spoke, his voice was moderately deep and pleasant.

"Good morning, everyone. Welcome to a new year at Carver. Upperclassmen and many of our faculty are, of course, returning. It is good to see you again. However, the freshmen and three teachers are new on campus. We want each of you to know how happy we are to have you join our family."

After his opening, Mr. Rodgers talked about the school, his hopes, and expectations for the Year. Then he introduced the faculty, starting with the new teachers sitting on stage and acknowledging those returning. He called each person by name and gave the courses they taught. They stood as he introduced them. There were only ten. After the introductions, he dismissed all upperclassmen and their teachers to go to their homerooms. When the noise of those leaving cleared, he turned to the four teachers on stage. He repeated their names and asked each one to stand to receive the students in their section of the freshmen class: A, B, C, and D. His secretary, Miss Waters, would call the names in each group. While his secretary made her way to a table up front, Mr. Rodgers expressed hopes that all of us would have a successful year and said he looked forward to getting to know each of us. Then he left.

Seated at the table with four stacks of paper in front of her, Miss Waters greeted us and explained: "Students' names have been assigned to the homerooms randomly. The letter for each group is for identification only." She smiled, announced section A, and began calling individual names. The students joined their teacher at the back of the auditorium and left. Next, she called the names for section B—the group to which I was assigned. When she had finished calling the twenty-five names in our section, we followed our teacher, Miss Adamson, to room 107, in the one-story building to the right of the gym.

That would be our homeroom and homeroom teacher for the next four years, although we would rotate to other locations on campus for our various academic classes. For example, Ms. Adamson was the French teacher and her language classes would meet in our homeroom when she was teaching. Most of the teachers had two or more duties. For example, Mr. Haines, the social studies teacher, taught, not only that subject but also health and physical education. Plus, he was the basketball coach for the boys' team.

When I learned about the teachers' myriad tasks, I couldn't help but wonder if individual teachers at the local schools for whites had as many varied responsibilities. This was of interest to me because my mother had said to me so many times: "Get your education. As a Negro woman in the South, if you can't do anything else when you grow up, you'll be able to teach in a Negro school. I don't want you to have the hard life I've had." Her remarks were not intended to be derogatory about Negro schools, but rather acknowledged reality concerning discrimination—the forced limitations placed on Negroes. I knew she was right because I hadn't seen any Negro professionals except teachers, preachers, and undertakers.

Miss Adamson stood beside her desk in the center front of the room. We, students, were all seated in single-armed desk chairs arranged in rows. Our teacher was a short woman with an unequally proportioned body— very small breasts and a round, protruding derriere. Her hair was an extremely short rust-colored curly mass that surrounded her pale, almost white, face. She spoke hesitantly in a soft voice with no accent I could detect. She introduced herself and explained the functions of a homeroom. "It is the classroom to which you report each morning, but more than that, it is your home away from home that serves to promote student cohesion as a support group while progressing through high school. It is also of value in planning and conducting school projects. In a few weeks after you've gotten to know each other, you will elect class officers. We will have class meetings on a regular basis. Once or twice a year, each homeroom class sponsors an assembly program for the high school. You may want to plan community projects to help others and/or social events. I want you to feel free to come to me to discuss anything of importance to you and especially any problems or concerns."

"Now," she continued, "I'd like for each of you to give us your name and tell us something interesting about yourself. It can be about your hobby, the kind of books you like to read, movies you've enjoyed, your interest in a particular sport—any number of topics. We'll start with the first person in the first row." She pointed to her right.

There were some moans, groans, and silly remarks among the students as she gave us that assignment. However, varied and interesting personal accounts followed: some funny, some sad, and many happy ones.

When my time came, after stating my name, I said, "There isn't very much interesting about me and my life. I do enjoy reading mysteries. With each story, I try to solve the puzzle before the author reveals the solution."

A boy in the back asked, "How well do you do in solving them?" I looked around at him. "Very well most of the time," I said.

"Good. We'll know where to go if we have problems we can't solve, even those in math," he retorted. Some of the students snickered and others laughed out loud. I didn't know if the boy was making fun of me or what. I managed to give a weak smile as I returned my focus to the front of the classroom. The student behind me was invited to speak. Thus, began the first day of my first year in high school.

The introduction exercise we had that first day helped me tremendously in getting to know my 24 classmates. Within a few weeks, I knew who the jokesters and teasers were. Manny, the boy who had made the comment about me solving problems, told me later that he was only teasing. I realized then that I needed to take such remarks less seriously. I soon identified the intellectuals, the sports enthusiast, the exceptionally quiet students, the shy ones, the socialites, and popular students. I don't know exactly where I fitted in—if I did at all.

We were not only a motley group in our interests and abilities, we were also varying shades of color that made up, and continue to form, the color spectrum in the Negro race. Obviously, I was not alone in my brownness nor in having artificially straightened hair. But everyone else seemed to accept themselves as they were—I did not. It was very hard for me to have an undistorted image of myself in the mirror of life because influences from my past obscured my view. Would I ever correct the erroneous effigy of the person I saw myself as being and develop into the perfect human being that I had set as my goal—one who would compete successfully with whites in every respect and who would, therefore, be evaluated by all to be a valid, worthwhile member in society? I knew I had two natural impediments in accomplishing this goal—hair texture and skin color.

But I could work on making my personal appearance appealing. That was something I hoped to accomplish as I simultaneously acted on getting the necessary academic background and training. I never stopped to wonder if these were attainable goals I was setting. I had to hold on to this hope. It was what gave me the motivation to keep going because sometimes, I felt so sad that I wanted to cease existing.

My desire to have a lighter complexion reached the point of desperation. One Saturday evening when preparing for my bath, I poured a half cup of Clorox in the water. It lightened clothes, why wouldn't it erase some of my skin coloring? I was enjoying just sitting in the comforting warmth and had not submerged the bar of Lifebuoy soap to begin washing myself when Mother came into the kitchen. She stopped suddenly, took a deep breath, and glared at me. "I smell Clorox! You didn't put that stuff in your bathwater, did you?" It was one of the few times I lied to her. "No, ma'am!" I replied with great emphasis. She added, "It's not meant for the body, and could mess up your skin." I quickly began rubbing my bath cloth over the bar of reddish-pink soap and lathering my body. The wet soap perfumed the air and weakened the smell of Clorox. Mother left the room. When I got out of the tub, I realized my skin color had not changed one bit. The experiment hadn't worked.

With few exceptions, I enjoyed high school. Taking various classes, meeting the challenges, and doing well were gratifying to me. Plus, things were going well at home. Everybody in the family was congenial with and helpful to each other. Even Aunt Clara's attitude seemed different and she didn't have quite as many sick spells. Thanks to the Rural Electrification Program started under President Roosevelt's leadership, we finally got electric lights. Mother bought an electric range for cooking, but we still had to use the outdoor toilet. Life was a little bit easier for Mother. Depending upon the season, she managed to work as a maid or in the fields nearly every day.

My most challenging courses throughout high school were the progressive levels of mathematics: General math during my freshman year, algebra I, then algebra II, and finally, geometry. I went home at the end of each weekday and after washing the dinner dishes, I would sit at the big round table in the dining room, spread my books out before me, and get to work on various assignments. Two other girls, Anne Faison (same last name as mine, but not a relative), Mary Winters, and I competed with several boys in each of our math classes. We were successful in doing the assignments and examples on the blackboard as well as, if not better, than the boys. I developed a casual friendship with Anne and Mary. However, they lived in Mt. Olive and did not ride a school bus. This situation and my reluctance to have close relationships prevented our being truly good friends. However, we were the only students from our school inducted into the National Honor Society (NHA) during our junior year. When we graduated in the spring of 1955, Anne was valedictorian of our class and I was salutatorian. Mary was third in the class academically.

Developing close friendships and feeling sincerely welcomed as part of any social group were two things missing in my high school experience. Everyone was friendly toward me, so maybe it was just my own thoughts that made me imagine I wasn't accepted by others. However, I had a big goal to achieve in life; therefore, my insecurity did not deter my participation in school activities: Namely, the NHA (New Homemakers of America), Student Council, Student Patrol, Dramatics, and the National Honor Society (NHS). Surprisingly, the student body elected me to some of the positions I held. Most significant among these was the editor of the weekly school newspaper, The Carver Tips. I was surprised to receive five medals awarded by the faculty during my four years at Carver. They included two for citizenship, two for journalism, and one for home economics. During our senior year, the class elected me Editor-in-Chief of the yearbook staff, The Tiger '55. Being suspicious of any recognition given to me, I thought the class' selection of me was because they knew I was a hard worker and no one else wanted to undertake the responsibilities involved in this project. However, it turned out to be a coup for me. I was able to demonstrate many skills, gain support of the staff, and together, we produced an excellent yearbook.

My accomplishments in high school should have made me begin to feel accepted and valued as a person. However, these recognitions were being given to me by other Blacks. While I appreciated and was happy about the attention I was receiving, it wasn't from an inclusive sampling of society—whites were, of course, not included. They were the people who could really give me validation. Or so I thought. I had more work to do to reach my goal of being valued in our dual society.

The concern that stayed with me all through High School was how we would pay for my going to college. Mother hardly had enough income to keep food on the table—as the saying goes. There were still five of us at home. The father, who was so proud of me and treated me so lovingly when we met while I was in elementary school, seemed to have forgotten about me. I never heard from him. He had not helped my brother Jim go to college although he had *always* known my brother as his son. So, I knew I could not count on *him* for any assistance!

One spring day in 1954, the school Guidance Counselor, Mr. McArthur, asked me to stop by his office that afternoon. He was also my American History teacher. I immediately thought he had found some problem with an essay I had turned in a few days earlier.

Mr. McArthur was easily recognized. He stood out from others because of his strange coloring: His hair, which he wore very short, and his skin were the same color—a true dull orange. Some of the students called him "the orange man" when he wasn't present. I thought this was rude and disrespectful. However, I personally wondered if he had some kind of health problem that caused his skin and hair to be the color they were. His general appearance gave no indication of illness. In fact, he was always the picture of health, very neatly dressed and well-groomed. He never smiled but was kind and easy for students to approach. His wife also taught at Carver.

His office door was closed when I arrived. I knocked on the wooden frame, which had an opaque glass in the upper half. He could not see me but probably guessed who it was.

"Come in, Anece," he said. He was seated behind a large brown desk with a folder open in front of him. "Have a seat." He gestured to the chair next to his desk. I sat down. He got right to the point. "I want to talk with you about college since you hope to graduate in a year." I smiled at his use of the word *hope*. "I assume you plan to go . . ."

I interrupted him. "I certainly do, Mr. McArthur, if I can get money for it." (The year was 1958 and tuition wasn't a fraction of the cost it would become, but the economy was not comparable to what it would be in the future either.)

"We may be able to help you with finances. I have received some information about a student loan program that is made available to students who meet certain criteria."

I listened, hardly breathing because I was afraid I might miss some of his words. He continued, "I know you're familiar with Nehi Orange soda."

I nodded in agreement.

"Well, funding for this program was made possible by the president and founder of the company that makes it. He was a Georgian named Claud A. Hatcher. He left provisions in his will for this trust fund to be set up in his name and in memory of a deceased friend and associate, DeWitt C. Pickett. So, the fund is called the Pickett and Hatcher Educational Fund. It's governed by a board."

"Mr. Hatcher was a white man?" I asked. "Yes," Mr. McArthur replied.

"Do you think they accept applications from Negro Students?"

"The application and instructions say nothing about race being a qualification." Mr. McArthur leaned over his desk, clasped his hands on top of it, and looked me straight in the eyes. "The Board of Directors for the Fund wants applicants who, among other things, have good academic standing in high school, plan to earn a bachelor's degree in a four-year college or university, who have no other means of going to college, and know adults with good credit who are willing to co-sign for the loan."

I met all those qualifications. It began to sink into my brain what this meant. I *could* possibly go to college! I felt like clapping exuberantly, like a small child getting her favorite ice cream on a hot day. It was hard to restrain myself and remain seated.

Mr. McArthur continued, now describing the application process: What a recipient could expect to receive, the small amount of interest on the loan, and his confidence that once out of college, I would repay it in a timely manner.

When he concluded, he asked, "Think you'd like to try applying for this loan?"

"Yes, Sir!"

In my joy, I spoke quickly and probably too loudly. I was anxious to get home and share my good news. *I'm going to college, I'm going to college,* ***I'm going to college!*** I intoned in my mind. We made an arrangement for additional counseling sessions for me to receive help if I needed it during the application process and in making plans for college. When our session ended, I left his office feeling as if I were floating on air. I was so, so happy! All the way home on the school bus, my brothers bugged me to tell them why I was so cheerful. I tried to pacify them by admitting I had a big secret. The bus route had changed by then. When the bus stopped in front of our house, the three of us rushed off and bolted up the steps, slamming the door as we entered the house. Mother and Aunt Clara were in the front bedroom where they had watched us through the window.

Mother said, "What in the world is all the racket about?"

George and John responded in unison: "Anece has a secret and she won't tell us what it is." Mother and Aunt Clara looked at me with questioning expressions.

I said most blithely with a big grin, "I just learned today that there may be money for me to go to college!"

"Where, how, what?" Mother stammered as she tried to form a question. I gave them a full account of my meeting with Mr. McArthur. They were as overjoyed as I.

Each took turns in hugging and kissing me. Then they spoke over each other as they expressed their opinions and asked questions. "That's wonderful news! Where do you think you'll go to college? When will you know that you've gotten the loan?"

The words were being fired at me like BB shots. I had to laugh. "Thank the Lord," Mother said as she kissed my forehead again. Aunt Clara and the boys applauded after I answered their questions.

The two women agreed with my decision to apply for the loan but warned me "not to count chickens before they hatched." They were afraid I would "get my hopes up" they said and then have something go wrong.

Each night before retiring, it was customary for me to kneel beside the bed, thank God for the day's blessings, and ask for His continuing care. That night, before my mother and brothers who shared the room decided to go to bed, I went into the dark, quiet bedroom, knelt beside the bed, and said my nightly prayer. I felt tears roll down my cheeks as I expressed gratitude to the Lord for providing a way for me to go to college. Despite my mother's and aunt's cautions, I believed everything would work out and my dream would be fulfilled.

The application process didn't go as smoothly as I had hoped. The main problem was finding a third man to cosign for the loan. It had to be a male. The signature of a woman was not acceptable at that time. My brother Jim and one of his friends gladly agreed to sign. In an attempt to find a third person, I approached two different men in Simmons Town, each was married to one of my distant cousins. They had the largest farms in our community and seemed fairly well off. Not surprisingly, each one gave me weak excuses for not endorsing my loan. After much thinking on the matter, I decided to contact a teacher from my elementary school, Mr. Began. He had taught me in sixth grade and had continued to show interest in my academic achievements. He was a young, single man—probably in his early thirties—who lived with and spoke lovingly of his mother. I thought he was in a good position financially to assist me. When I asked, he agreed without hesitation to cosign the loan.

There were no delays after that. I was approved for the educational loan. At graduation, I received three scholarships: One from the local Chapter of the AKA, Alpha Kappa Alpha Sorority, a national sorority of Black women; the second from the Eastern Star organization, and the third from the school to which I had been accepted, Bennett College. I was so happy during this sunny period of my life that I never imagined dark times loomed and would begin about two years into my future.

Chapter 9

The summer following graduation from high school, I went to Atlantic City to work as a "mother's helper" for a Jewish Family. However, I thought, a maid by any other name is still just a maid. The family consisted of three generations: The two grandparents, Mr. and Mrs. Baumgartner, two married daughters, Hanna Cohen and Judith Kruger, and their families. The older sister, Hanna, was married to a lawyer like his father-in-law. They had two sons, Nicholas, and Jacob, ages nine and six respectively. The Baumgartner's younger daughter was married to a doctor, and they had one little girl, age four. Her name was Carol. The three families lived separately in their own homes in Philadelphia during fall, winter, and spring but shared a large three-story house near the boardwalk in Ventnor City during the summer months. Ventnor was what I considered a suburb of Atlantic City, New Jersey. The beach was not so crowded there.

My cousin, a teacher, who was also my godmother, had worked for the Baumgartner family as a teenager and recommended me to them. They resided in one of the more affluent neighborhoods. I was the only hired help in their beach home. My primary responsibility was caring for the three children. However, I also did light housework, helped serve meals, washed the dishes, cleaned up after each meal, and did some ironing. I had Thursday afternoons off and went to a movie or to visit my godmother at that time. She introduced me to some of the local black girls of my age, but I did not enjoy socializing with them. They seemed much more sophisticated than I. Once again, I found myself outside the group. As sensitive as I was about my status—being black and poor—it seems that I would have resented working as a maid for the Jewish family. But I wasn't resentful for several reasons: First, I was familiar with the derogatory way this group of people was treated in my hometown and other locations in the south. Descendants of other white Europeans called them insulting names and told disgusting jokes about them just as they did about Negroes. Although this family was much better off financially and socially than we Blacks, I felt our lack of social acceptance made us somewhat synonymous in the white world.

All the family members were kind to me. I can recall only once when one said something that I considered a putdown. I was helping in the kitchen on a Friday evening while Mrs. Baumgartner and her older daughter were preparing the Sabbath meal. Mrs. Cohen stared at me for a few seconds while I dipped matzo balls soup into bowls. Finally, she said, "You are such a pretty color." Before I could say thank you, she added, "I'd like to have my dining room painted your color." I clamped down my teeth, didn't say a word, and continued with my work.

I learned from the Jewish family how to use more appropriate expressions and many other refinements. For example, one evening, Mrs. Cohen's younger son, Jacob, was fretting and stomping his feet in anger because his mother wouldn't let him have his way. He wanted to stay out longer to play. I watched this struggle between mother and son and said, "Boy, he's really raising sand."

Mrs. Cohen gave me a puzzled look and said, "He's what?" I realized I had used a southern (maybe southern black) expression she didn't understand. I quickly responded, "He's really acting up."

The summer ambled along, each day seeming longer than the previous one. However, it wasn't an intolerable situation—far from it. In fact, I returned to Atlantic City and worked for the Baumgartners, Cohens, and Krugers during the summers following my freshman, sophomore, and junior years in college. They began to seem like a second family to me.

It was good to be home again at the end of that first summer. Late August was a happy but anxious time for me. I was to leave for college in about two weeks. Since I was the first member of our family to attend college, there was no one to advise me about what to expect or how to prepare. Common sense told me to get clothes ready for fluctuations in the weather. I inspected, mended, washed, or had clothes cleaned to take with me. Mother and I made a trip to Goldsboro to shop for some underwear and toiletries. Finally, I packed everything in a shabby old suitcase and the new footlocker my godmother had bought for me before I left New Jersey.

Mother and I planned to take the greyhound bus from Dudley to Greensboro and wondered how we would manage my luggage. We discussed asking a neighbor to take us up to the Smith Brother's store to catch the bus. This way, all my stuff would be loaded there and we wouldn't have to worry about it again until we arrived in Greensboro. Once there, we would take a taxi to the Bennett College Campus–at my expense, of course. I could see the money I had saved during the summer finding its way into other hands.

Nonetheless, I was excited about seeing the Bennett College campus for the first time. I had read the registration packet sent to me numerous times. I had also studied other sources and, therefore, knew a little of the college's history: The land on which it sits was purchased by a group of emancipated slaves in approximately 1873. The school was coed in the early years and converted to a college for young black women in 1926. By 1954, when I enrolled there, Bennett had the reputation of providing excellent education and an environment in which young ladies could reach their fullest potential. That was for me!

One of my high school classmates, Jean, was going to Bennett also. She lived in Mt. Olive, but we knew each other well through school activities. My mother had met her parents and conversed with them at school plays, etc. Her parents invited Mother and me to ride with Jean and her father to Greensboro. They reasoned that doing so would allow each of us girls to have one parent with us. Mother accepted the offer with great appreciation.

Jean and her father, Mr. Morris, arrived at our house at seven o'clock that Wednesday morning. The distance from Dudley to Greensboro was about one hundred and fifty miles, a two-and-a-half to three-hour drive. It was a beautiful day for the trip. The sky was cloudless, an uninterrupted light blue and the sun made everything seem especially bright, although the autumn breezes were a little chilly. Mr. Morris struggled to get my bags in the car truck with Jean's. It was a large car but the trunk lid had to be tied down. Some of the smaller things, like makeup bags, books, and other sundry items were put on the floor of the back seat.

Jean and my joy over this trip showed in our wide smiles and cheerful greetings as Mother and I got into the car. She sat in front and I crawled over our stuff on the floor onto the back seat next to Jean. I was surprised to see that Jean was dressed very casually for the trip. She wore a red, white, and green plaid, pleated skirt, with a white blouse and a red, V-neck, long-sleeved, pull-over sweater. Brown oxfords and white shocks completed her simple outfit. I, on the other hand, had dressed to impress. I wanted the Bennett College community to think that my family was economically well off—not wealthy—but also not as poor as we were. So, I wore my Sunday best: a lightweight, soft gray suit which had a small colorful ornament sown on the jacket's upper left pocket, small rhinestone earrings, stockings, and low-heel black pumps. Bad choice!

When we arrived on campus, I found all the students were dressed casually. Dorm counselors helped freshmen find locations and chatted about their experiences on campus. One who was accompanying us leaned close to my ear at one point and whispered, "It's inappropriate to wear rhinestones before six P.M." I thanked her for warning me and felt so embarrassed that I probably would have turned red if I could've. There were some advantages to being brown-skinned after all.

The college campus was more beautiful than I had anticipated. Redbrick buildings, including several dormitories, the science hall, the administration building, and the chapel surrounded a large grassy quadrangle in the middle of the campus. At the quadrangle's center, a tall flagpole hoisted an American flag that waved leisurely in the gentle breeze. A concrete platform encircled the pole forming a seating space. At the front end of the campus, across from, and directly in line with the chapel, was a black, ornate, double gate. Our student guide told us that it was opened only once a year for the graduation processional.

I thought, in four years, my classmates and I will walk through that gate wearing academic attire. My family, especially Mother, will be so proud of me. She had made so many sacrifices for her children. I planned to get my degree, find a good job, and invite her to live comfortably with me for the rest of her life. I looked over at her and smiled. Perhaps, she was having similar thoughts. She was looking at me and smiled back.

Later, Mr. Morris, Mother, Jean, and I struggled to remove our heavy luggage from the car which was in the driveway in front of Jones Hall. We then went up the wide steps into the building and to our rooms. Jones Hall, a two-story, brick building that looked older and appeared larger to me than the others, was the freshman dorm.

We checked in and were directed to our rooms. Mine was on the first floor, just around the corner from the main hallway and the dorm Mother; Ms. Johnson's, office. After dropping my bags in front of my door, Jean and her father took her belongings up to the second floor and her room.

I opened my room door and found a long, rectangular room shadowed in a ghostly gray. I stepped aside so Mother could see. The shade covering the window at the other end of the room was completely closed and the light was off. I heard a faint moan coming from the single bed to our right. In the dimness, I watched a blanket-covered lump turn toward us and grow longer as a body stretched out full length. A girl sat up on the bed and looked at us.

"Oh!" she said in surprise.

"I'm sorry we woke you," I said.

She stood and switched on the overhead light which flooded the room like a bright noonday sun. "That's okay," she said with a smile. "I guess we're roommates." She continued, "My name is Isabel."

I introduced Mother and me.

Isabel explained, "My Dad brought me early and left because he had to get back. I was tired and decided to take a nap. 'Guess I slept longer than I should've. It's time for me to start unpacking. Welcome, roommate," she said while grasping my hand and then shaking Mother's. She glanced at the bed behind her. "I plopped down on this bed when I came in, but if you prefer it to the one over there, I don't mind switching."

I smiled and responded, "That's okay. I'll be fine on that one." I liked her!

I looked around the room and observed a desk and ladder back chair in front of the window. An armchair was on each side of the desk. A bookcase occupied one of the sidewalls and a dresser with a mirror was on the other.

There was a curtain-draped closet at the head of each bed. The room didn't look very inviting—we would have the fun of decorating it.

After Isabel stood, I could see she was plump, although not fat. She had very light skin with a few freckles around her nose. Her reddish-brown hair was short and curly, but I could tell it had been styled using a hot comb and curling iron.

The three of us chatted for a while. She told us she was from a small town north of Greensboro. Her father was a farmer and that was the reason he left early—to do some chores at home and to check on her younger brother and two sisters. All three were in their teens, but the father didn't expect them to finish their work if he was gone too long. She didn't mention her mother, who I learned later was hospitalized.

There was a knock at the door. I opened it to find Jean and her dad. He was ready to drive back home. Jean and I walked with him and Mother to the car, gave them big hugs, and watched them drive away. I saw Mother continue to wave at us until the car turned the corner and was out of sight. I felt sad seeing her leave.

That evening, the dorm mother, Miss Johnson, six upper-class dorm counselors, and the freshman residents crowded into the parlor for our first meeting. The group was too large for everyone to be seated in the room. Some students squeezed together on the sofa and other various parlor chairs. The rest, including me, sat on the carpeted floor with our legs crossed in front of us.

Following my usual habit when part of a new gathering, I scrutinized the group. We were all Negro women—the word *black* was not used yet in referring to members of our race. In fact, in some places, describing someone as being black was considered an insult. Anyway, the group present that evening consisted of people who were gradations of color— from what could have passed for white to dark, rich chocolate brown. Most had hair that looked like it had been straightened and styled, while a few had naturally straight or curly hair.

At the beginning of our meeting, the staff gave welcoming messages and asked us to introduce ourselves. Most of my dorm mates looked affable, but a few seemed sad and bored. I felt anxious over all the newness experienced that day and evening. I wanted the meeting to end almost before it began. Then things became a little more interesting because after introductions, our leaders began to give us the general rules of Bennett. The discussion included the following:

• First and most important, we would always conduct ourselves like ladies. This included not being loud and boisterous. We were to treat each other with kindness and respect. Sisterhood was a big thing at Bennett. Every freshman would be assigned to an upperclassman—a Junior—who would serve as her big sister for guidance and comradery.

• We were told to wear girdles and to wear hats and gloves to Sunday services, both on and off-campus. We were also to wear hats when going downtown.

• We were required to attend chapel services on campus every Sunday and Wednesday morning. Demerits would be given for missing these services and we were allowed to have only a certain number of absences each semester. Checkers, sitting in the balcony with seating charts of attendees in the pews below, made notations of those who were absent, then turned the report into the Registrar's office. While I didn't know at the time, this was a job with which I would become very familiar during my junior and senior years.

• Freshmen were to go off-campus in groups of two or more. Of course, we were to sign out of the dorm when going to places off-campus during the day and to *any* place at night, on or off-campus, then to sign in upon returning to the dorm.

- All students, including upper-classmen, would observe a one-hour break following lunch. We were expected to be in our rooms resting during that time. In the evening following dinner, we would observe quiet hours for studying.
- Lyceum programs, featuring notable speakers, concerts, or other entertainment, would be held in the chapel on some evenings. While these were not mandatory, we were encouraged to attend.
- All students would rotate in and out of "beauty work" assignments for the purpose of cleaning the dormitory common areas. We were expected to keep our rooms clean and tidy—there would be daily room inspections by the dorm counselors. Once a year on parents' weekend, we would have an open house and display our creativity in decorating our rooms.
- Three meals a day were served in the dining hall. The costs of meals were part of our tuition and fees, so everyone ate there most of the time. Students were assigned periods of time to assist the kitchen staff in serving meals and cleaning up. This was equitable because every student, including upper-classmen, had dining hall duty at various times.
- There were rules concerning dating and other social behavior. *I attended Bennett from 1955-1959. The rules listed above could have changed since then.*

Bennett College was and is still a Methodist Institution. I had no problems with the expectations and responsibilities the staff had explained to us. I realized the guidelines were founded upon the doctrines of that denomination and with the objective of molding us into intelligent, strong women who would respect the work ethic.

Classes began the following Monday. During the interim, I registered and declared Home Economics, with an emphasis on foods and nutrition, as my major. I didn't have to decide on a major that early, but I knew what I wanted to do, so I thought why wait? Home Economics was the high school course in which I had received all 'A's. Emphasis on foods and nutrition would start me on a career as a nutritionist. After getting my bachelor's degree, and while working on additional requirements for that profession, I planned to teach in a junior or senior high school.

The freshman year proceeded very well for me. My tuition and fees were paid promptly by scholarships and the Pickett and Hatchett Educational Fund. After buying books and other school supplies, I had some funds left for small necessities and to travel home. Isabel, my roommate, became my best friend. She was a pre-med major. We were compatible in several ways. Most importantly, we shared a serious attitude about studying and wanting to make good grades. She would continue to be one of my best friends after finishing college and going our separate ways. I saw my "homey," Jean, often, although I wasn't in her social group—dorm mates who played pinochle and watched soap operas together during much of their free time.

Classes during my first semester consisted of core courses in language, arts, and the sciences, as well as first-year foods and a beginners' clothing class. College was everything I had hoped it would be—enlightening, challenging, and fun. I began to lose some of the focus on what I considered my physical deficiencies. I liked all my classes and the professors. However, Dr. Bullard, my clothing and design instructor, was the person who became my most staunch supporter. She became my mentor and advisor during my senior year when I decided to do a very special project in the design class. She treated me as she would have her own daughter. She and her husband never had children.

I went home for Christmas break as excited as a young child who sees everything she wants under the tree on Christmas morning. Mother had a neighbor pick me up at the bus stop in Dudley. I stepped off the Greyhound and saw the familiar buildings that I had left four months earlier. Except the Smith Brothers' store, the corn mill and other structures were dressed in gray under an overcast sky, much different from the sunny day of our departure.

But once in our house, greeted warmly by my mother and brothers at the front door, the cloudiness outside didn't matter. There were joy and sunshine in our hearts from seeing each other. I went over and kissed Aunt Clara who was, as usual, sitting in her rocker in her bedroom. The pot-belly stove next to her was radiating warmth that day. As I greeted her, the others followed me into her room where they began to ask me about college. It was astounding how my family was living the dream of higher education through me.

My only concern during Christmas break was my mother's health. She was very pale and seemed weaker than I had ever known her to be. Several times during the holidays, I asked, "Are you sure you're alright, Mother?"

She would always respond, "Yeah, I'm okay." I'd continue, "Have you been to a doctor?"

"No," she'd say. "I don't think I need to—I'm still able to get around—maybe a little slower than usual and with shortness of breath sometimes, but these things are due to getting older." She was only 43.

One time during the holidays, she said to me, "If anything happens to me, I want you to take care of my boys." George was nine and John was seven.

I looked at her, feeling furrows on my forehead as my eyebrows shot upward. I said, "Of course, I will!" I was perplexed by her request but decided not to question why she had asked me that just out of the blue, without any provocation. A few days later, I returned to Bennett. I tried not to worry about Mother's health, but she remained in my thoughts. I hoped she would let me know if she needed me to return home and help the family.

Much to my surprise, I felt good about being back at college. I was not as uncomfortable in the group on campus as I was among the citizens in my hometown. Of course, not everything was perfect for me at college. I still paid a price for not being outgoing or as worldly-wise as most of the other girls. I hadn't been to many movies. We didn't have a television at home, so films and T.V. programs weren't very familiar to me. I was also unable to join in when other topics of interest to them were being discussed. However, my personal values were changing. My obsessive desire to be light-skinned, have "good" hair, and my feeling that I had to be liked by whites to prove my worth were diminishing. I attributed this change to not being confronted each day with the erroneous belief that the more nearly a Negro person looked and acted white, the more superior she or he was. That had been the prevailing ideology in Dudley.

I felt a degree of relief in knowing that I didn't need those physical features to be acceptable or accomplished in the general society. I witnessed evidence of this in the various speakers, such as Dr. Benjamin Mays, a black opera star Leontyne Price, and many other Black performers in various arts and other professions. I also noticed the cordiality and respect shown to black students, faculty, and administrators by whites when they visited the campus. The environment at Bennett was helping my self-confidence to develop slowly like a balloon receiving a little air at a time. But it would require more years and other experiences to fully eradicate the effects of the ugly attitudes toward race and color differences I had witnessed during my formative years. The low opinion lighter skin Negroes had toward the darker ones was especially hard to reconcile and remove from my thoughts.

My courses during the new semester were continuous, the second half of those I had taken during the previous term. Again, I studied hard. Spring came early that year. The trees on campus changed to their green attire. Flowers of various kinds and colors sprouted, giving strips along the front of buildings a multicolored display of beauty. Before long, we started planning for summer break. The students in my dormitory were very excited. We had gotten through our first year successfully. *We were sophomores!* My studiousness paid off. I had a B+ average.

The next year, I would surely earn an A grade point average.

Chapter 10

I went home for a brief break when school was out. The plan was for me to spend a week or so with the family before leaving for Atlantic City and my summer job with the Baumgartners. However, I considered not following through with those plans and staying home. I found my mother looking more ill than she had during the Christmas break. She had never been large, but she had reached the point of looking emaciated. She had circles under her eyes. She was often tired and moved more slowly than usual. Yet, she still had not gone to a doctor. I knew the major reason for her delay was the lack of money. It saddened me to see her sick, in need of money, trying to care for an invalid sister and two active boys. I suggested my staying home to help her and doing local work when it was available. She wouldn't even listen to that plan. "No! *You* have to finish college!" she said very forcefully.

I left rather reluctantly for Atlantic City. During the train ride to Philadelphia, my thoughts lingered on the family back home. Mrs. Baumgartner had given me her home address and told me to take a taxi, which I did. She paid the driver when I arrived, then gave me a welcoming hug. We spent a few days at her house in the city, preparing for summer at the beach. Within four days, the three women, three children, and I were getting settled in their summer home. Their husbands worked in the Philadelphia offices during the week and joined their families on Friday evenings in time for the Sabbath meal. They remained in Atlantic City for the remainder of the weekend.

My bedroom and small bath were in the attic, the same location I had had during the previous summer. I settled back into my work routine but continued to be concerned about things at home.

Mother and I corresponded by letter weekly–she didn't have a telephone. During the middle of July, she wrote: "Clara's behavior has become intolerable.

The other day, she was in a rage over something and threw a dish, just missing my head. Another time when I had come in from grocery shopping, she quickly bumped into the kitchen on her single crutch, picked up the few meat I had bought, and threw them out to the dog. I went to my room and cried. I had scrimped and saved the little money I had for shopping that day and I don't know how I will replace it. I hate to leave her alone, but the boys and I have to get away from Clara!" The next week, I received another letter from Mother informing me that she, George, and John had moved to Wilson, North Carolina and were staying with a spinster cousin named Lucinda. My mother's side of the family had so many levels of cousins, i.e. first, second, third, and so forth, that I didn't know where or how this one fitted in. The relatives in Simmons Town had promised to check on Aunt Clara every day and help her get whatever she needed. This arrangement was to be temporary until mother's health improved. She had finally gone to a doctor, and he said she had a heart problem. He gave her some pills and instructed her to "slow down."

I still thought it would be best for me to devote my time and income to help the family. On the other hand, my mother's main objective was for me to finish college. I couldn't do both. Lessons from Sunday school and Church during my youth reminded me to turn to God for help. I prayed and concluded that the deciding factor would be for *Mother* to *ask* me to help her. I doubted she would ever do that. But this would be a definitive answer to my prayer.

Worrying and trying to decide what to do began to have a visible effect on me. I became more somber and less pleasant than I had been the previous summer. With a frown on her face, Mrs. Baumgartner said one day, "You're a different person than you were last year." I didn't have an answer for her. I didn't tell her about our family problems.

A few days later, I received a letter from Mother describing how she and the boys were struggling to meet their daily needs. Cousin Lucinda was not charging her as much rent as a regular apartment owner. Still, she did have to pay a little for their room and for food. Plus, she was concerned about buying school clothes for George and John. In her last sentence, she wrote, "Please consider not returning to college this fall and try to get a job up there for the winter to help me financially, just until I'm better."

I couldn't believe the request she was making! It made me sad to know that I wouldn't return to college in the fall, but at the same time, I was amazed and thankful that my prayer had been answered so directly and clearly. My dilemma had been resolved. I would be happy to assist Mother and my brothers. I could return to school another year when things were better. Another letter arrived from Mother two days later asking me to disregard her last one. She said she was sorry she had written it. She wanted me to return to school in the fall. She said for me not to worry about them—they would be okay.

I responded that I wanted to help, not to feel bad about my missing some time from school, that I would return when things were better. "Please, please do as your doctor says. I look forward to you fully recovering soon. Give my brothers a kiss for me."

I contacted my oldest brother, Jim, in New York. I told him that I needed a job and asked if he and his wife, Josephine, could help me find one up there. He was disappointed to learn that I wasn't returning to school but was glad to know I planned to help Mother. His own family responsibilities would not allow him to do very much for us, although he had helped the family financially when he was first employed.

Josephine, Jim's wife, had a friend who worked at the New York telephone company and thought I could get a job there as an operator. Of course, I would have to make an application and be interviewed. I asked Mrs. Baumgartner for three days off so that I could go to see my brother and his family. She thought the break would be good for me and graciously agreed to my taking time for the brief trip to Brooklyn.

Jimmy met me at the train station and took me to his house. He and Josephine had two young daughters. It was good seeing his family and with the excitement, some of my worries seemed to melt away.

Josephine and her friend had scheduled an appointment for me on the next day at the phone company. Around eight o'clock that morning, I dressed in a light blue, sleeveless dress with a short sleeve bolero, stockings, black patent leather, low-heeled pumps, and a matching small purse. When I left the house, I carried a little spiral notebook in which I had written instructions Josephine had given me concerning subway connections. With this, I found the right subways to take me to the stop for the New York telephone company and its Plaza 4 Office. The whole experience was new, exciting, and at the same time so intimidating that I wanted to *run* back to little, rural Dudley, the territory I knew best.

However, everything went well. I was nervous during the interview but managed to keep myself from shaking visibly. The older woman who interviewed me, Mrs. Gardner, was very pleasant. In addition to asking questions about me personally, she explained the duties of a telephone operator.

She said, "The exchange—Plaza 4—is where long-distance calls from some of New York's largest and most elite hotels and businesses originate. Therefore, our girls have to be very competent. All our new operators go through a training period and must pass it to be hired permanently. Of course, you will be paid during training." She smiled and invited me to accompany her on a brief tour of the training station and the rest of the area. Before I left, she told me that within seven to ten days, I would receive notification as to whether or not I was accepted. I thanked her and left feeling very hopeful. The next day, I boarded a train back to Atlantic City and my summer job.

The day after getting back to the Baumgartner's, I wrote Mother to tell her about the possibility of me getting a job in Brooklyn. She was somewhat relieved about the help she would receive but sad about my having to miss a semester of college. I wrote Bennett College and the educational fund in Georgia to inform both that due to my mother's health and her need for my help, I would not return to college in the fall. However, I told them that I planned to continue my education as soon as possible. Both granted me a leave of absence. Of course, I would have to make small monthly payments to Pickett and Hatcher Educational Fund while I was out of college. This was stipulated in the contract, but no amount or percentage was mentioned. In the fall, I sent them six hundred dollars from my summer employment. To my surprise, the Fund treasurer accepted that amount and applied it as my payment for the entire first semester.

Within a week, I received a letter of acceptance from the phone company. I had given my brother's Brooklyn address when I applied for the job, so he forwarded the letter to me. The family I was working for still didn't know about my plans for the fall. They were almost as pleased as my family about my attending college. I was concerned that if they knew about my plans to take some time off, they would try to talk me out of them and perhaps even offer to help my family in some way. We were a very private and proud family; therefore, I thought it best to keep our problems and my plans to myself. I was scheduled to begin working for the phone company the first week in September. I was so happy and excited that I buzzed through the remainder of the summer at the Baumgartners like a bumblebee during the first warm days of spring.

In the last week of August, I left New Jersey to go to Brooklyn. The Baumgartners thought I was going to visit my brother before returning to Bennett. I was sorry to mislead them and I also felt tinges of anxiety over starting a new job in New York, a big city I hardly knew.

Chapter 11

Jimmy and his family welcomed me when I returned to Brooklyn. They lived in an apartment. I slept in a narrow room at the end of the hall. I would not have to pay them rent or for food. While it wasn't a formal agreement, I decided to help with chores in the apartment and babysit for them whenever possible.

I was excited about starting a new job and having to find my way around New York using public transportation—usually subways. My sister-in-law, Josephine, who was very familiar with the transportation system, gave me explicit instructions each time I was going someplace in the city that was new to me. I kept all her notes in my small spiral notebook and used them frequently. One day, I became confused and went up to the token window to ask the man for clarification. He was a heavy-set black man who, when he saw me and my notebook, teased in a low, solemn voice, "The bigger the notebook, the less they know." My notebook was small. I looked at him somewhat puzzled but proceeded to ask my question. He showed a big grin and gave me the directions I needed. I thanked him.

The first weeks on the job were spent in training as the interviewer had promised. Our supervisor, Mrs. Whitehead, was the grandmotherly type—a white woman, not fat but thick around the waist. She had gray hair styled in short curls. Her voice was soft and stern yet friendly. The only other person training with me was Irene, an Irish girl, who had shoulder-length, reddish-orange hair and freckles. She was about my age and size. She was amicable and talked very fast. We became close friends. I noticed there were only a few black women seated at the large boards.

Irene was my first white friend. The difference in our race didn't seem to matter to either of us. We never discussed it. My time and thoughts over the summer months had been so full of other concerns that I had stopped comparing

Seeking Personal Validation

my skin color and hair texture with that of other people. I tried always to be well-groomed and pleasant. I felt accepted in most places I went. And no one, in stores and other public places, told me to go to the back door. However, I persisted in my desire to be acknowledged and respected by members of the general society—whites and blacks. Although it had not been planned with my long-term goal in mind, working as an operator in the New York telephone company was my first step in being an "equal" member of a mostly white group of people. Now all I had to do was prove myself capable of doing the job.

One of the first things Mrs. Whitehead told us in training was, to be good operators, we had to learn to work fast and accurately. Irene and I sat in front of our individual switchboards: a medium-sized board with small, single outlets which had tiny lights immediately above each. A flashing light signaled a call was coming in. There were various colored cords along the bottom of each board, even on our training ones. Irene and I, working separately, learned to quickly plug in a colored cord below the blinking light. This action made the connection. Then we would speak with the switchboard operator through our headphones while making notes of her instructions on where to forward her call and any other information we needed. Each of us plugged another cord into the outgoing location, connecting our party to whomever they were calling. Some of the operators at the large switchboard were so fast in responding to the lights that they had multiple connections with so many lines crisscrossing that their boards looked like works of art. Irene and I had many practice sessions and other lessons to complete in training before we would be ready to work at the large board.

Finally, we came to the last day of training. The next day, we were to be tested on all the procedures. I was so excited and nervous the night before that I hardly slept. Each time I drifted off to sleep, I'd awaken from a dream about getting something wrong on the test. After experiencing a night of twisting and turning in my bed, morning finally arrived. It had snowed during the night. The scene outside my bedroom window was beautiful, but I hardly noticed it. I showered, dressed in warm clothes, and boots. I said a quick goodbye to the family, who responded, "Good luck." Then I rushed out the front door.

I smiled nervously at Irene when we arrived at our desks and said good morning. Her facial expression showed as much apprehension as I felt. Mrs. Whitehead was less austere than usual. Perhaps, she was trying to calm our fears. She told us that the test would only cover what we had studied during training. We sat at our desks and began working on the written part, which consisted mostly of problem-solving—the description of various situations and questions about how we would handle them. Then we were accompanied to the big switchboard. There we sat and handled several incoming calls without assistance from Mrs. Whitehead. But she was watching us as closely as a mother monitoring her young child's first bike ride. She also made notes as we worked. When everything was over, she told us to wait in the lounge while she reviewed our test results.

The lounge was a comfortable room with a soothing light blue color scheme. It was used mainly as a break room where operators could relax during their ten minutes away from their busy, pressure-driven duties. Irene and I plunked down on opposite ends of a light blue and crème-striped sofa. We folded one leg under our body so that we could face each other. During our free time together, we were usually very talkative. But that day, for a while at least, we stared pensively around the room and at each other. Irene was first to break the silence:

"I'm sure we passed that test. *We just had* to! I want to save up for getting my own apartment."

"If one of us passed, I hope both did." I said, "It would be nice to continue working together." Irene's face seemed to brighten as she said, "Whether we passed or not, let's go to a nice restaurant and have dinner before going home. We can at least celebrate completing the training."

I caught her renewed spirit and responded excitedly, "Okay, that's a good idea."

In about an hour and a half, a secretary interrupted our casual chit-chat to announce, "Mrs. Whitehead will see you now." We followed her to our supervisor's office. Two carved back-office chairs were in front of Mrs. Whitehouse's large desk. She opened her hands, palms up, and spread them apart indicating we should sit. We sat down but maintained our rather solemn expressions as we looked expectantly at our supervisor. She shuffled some papers on her desk and seemed to take forever before speaking to us. Finally, she gave a slight smile and said, "Congratulations, young ladies, both of you passed the test successfully." Irene and I sat taller in our seats and put on happy faces while murmuring, "Thank you." We were so elated, proud, and filled with excitement and thankfulness that we found it hard to articulate our thoughts.

Mrs. Whitehouse continued, "There were a few things each of you missed or could have done better, but all in all, you did well. Improvements will come with experience and the floor supervisors will continue to work with you if you have a problem at the big board. Today is Friday, so you will begin regular hours on Monday. This afternoon, I need you to go to the Human Resource Office and take care of the paperwork to finalize your employment. I've enjoyed working with both of you. You were very attentive and eager students. Do you have any questions for me?"

Both of us said "no." Before getting up, I said, "Mrs. Whitehouse, we really appreciate the care and patience you showed while teaching us." Irene added, "Ditto that—thank you very much for everything." The white-haired lady accepted our expressions of gratitude with a dry smile, told us where the HR office was located and promised to see us later in the afternoon.

Irene and I did go to dinner that evening to a much fancier restaurant than we would have without being assured of our job. We had an enjoyable time. We, two young women sitting across from each other at a white cloth-covered table, with the warm glow of a candle reflecting on our faces. Two young women at the dawn of adulthood, discussing our hopes and dreams for the future. Two young women, one white and one black, from different backgrounds and cultures. How divergent would our paths be in the future? At that moment, we didn't think or wonder about differences. We were just glad to have each other's company as we celebrated getting our first real job. That was a goal we had shared.

The night was beautiful when I walked up the steps from the underground subway. Large snowflakes fell from the dark sky and seemed to shimmer as they danced around the bright streetlights. With each step, I kicked up snow on the ground causing it to make a small fan-like design in front of each foot. Two heavily bundled black men who had apparently been complaining about the weather passed me. I overheard one say to the other, "Look at her, she's even playing in it." I chuckled to myself and ran the short distance home.

Jim and his family met me with congratulatory greetings, hugs, and kisses as I entered the apartment. I had called them before Irene and I went to dinner, shared the good news, and explained why I'd be later than usual getting home.

The first six weeks at my new job went very well. I eagerly anticipated sitting at the big board each day. Of course, I encountered a few problems, but when help was needed, I'd put on a signal light and a supervisor would come to my rescue. One day, an operator called in from a hotel exchange. I plugged in and answered in what I thought was a normal, pleasant voice, "Plaza 4, may I help you?" She laughed and said mockingly,

"We're from the south, aren't we, honey?"

With a smile, she couldn't see but I hoped she could hear in my voice, I said, "Yes, we are. How can I help you?"

We resumed business related to the call, she with her New York accent and me with my southern way of speaking. I was very pleased with myself for not being intimidated by her joke and for continuing my job in an unsettling manner. I was becoming surer of myself when interacting with others.

As I worked to perfect my skills, I also spent a lot of time thinking and worrying about Mother and my brothers back home. When I had saved enough money, I went to Macy's and bought some packaging tape before selecting several school outfits for each of the boys. I had a large collection of long pants, matching knitted shirts, two heavy sweaters each, socks, and underwear. I went to a department where new shipments were being unpacked. I asked for one of the larger empty boxes, which a clerk willingly gave to me. I went to the ladies' room, folded the clothes, and put them in the box, sealed, addressed it, and managed to get it to the front entrance. I hailed a taxi and asked him to take me to the nearest post office where I mailed the box. I imagined my mother's joy and relief upon receiving the clothes. She had told me in one letter she was so weak that she feared taking my brothers shopping. Plus, as always, there was the problem of having money for the clothes.

Back at work, everything was still fine. But one day around midmorning, the head supervisor called me to her office. Her name was Mrs. Brooks. She was a tall, medium-built, white woman who wore her auburn hair in a short, very fashionable style. Her oblong face looked exceptionally somber as she invited me in and told me to sit down. I stared at her with anticipation. After I was seated, she said, "I'm very sorry to have to tell you we received a call from your sister-in-law in Brooklyn." Bad news was coming. I looked down as if I were fascinated with the floor and tried to keep from showing the anxiety I was feeling. She continued, "She wanted us to tell you that your mother collapsed [I looked at her and gasped] at home this morning and has been taken to the hospital emergency." I started sobbing. She came around the desk to me and gently caressed my back. "I'm sure this is very painful for you," she said.

I managed to respond, "Mother hasn't been well for some time." Mrs. Brooks sat down in the chair next to mine and gave me some tissues. I said, "I have to go to her!"

"Of course, you do," she replied. "We have procedures in place to accommodate employees in your situation. You may leave work now if you wish. Take the time that you require to help your mother. Once you know approximately when you will be able to return, give us a call. Call also at any time we can be of help. I hope your mother is better when you get home. Will you be going to North Carolina by plane?"

I answered with a barely audible "No, by train." She looked at me, smiled slightly, and stood. I took that to mean our conversation was over. I stood also and we shook hands as I thanked her for her understanding and the time she was allowing me to take off.

Actions proceeded very quickly. After stopping briefly by Irene's station to let her know what was going on, I called my sister-in-law to tell her I was on my way to her apartment. I asked her to check on the train schedule for me. At her place, I packed hastily, then went to the train station and purchased a ticket. By one-o-clock, I was on my way to Wilson, North Carolina, and Cousin Lucinda's house.

As I walked in the front door when I arrived there, I saw my elderly cousin, but before we could greet each other, I looked at the man standing in the center of her living room. I recognized him as the undertaker who conducted my grandmother's funeral. I knew right away why he was there. I let go of my suitcase, dropped to my knees, wailing, "No, no, no!" and started crying uncontrollably.

The two adults helped me up and tried to comfort me as they guided me to a faded green sofa where I sat between them. I leaned on Cousin Lucinda's shoulder, still crying, while they explained how mother had succumbed to death. Cousin Lucinda was visiting Mother when she died, during the time I was on the train traveling to be with her. My cousin said the last thing Mother said before she passed away was, "Get my daughter." The doctor said she died of a coronary thrombosis; in other words, a heart attack. I caught the essence of what my cousin was saying; however, I was so heavy-hearted that her words didn't fully register in my mind. The undertaker said my brother, Jim, contacted him as soon as he received word of Mother's death. Jim asked him to pick up the body and plan on arranging the funeral. Jim also told him that his sister was on her way to Wilson and for them to please take care of her until he arrived. He said he and his wife were driving down later that night. I had stopped crying and was wiping my eyes.

"My brothers, where are my baby brothers!" I asked in a trembling voice as I raised my head from Cousin Lucinda's shoulder.

She patted my arm and said, "Don't worry, sweetheart. They're alright, across the street at Mrs. Camp's house. They understand that your mother is gone and they are very sad. I thought it would be better for them to be over there playing with her children. They'll be back in a little while. I want you to eat something now and afterward, try to get some rest." She went into the kitchen to fix me a snack. The undertaker said he was leaving, but he wanted me and Jim to stop by his funeral home the next day to make arrangements for Mother's funeral. I promised we would.

After I had eaten and was lying down on a bed upstairs, I heard the front door close, some mumbled words, and two pairs of feet running up the steps. In a few seconds, George and John were tumbling onto the double bed with me. They hugged and kissed me as the three of us cried. They stretched out, one on each side of me. We talked between sniffles.

George said, "We miss Mother so much! Are you going to stay with us and take care of us now?" John, the younger one, looked at me with wide eyes, tears still running down his face.

My heart felt like it would burst, but I had to stay as steady as possible for them. "Yes, I am," I replied. "We're going to move back to Dudley to Momma's house and I'm going to care for you, as much like Mother did as possible." I tried to sound as spirited as I could to ease their grief and concerns.

John said, "But, Aunt Clara . . ."

I interrupted him because I knew what he was going to say. "Aunt Clara will probably welcome us because she's doubtlessly tired of being alone. We'll be helpful to her. If she has days when she's hateful, we'll just leave her alone and stay away from her. How do you feel about going back to your old school in Dudley?" I asked.

Both said they didn't care. We talked about Mother and what her last days were like. The gloominess was lifting to some extent. We switched our conversation to the topic of T.V. shows and movies. Then I started describing what New York was like. They began to yawn and before long, both were sound asleep.

I lay between my two young brothers, listening to their soft breathing, and I thought about how my future would be changed. I would have to notify the Plaza 4 office, Bennett College, and the loan fund that I *would not* be returning to work or school. I tried to think of ways I could pay expenses during my new role as a young single "mom." My mother's words resounded in my mind, *Get your college education. I don't want you to be like me!* She didn't plan on dying and she couldn't help the way things had turned out for her and me. I thought of how much I loved her and what she had sacrificed for all her children. I remembered some of the more pleasant times we had shared and while having those happy thoughts, I drifted off to sleep.

Around 3:00 A.M., I was awakened by voices from the first floor. I knew right away that Jim and Josephine had arrived—but who was the second male voice I was hearing? I slid from between my two brothers, who were still asleep. (The three of us were so tired and drained from the shock of the previous day that we had gone to sleep still dressed.) By the time I stood and was putting on my slippers, I heard heavy feet coming upstairs. Jim entered the bedroom first. I ran into his arms and we clung to each other sharing the pathos of the moment. The boys were awake by then, sitting up and rubbing their eyes.

A handsome, tall, dark Negro man stepped around Jim and me. He went straight to the two boys on the bed. I turned around and was surprised to see Mr. Winters hugging his sons. I said, "Mr. Winters, what a surprise to see you!"

He gave a slight smile as he turned, embraced me, and kissed my cheek. "I'm very sorry about your mother's passing," he said. "When Jim called and told me the news, I asked to ride down here with him to get my boys." George and John looked at us wide-eyed. George started, "But Anece is going to . . ."

I interrupted him, "No, George, Mr. Winters is your father and his wanting you to live with him is right—the right thing to do. I love you both dearly. If you didn't have him, I would gladly keep you with me and take care of you the best I could. Although we have Momma's house in Dudley to live in, there is the question of how we could pay for food, clothing, etc."

Jim and Mr. Winters began talking with them gently but persuasively. Finally, George and John understood and accepted what we were telling them. Plus, they became a little excited about going to New York City where their dad lived.

I regretted not fulfilling my mother's request to take care of her boys, but at the time she asked me to do that, she probably didn't consider Mr. Winters at all. He had never been a caring father, why should she expect him to be any different in her absence? I had a suspicion that Jim had something to do with Mr. Winters coming forth to assume his responsibilities.

The four of us joined Josephine downstairs in the living room. Cousin Lucinda was in the adjoining kitchen cooking breakfast. We were aware of the bacon and other smells coming from the kitchen as we sat around in the living room trying to converse. But an air of melancholy filled the room and seemed to freeze our words. We were all sad. Yet, there was a lot of love felt, especially among Mother's four children. We remembered the hard work, gentleness, and love she had put into nurturing and raising us—despite her many hardships.

Later that morning, Jim, Josephine, and I left to go to Dudley and Simmons Town, specifically. It started drizzling rain. The clouds were a purplish blue, hanging low against the background of an angry gray sky. It seemed that nature was mourning with us.

The old home place looked good when we arrived. During my last few years of school, Jim, who was working in New York, helped Mother pay to have the front porch fixed and the house painted. Aunt Clara saw us drive up and was standing in the doorway when we ran a short distance through the rain to the porch. She was very glad to see us. We took turns hugging her. I noticed she was the same, small, woman with a single crutch and curved hip that she had been when I left home to go to New Jersey in early summer. We went into her bedroom and sat down. All the while, Aunt Clara rattled on about how good we all looked.

"What are you doing here in late fall like this? I was hoping to have a visit at Christmas but didn't expect you all this early. Of course, I'm always glad to see you . . ."

Jim interrupted her and said, "I'm afraid we came with bad news." He gave her a few seconds before continuing. Her pale skin seemed to turn gray and she started trembling. I went over to her and put my arm around her shoulders. Jim said in a broken voice, "Mother passed away yesterday morning."

Aunt Clara screamed, "Oh, God, no! Not my only sister! No! No! No!" The three of us started sobbing. She continued, very loudly exclaiming words that echoed feelings of hurt and sorrow. We tried to calm her. She was too deep in her grief to hear us. There was probably lots of guilt mixed in with the grief because it was her hateful behavior that had driven Mother away—away from a home that belong to both of Momma's daughters and her four grandchildren.

Through all the noise, I discerned a knock on the front door and went to answer it. One of Mother and Aunt Clara's first cousins, Georgia, who lived on the corner where the two neighborhood roads met, was at the door. We exchanged greetings. She could hear Aunt Clara crying. "What's going on?" she asked. Before I could reply, she continued by explaining, "I saw the car out front and thought I should see if Clara is okay."

"I was finally able to explain my mother passed away yesterday morning. She was living in Wilson and we've just informed Aunt Clara. She's taking the news very hard."

"Lord have mercy. I'm so sorry about your mother! Let me go in and see

Clara." She rushed into the front bedroom and I followed. Cousin Georgia joined the other two in talking to Aunt Clara and trying to console her. I felt very sad, weary, and tired.

After Cousin Georgia volunteered to stay with Aunt Clara, Jim, Josephine, and I left to keep our appointment with Mr. Barnes, the funeral director. The rain had almost stopped and the sky looked a little brighter as we headed south to Mt. Olive. Mr. Barnes was waiting at the funeral home and invited us into his office shortly after we arrived. After some general discussions, Jim and I decided Mother's funeral would be in three days, on Thursday of that week. That would allow time to notify all relatives and friends. Josephine was silent, mostly leaving the decisions up to her husband, Jim, and me. We agreed Mother's body would be taken to the Congregational Church in Dudley at 12:00 noon on Thursday, where it would repose in state. Those who wished could visit and view the body during the two hours before the funeral service, which was to begin at 2:00 P.M. We told Mr. Barnes that we wanted a simple service, similar to what our grandmother's had been a few years earlier. He understood and said he would talk with Rev. Greene and they would do the necessary planning. Then he took us to the display rooms where we selected a casket, shroud, and a floral spray from the family. We were pleased that our mother would look as nice at her funeral as our grandmother had at hers.

Thursday was sunny and cold. Many relatives, neighbors, and friends had gathered at the church when the family arrived. Some had gone earlier to view the body. As the family entered the church, Mr. Barnes closed the casket. Flower girls placed a variety of wreaths and flowers around it. The service began. There were a few vocal mourners, including Aunt Clara. The rest of the family and others sobbed quietly.

After the service, we formed the procession which followed the casket and flower girls. Aunt Clara was first in line with Jim and the nurse assisting her. She seemed so grief-stricken that I knew she wasn't pretending. George and John walked beside me. We held hands and were second in line. Josephine and Mr. Winters were third. The rest of the attendees followed in twos. We boarded vehicles and took that last journey with Mother to the church cemetery. Her grave had been prepared next to Momma's. Once Reverend Greene said his last words, the casket was lowered into the ground, the grave refilled, and flowers were placed around the new mound of dirt. I stood alone watching the total process while engaging in many sad thoughts. I was saying goodbye to the individual who had been the dearest to me and the most loving throughout my life. I felt like my heart was badly damaged and would never heal or be normal again. Tears streamed down my face as I used my hand to put a kiss over her grave. Then I turned slowly and went to join the rest of the family in the undertaker's limousine.

The next two days were so busy that I felt like I was in a whirlwind. It was Friday, the day after Mother's funeral. Jim, Josephine, Mr. Winters, and the boys were leaving early Saturday to return to New York. George and John still had mixed feelings about me. I tried to reassure them that their father would take good care of them—I didn't say but I knew Mr. Winters was living with what was then called a "common-law wife." I had met her and had confidence that she would care for them.

Then John wanted to know, "But what about you? We want you to be okay, too. Who will take care of you?"

I smiled and responded, "I'll be fine. Of course, I'll miss you both and the family life we had with Mother and Momma. However, the thing Mother wanted most after your being cared for was for me to return to college. That's what I'm going to do at the beginning of the second semester in January. I'll go to New York to see you from time to time and if either of you feels neglected or need help, do let me know. Okay?"

They said "yes" in unison and each gave me a big hug. They seemed consoled and ran away to some other room in Cousin Lucinda's house to play. I thought about our conversation, about Mother, Momma, and me. I felt very sad but managed to hold back the tears. I lifted my head up high and silently prayed that God would be with all of us.

I packed my brothers' clothes that Friday morning and gathered all of Mother's things. Jim and I took hers to Dudley, where we stored them in two old trunks in Momma's house. Once that task was completed, we talked with Aunt Clara for a short while before saying our tearful goodbyes. We loved her and hated leaving her alone again. However, relatives in the neighborhood had monitored her daily after she chased Mother out. Cousin Georgia had promised me that they would provide help and care when needed.

The family members going to New York with Jim left around at 5:00 Saturday morning as planned. I had a round trip train ticket back, plus Jim's car was filled after he and his four passengers boarded it. So, I left Wilson later that morning by train.

Chapter 12

By the middle of December 1956, I had completed all the duties necessary for returning to Bennett College. These included going back to the N.Y. phone company and giving notice that I would resign in three weeks for the purpose of returning to college, writing the Bennett registrar that I wished to reenter in January at the beginning of the second semester, notifying the Pickett and Hatcher Educational Fund that I would return to school in January, and finally writing the Baumgartners to tell them about my Mother's death and to ask them to forgive me for misleading them. I told Mrs. Baumgartner my reasons for not telling them about our family problems at that time. She said they understood and wanted to know if I would be back the following summer. Of course, I would!

I went back to Dudley for Christmas. Aunt Clara and I spent a quiet holiday season alone in our old home. She was very happy to have me there. It was a bittersweet experience for me. I kept remembering past years when all of us were together and the fun times we had, especially at Christmas. Mother had bought our first television the year before being driven from home. Aunt Clara and I never mentioned the trouble they had with each other, but we sure watched a lot of black and white T.V.—thanks to Mother. When the day came for me to leave for college, I was definitely ready to go.

The campus looked good dressed in its winter apparel. It had snowed the night before. I was a sophomore and was therefore assigned to one of the upperclassmen's dorms. I had a roommate I hadn't met before. She was a transferred senior. But she seemed okay. My former roommate, Isabel, was living with a different person in another building. My friend, Jean, from the same high school, was also living in a third building. I saw her sometimes. But we had not been buddies during our freshman year and I didn't expect us to be very close that year. Everything seemed so different from what it had been during my freshman year. I didn't mind. I was never a social butterfly anyway. And I had a much more serious objective in mind.

It didn't take me long to realize I had changed. Differences in the color of people did not matter to me anymore. I had grown beyond the idea that being white was a goal worth wishing for or wanting to achieve—even if I could. I still admired women, both black and white, whose hair could be styled beautifully without using a hot comb. But this admiration was due more to convenience—Afros and long, natural wrinkly curls had not yet come into vogue, and trying to make other hairstyles with kinky hair required more time and work. The goal I had to achieve now was to accept *myself* as a worthwhile human being. I had to learn to *love me*.

I had lost a half year of college by missing the first semester of my second year. I was determined to finish and walk through that gate with my original class on commence day in 1959. I had a lot of courses to complete in the two and half years remaining. Graduating on time with a good GPA (grade point average) was my most immediate objective. Making notable contributions to society after finishing college became my long-term goal. I determined I could do both!

The Bennett College registrar helped me in accessing my academic record to determine the credits I needed and the best order in which I should take them. It was clear that I was going to have to take an overload during one semester and two courses in summer school. Since Bennett didn't have summer classes, I would have to go elsewhere for the courses. I decided on New York University, the Washington Square College of Arts and Sciences. The registrar agreed with my choice. I could save money on room and board while in school by staying with my brother's family. Picket and Hatcher had resumed the loan I'd received from them my first year, but it did not include summer school. I planned on returning to my previous summer job during the first month of vacation. I hoped to earn enough to pay summer tuition. Meanwhile, I took four courses, 12 credits—a normal course load during the spring semester of my sophomore year. That was my first term back at Bennett. I would take the 6 hours at NYU during the summer. The courses there were to be in English Literature and Child Psychology.

Things worked out well for me in finding time to work that summer. Judith, the second of the Baumgartner daughters, was pregnant with her second child. The baby was due in July, the month in which I was to start classes.

The Krugers were not going to Atlantic City that summer and stayed in their Philadelphia home. The three-family group decided I would assist Mrs. Kruger with housework and care of their little girl until leaving for summer classes. So, I joined them in Philadelphia. A nurse was hired to help after the birth. A girl, who worked for the Baumgartners two days each week when they were at their regular home, was hired to replace me in Atlantic City.

I went to N.Y. the first week in July and started my summer classes right away. Once again, I braved the subway system each day. This time, I did so in hot sweltering weather rather than in snow and ice. I thought of Irene and the other people in the Plaza 4 office, but between going to school, studying, and helping my sister-in-law and her family, there was little time for visiting.

The NYU campus was bigger and, in my estimation, wasn't as beautiful a setting as I had become used to at Bennett. But the classrooms were comfortable and there were only a few students in each—approximately fifteen. I enjoyed the classes and observing the different demeanor each professor showed his students. The one who taught literature was the younger of the two. He spoke with a slight British accent, was very business-like, and seemed to dare his students to even breathe loudly when he was lecturing, much less ask a question. The other professor was a bit older. He had a mid-western air about him and seemed very approachable. I passed both courses but did better in Child Psychology than Literature. I talked with George and John frequently by phone and saw them several times while in New York. They were doing well. Classes ended the third week in August and I left Brooklyn within a couple of days. On my way to Dudley, I stopped by the Krugers in Philadelphia to see the new baby. Aunt Clara was, as usual, glad to see me when I arrived home. I had time to spend a few days with her before leaving for Bennett.

Chapter 13

After only one and a half years, plus the two summer classes, I was classified as a junior. However, that was the year the registrar and I had decided I should take an overload. During the first semester, I took eight classes including chemistry, two clothing classes, principals of nutrition, two home management classes—one included living in the home management house where two other girls and I alternated in doing home management activities; in other words, running a household. The two remaining classes were child development and physical education. It was a struggle but at the end of the semester, I had passed all the classes with fairly good grades. In the second semester, my course load was nearly normal with six courses. I became more socially active during my junior year. Jean, my friend from high school, and I had elected to be roommates. Isabel, with whom I had lived our freshman year, had a young sister who was an upperclassman then, so they roomed together. These were my best friends.

For six weeks in the fall, two other home economic majors and I lived in the home management house. They became special friends, also. The Agricultural and Technical College (A&T), a state school that later became a university, was only two blocks from Bennett. Many of the men from A&T dated women on our campus. Joan, one of my housemates, was engaged to Thurgood, a senior at A&T. One day when he was visiting her, I mentioned not having a boyfriend. That wasn't exactly true because a fellow who lived in Goldsboro and had dated me when we were in high school still considered me his girlfriend.

Anyway, Thurgood said, "You want a boyfriend? I'll get you a boyfriend."

I thought he was joking until one afternoon, I opened the front door of the house and saw a man whom I didn't know sitting on the couch in the living room. I asked if I could help him.

He said, "Your house mother invited me in. Thurgood told me to come over and meet Anece Faison."

I smiled and said, "Well, you're meeting her. That's me." We both chuckled.

He stood and shook my hand. He said, "My name is Verable McCloud." I said, "Nice to meet you, Verable. Let me put my books in my room and I'll be right back. Can I get you some water or something else to drink? We have cokes and other soft drinks."

He said, "No thanks, I'm fine." His voice was masculine but soft and pleasant. He sat back down as I turned and left the room.

I couldn't help thinking about how handsome he was— six feet tall and slender. He had one of those fresh-pealed banana complexions and a black mustache. His dark hair was cut short and neatly groomed. The Air Force ROTC uniform he was wearing enhanced his appearance. I put my books on the desk, took a quick look at myself in the bureau mirror, and casually walked back into the living room. He stood as I entered, then we sat down on the sofa. He was such a gentleman!

We talked for about an hour before he had to leave. He said he had enjoyed meeting me and would like to call me sometimes. I said that would be fine and gave him the phone number for the house. That was the beginning of our courtship which would last our remaining two years in college and beyond.

Verable and I didn't lose any time in becoming good friends. I worked studying in between dates. Being an "A" student himself, he understood and appreciated my taking studying seriously. He took me to football games and a special dinner at A&T. I invited him to the management house to have dinner with Mrs. Kook, the other residents, and me. There were only four of us, plus the one guest. The University photography took a group picture for one of the newspapers. The accompanying article told about our home management course, gave our names, and identified Verable as an onlooker. We often had dinner at a nearby restaurant which Verable and I labeled the greasy spoon. They served the best pan-fried chicken in town, but it was very greasy. I enjoyed being with him *and* I think the feeling was mutual.

Christmas of 1956 rolled around. Verable gave me a box of candy for my Christmas present. Unfortunately, I didn't give him anything. I just didn't think about getting one for him. I spent the holidays with Aunt Clara. It made me happy to see that my being there was bringing her so much joy. I told her about Verable's Christmas present. She said, "That's what a young man should give a lady as his first gift to her." I smiled and thought to myself, *How does she know?* I went alone to visit Mother and Momma's graves a few days after Christmas. While standing there, I thought about holidays of the past and couldn't keep from crying.

Chapter 14

I was happier than usual returning to campus. Verable stopped by for a short visit the first day we were back. Since my course load was a little lighter the second semester, life was less stressful for me and I enjoyed being alive more than I had ever before. Of course, Verable had a lot to do with the change in my feelings.

Our six weeks in the Home Manage House ended before Christmas break, so I joined Jean in our dormitory room upon returning to campus. I became engrossed once more in my college courses. Chemistry was again the course I disliked most. I struggled with it but everything else was going well. Verable came to see me nearly every day or we talked by phone—most days, we did both.

For Valentine's Day, Verable gave me a box of chocolates with a pretty porcelain doll on a heart-shaped box secured in place by plastic wrap. The doll wore a pink dress with blue ribbons surrounding its fully gathered skirt. The ruffled skirt was spread over the lower two-thirds of the box. He included a small envelope with a love note. There were three other Home Economics majors in the sewing room with me. They saw the box of candy when it was delivered but only noticed the note when I opened the envelope and started to read its contents.

Then they playfully surrounded me saying, "What did he say?" "Let me see."

"Give it here."

So, I dodged them and began running around the cutting table. They followed me until I stopped and said very forcefully, "You'll only get this note over my dead body." All of us had a good laugh. I thought, *Verable and I are becoming recognized on campus as a romantic couple. How nice!*

Verable wanted me to visit his home in Mt. Airy, North Carolina and meet his parents. I was flattered. His mother would have to send a letter of invitation for me to the college, and my aunt would have to send one granting me permission to visit his family.

Mt. Airy is in the northwestern part of the state and much hillier and more mountainous than the flatlands where I had grown up. Verable told me, "When you get to my parents' home, don't go to the edge of the back porch because if you fall off, you'll roll down a steep hill."

I said, "Really? Okay." When we arrived at his home and after meeting his mother and father, I stole out to the back porch. Surprise! The backyard was *not* steep at all. Verable had been quietly following me. When I turned around and looked at him in surprise, he began laughing. Afterward, he explained to his parents how he had tricked me.

I laughed too and said, "You'll know payback when you get it." To this, he responded, "I'll accept that."

His parents were very congenial and made me feel at home. His family reminded me of the people in Simmons Town—in looks but definitely not in attitude. In other words, they did not seem color conscious. They had true, traceable Indian ancestry. There were 12 children in his family and all the females had long, naturally beautiful hair. Verable's grandfather was half-Indian and therefore, his surname, Cloud, was of Indian origin. This presented a problem when his grandchildren were ready to attend school. Indian children were not allowed to go to the Negro or white schools in that area. Verable's father added Mc to their last name, making it *McCloud*, which was more in keeping with the names black people had obtained from the white masters during slavery. The name change made it possible for the children to attend the black school. His family, like many blacks in N.C., had some white ancestry, also. However, even after I had gotten to know Verable's family very well, I never heard a derogatory word said by the family members about anyone because of their complexion or color.

We had a wonderful Easter holiday. We spent Saturday lounging, watching T.V., and talking. After church that Sunday, Verable's sister, Jesse, and her husband, James, took us to have dinner with one of their friends, Ms. Amelia Smith. She was a high school teacher. Her home looked like it had been professionally decorated. The meal was delicious, too. It consisted of honey roasted ham, cranberry sauce, and a variety of fresh garden vegetables. We talked about current activities in the neighborhood. Verable asked about some of his old high schoolmates.

Following dinner, Jesse and James gave us a ride through some of the mountainous regions near the city. It was so beautiful. Afterward, they dropped us back at Verable's parent's house where we spent time conversing with them in their cozy living room. They told me about having twelve children—six boys, six girls—and how things were when they were growing up. They had lived in Virginia for a while but had been mostly in N.C., in the same house. It had four bedrooms, a dining room, living room, kitchen, and bathroom. Mr. McCloud had worked in lime mines as well as farming. They talked about how hard life was back then and how they survived. At times, some of the younger children stayed for a while with the older ones who were grown and married.

Soon, each of us decided it was bedtime. The McClouds were early risers, they said. Verable and I were leaving the next morning to take a bus back to Greensboro. Before I wished them good night, I thanked them for the visit and told them how much I had enjoyed it.

There were many good things going on in my life. But one experience I was having puzzled me. Infrequently, when I was in my room alone studying or just resting, I would be overcome by a very deep sadness with no identifiable cause. Eventually, I would start crying, and I didn't know why. After 10 or 15 minutes, the feeling would begin to diminish like a heavy fog gradually thinning out and finally floating away. I would wipe my eyes and go back to my homework or find something else productive to do. I found it hard to concentrate. I never told anyone about these episodes. But I couldn't help wondering what was causing them and if they continued, what effect would they have on my life.

The end of the school year was approaching. Verable and I discussed his going to Georgia for several weeks of cadet training during the summer.

We also wanted him to meet my aunt living in Dudley. He said that the best thing would be for him to stop in Dudley for a weekend on his way to Georgia. So, I wrote Aunt Clara and asked if it would be okay for Verable to spend the first weekend in June with us. She answered immediately. Her answer, written the same day she received my letter, came as quickly as mail delivery allowed. She was more than thrilled for him to come that weekend. I had told her that I would help buy food for that weekend and could get home a few days before his arrival to help with cleaning.

She responded: "I'm so glad you are coming home for a few days I don't know what to do. I'm so happy McCloud is coming for the weekend so I can meet him. I cleaned for Mother's Day [Jim and his family, George, and John had visited.] so there won't be much cleaning to do. It will be my greatest pleasure feeding both you and him if you all will just come. We will go to church as I would like the Dudley people to meet him."

One of the Dudley people did meet him before noon on Saturday, his second day there. We had finished breakfast. I was cleaning up the kitchen. Aunt Clara was relaxing in her rocker. Verable was sitting on the bare boards of the front porch. There was a swing he could have used, but being the country boy he was, he preferred the floor. Mr. Powell, cousin Evelyn's husband, came by in his car. He saw Verable and stopped to introduce himself. When I finished in the kitchen, I joined them on the front porch.

I greeted Mr. Powell with, "Good morning. I didn't know you were out here. Come on up and have a seat."

"No, Anece," he said, "I've got to be getting on to the store. 'Just saw your young man here n' thought I'd come over n' meet 'im. He looks like one of us."

We three talked a little more, then Mr. Powell left. Once he was in his car, Verable looked puzzled at me and said, "What did he mean when he said 'he looks like one of us'?"

I laughed and said, "He meant you look like the people in Simmons Town and their relatives." To which Verable said, "Oh?" He still didn't understand.

I said, "He meant that you are of a light complexion like the people of this neighborhood and their kinfolk."

He said, "You mean the people here are color-conscious?"

I said, "Yeah, they are as prejudiced against dark-skinned blacks as whites are against all of us people of color."

He shook his head in disbelief.

I sat down beside him. He put his arm around my shoulders and said, "When do you think we should get married?" That question came unexpectedly at that particular moment. He had not asked me *if I would* marry him. I wondered, *Is that what he was thinking about while sitting out here alone?*

I had thought about our having a life together, too. I had expected him to mention it first but not now. I said, "I don't know. When do you think?"

He said, "How about next summer?"

I began to get excited. I turned around and hugged him tightly. He stood, pulled me up from my seat on the floor. We embraced and kissed while intermittently exchanging expressions of love. I was very happy.

I looked at my watch and realized it was time for me to go in and help Aunt Clara prepare dinner. We were going to sit in the dining room at the large table. The menu consisted of a garden salad, fried chicken with gravy, rice, French cut green beans, her homemade biscuits, and chocolate cake for dessert. Of course, there was coffee, tea, and/or water to drink. The food was very good and we had plenty. My two companions ate heartily.

Later when Verable and I were talking, while taking a walk around the neighborhood, he said about Aunt Clara, "I've never seen such a *little* woman eat so much! Where does she put it?"

We laughed about that. I guess I was too exhilarated from our earlier talk, I didn't have much of an appetite and had eaten very little. Verable and Aunt Clara chatted in the living room while I cleaned up the kitchen. They seemed to like each other. Great!

Sunday was another enjoyable day. We didn't go to church after all. We took care of the necessary things, like cooking, eating, and cleaning up, but most of the time, we sat around and just talked. Aunt Clara was an avid conversationalist when she had an attentive audience. Verable was being a good listener, not just to be polite, but also because she told him about when I was growing up. I mostly listened but had to graciously correct her once in a while. We were sitting in the swing and chairs on the front porch. Soon, she went into the house. We didn't tell her that we had decided to get married. That was our secret to keep for a few months.

Sitting cuddled in the swing that afternoon, we discussed possible plans. We agreed that the wedding should be in the summer of 1959. Since we knew our graduation ceremonies would be June first—mine in the morning at Bennett and his in the afternoon at A&T—we discussed having the wedding that evening in the Bennett Chapel. That became our final decision, depending, of course, on our ability to get permission to use the chapel. We sealed the decision with a kiss.

The next day, Monday, I felt a glow in my heart that was matched only by the brightness of the sun. He had asked me to marry him! A cousin was taking Verable to get the bus to Georgia that morning. I hated to see him go but could be happy because I knew I would see him in six weeks. I think Aunt Clara felt a little sad about his leaving. In her earlier letter to me confirming our invitation, she had written, *"If you will come, I'll do everything in my power to make it pleasant for both of you."* She certainly fulfilled her promise. We had both enjoyed it tremendously. I would spend a few days with her in the fall when returning from my summer job in New Jersey. We had no way of knowing that the special spring visit we were just concluding would be the last time the two of us would see her together.

Chapter 15

A few days after Verable left, I boarded a train to Philadelphia where I joined Mrs. Baumgartner, her two daughters, and their children to go to Ventnor, N.J. There I resumed my regular duties—only there was one additional child—the baby boy who had joined the Kruger family during the previous summer. Since he was still quite young, his mother mostly took care of him. The older children and I (when my chores allowed) had lots of fun on the beach, building sandcastles and splashing in the clear blue water. Most of the days were nice and sunny. Much to my surprise, summer seemed to be passing very fast.

Verable arrived in Atlantic City in August, a few days before I was scheduled to leave. He had timed it so we would be able to take the train back to N.C. together. I was so glad to see him and proud to introduce him to my employers. He made a very favorable impression. It was Thursday morning, the day when I had an afternoon off. Mrs. Baumgartner suggested that I take off early to go out with Verable. Both of us thanked her. I rushed to my room, changed my clothes, and freshened up. We caught a downtown city bus at the corner and went sightseeing.

What a great time we had that day. First, we went to a different part of the boardwalk—closer to downtown than to Ventnor. It was much busier than the section to which I was accustomed. There were lots of shops displaying some crazy and unusual things. We bought a wrapped breakfast sandwich at one of the food stands and ate as we walked, then stopped at another place to buy cups of coffee. The boardwalk and beach were becoming more crowded as time passed. After visiting Steel Pier, we spent the rest of the afternoon downtown. Among other sights, we saw the Greek Temple Monument. Of course, we spent time looking in clothing stores at the different ladies' and men's styles. We saw the grand casinos and took pictures of some. We had a delicious dinner in a seafood restaurant that evening and returned to the Baumgartner's around 9:00 P.M., very cheerful and with full tummies.

That Friday, Saturday, Sunday, and Monday were my last four days of work. Verable called me every day from his hotel. We were scheduled to leave on Tuesday morning. Verable arrived early by cab. The driver waited to take us to the bus station. I felt a little melancholy saying goodbye to the three families. It was my last summer working for them and they always had been very congenial to me. A few tears were shed by the three women and me. Mrs. Baumgartner asked me to stay in touch with them. I promised I would.

Following the bus ride to Philadelphia, a brief transport to the train station there, and boarding the colored folks' car of the train to North Carolina, Verable and I settled comfortably on an isolated seat. There were only a few passengers in our section of the train. It was quiet except for the iron wheels bumping rhythmically on the rails. That sound had the effect of making me sleepy. Before long, I snuggled close to Verable. He put his arms around me, smiled, and kissed me on the forehead. I drifted off to sleep. The train made a few stops en route for passengers to disembark and others to board. Finally, I awoke. Once my head cleared, we talked about our visit with Aunt Clara.

Verable said, "I sent her a very sincere thank you note after arriving at the base in Georgia."

I said, "That was so *sweet* of you!"

To which he replied, "I'm a sweet guy. Haven't you noticed? My mother certainly thinks so."

"Most mothers do," I said and laughed.

He smiled, "I know you're kidding because *you* think I'm sweet, too."

I said, "I'll have to reserve my opinion about that until I know you better." We continued talking nonsense and some serious topics like school and marriage.

Soon, the conductor came through calling, "Mount Airy! All off for Mount Airy, North Carolina, Mt. Airy, all off . . ."

Verable said, "Well, I guess this is it, Love." He gathered his personal belongings. We kissed and said goodbye. As he was walking away, he turned and said, "Give my love to your Aunt Clara. I'll see you in Greensboro next week."

I was alone for the final leg of my trip to Dudley.

Aunt Clara knew the train's expected arrival time. She had made arrangements for our Cousin Charley to meet me at the Dudley train station. When I arrived home, I noticed she looked ashen, not as well as she had when I left in June. She was glad to see me but didn't seem to have her usual enthusiasm. When I asked about her health, she responded, "I just generally feel bad. I'm sorry, sugar." I told her, "Don't worry, I'm home and will do whatever needs doing. You go lie down on the bed or sit in your chair." She preferred sitting in her rocker. I stayed in her room and we talked for a while. She began dozing.

I quietly went into the second bedroom where I paused for a few minutes to think about Mother and my brothers. I missed them. But there wasn't time for me to reminisce. I unpacked my bags and put my clothes and a few toiletries away. After changing into one of my old dresses, I went to the kitchen to see what was available for dinner. There were bacon, eggs, and some cold biscuits in the lower part of the icebox. In the upper, colder part, I found meats: cut-up chicken, pork chops, calf's liver, and hamburger meat. I knew there were probably rice and white potatoes in the kitchen. If we were lucky, there would be some cans of vegetables there, too.

I guess my moving around must have awakened her. Into the quietness, I heard, "Anece," then louder, "Anece!"

Moving rapidly when I first heard her, I was near to her room by the second time she called out. I said, "Here I am. What's the matter?"

She said, "I could hear you and wondered what you were doing."

I explained, "Oh, I was just checking to see what there is that I can fix for dinner. You know what's in there. What would you like me to cook?"

She looked at me frowning. "I can fix dinner," she said.

I spoke up quickly before she could protest, "No, you are not going to cook or do anything else while I'm here, except rest. You aren't feeling well, so while I'm here, I want you to take it easy. Can you do that for me?" "Yes, ma'am!" she said and smiled. I hugged her and kissed her on the cheek. Then I went back to the kitchen where I decided to cook liver and onions with gravy, rice, canned green peas, and the leftover biscuits. I cut them in half, put butter on the halves, and toasted them for her. I chipped some ice off from what was in the box and made iced tea. I went to the bedroom to get her when I was ready to serve dinner. We walked to the kitchen together. I served her plate, set it in front of her, and she said, "Oh, sweetheart, this looks very good." I was pleased that she ate a good size serving, seemingly enjoying the food.

I felt very sorry for and worried over Aunt Clara's situation. All the fire had gone out of her. Whether she approved of what I was doing or not, she never criticized or raised her voice at me while I was at home. She never used a curse word or acted angrily. She seemed like a different person. She lived alone. Of course, the relatives and neighbors continued to look after her when I wasn't there. But that wasn't like having someone living with her. I thought, *I can't be in two places at one time. It'll be better for me and her if I finish my last year of college. At least, I will be in the position to get a steady job; maybe she can even come wherever I am and live with me.* I would recall that possibility when I felt especially concerned about her.

I did as much as I could during the time I was at home like giving the house a thorough cleaning, washing clothes, cooking all meals, and cleaning up afterward. I left to return to Bennett on Wednesday, one week after I had arrived.

Verable visited me that evening on campus. I was delighted to see him. As we sat close to each other on the sofa in the dormitory parlor, I asked what was going on back in Mt. Airy and how his parents were doing.

He said, "It's the same old same old, but health-wise, everyone seems fine—I missed you," he whispered, close to my ear.

"I missed you, too" I responded quietly. We returned to our normal voices and I told him my concerns about Aunt Clara's health. He was sorry to hear she was sick. He didn't want me to feel that I was alone, that he was with me, and would help us in every way possible. With tears rolling down my cheeks, I thanked him.

I wrote Aunt Clara a letter that night, letting her know I had arrived safely and that Verable joined me in sending love. In less than a week, I received a very disturbing response from her, acknowledging she had received my letter and explaining how sick she had become. Different neighbors were sitting up with her every night. She said she and others thought the doctor had given her the wrong medicine. She concluded with: *I swell all over and the worse hurting is in my chest and shortness of breath. I can't do any talking or lying down. I have given up. Thanks for everything. All my love, Aunt Clara.*"

The next morning, the Dean of Women asked me to come to her office. When I got there, she told me that she had just received a call from one of my relatives in Dudley. They wanted her to tell me my aunt had passed away early that morning. She said, "I'm so sorry. If there is anything the administration can do to help you, let us know. I'll tell the registrar who will notify all of your teachers to excuse you from class until further notice."

I thanked her and left her office crying. I was not too surprised about the news, but to know that she was gone hurt. My poor Aunt Clara.

I went directly to my dorm and called Jim to give him the sad news. He wasn't very surprised either. He said he would meet me in Dudley as soon as possible. I called Verable. Fortunately, he was in his room. He sounded sincerely sorry about the news. He asked if there was anything he could do for me at that time. I said, "no," that I was going to get my things packed and call about getting a bus home as soon as possible. He asked me to let him know when the funeral would be and he would come down.

After checking the bus schedule, learning what time I would leave Greensboro and could expect to arrive in Dudley, I called Cousin Georgia. I asked her if someone could please pick me up, and I told her the time I would get there.

"Sure, I'll get David—don't you worry. Where are you staying tonight? I'm sure you don't want to stay in your aunt's house alone. Why not have David bring you here and spend the night with us?"

"Thank you very much. I appreciate your help and what all the neighbors did for my aunt," I said. Then I remembered to ask, "Has her body been taken to the funeral home?"

She said, "Yes, Honey, Fred (her husband) called the Barnes Funeral Home in Mt. Olive as soon as I went over to check on her this morning and found her body. She was in the bed. It looked like she had tried to get a drink of water. The glass pitcher she kept on the bedside table was shattered on the floor beside her bed in a puddle of water. I'm so sorry, Alice."

"Thank you. I'll see you when I get to Dudley," I said and hung up. The bus was right on time and David was there to meet me.

After we greeted each other, he took me to his parent's house. He and his family lived on the corner across the road from his parents. His mother, Cousin Georgia, was the daughter of one of the original Simmons brothers; therefore, David was his grandson. My mother had been the daughter of another Simmons brother, and I am his granddaughter, but I never *felt* like I was part of that lineage. Perhaps, that feeling was derived from my erroneous thoughts.

I hugged Cousin Georgia and Mr. Fred when I entered the house. She was the peeled banana color I have often described and had "good" hair. He was darker but with a red tone that made his color like an amalgamation of brown and red. He had shiny, straight black, and gray hair. She asked me if I wanted something to eat. I thanked her but said, "no." She showed me where I would sleep and where to find the bathroom. I gave apologies for saying good night and going to bed early.

I ate breakfast with the couple the next morning. Afterward, I offered to help clean up the kitchen. Cousin Georgia said, "No, I think you will have enough to do today."

"You're right. I think I'll walk down to our house now and get started. Jim will arrive sometime this morning. He's driving down by himself, I think. He and Josephine didn't want to interrupt their children's or my younger brothers' school schedules. We should be able to sleep at our house tonight. Cousin Georgia, I made up the bed I slept in so you wouldn't have to do it until you're ready to change the sheets."

"Thank you, Sug," she responded.

I called back to her as I opened the front door, "Thank you so much for allowing me to stay last night."

She said, "You know you're welcome, Anece, anytime." I said, "Bye for now," and left.

It was a sunny day and not cool at all for mid-September in eastern North Carolina. While walking, I thought about the times and various stages of my life I had traveled this route. I was only 18, but somehow, I felt older. It didn't take me long to walk home. The distance was the length of Momma's now weedy, five acres, which lay between Cousin Georgia's house and ours.

Once home, I ran up the front steps, unlocked, and opened the door. I took a few steps inside, listened, then stopped suddenly. The house was so quiet and cold. My body felt paralyzed. I looked around, literally staring at each section of the living room and the part of the front bedroom that was within my view. A feeling of queasiness enfolded me. I felt dizzy, confused, and sad. This was my home and yet, it *wasn't*: the furnishings were the same, but my crippled aunt wasn't in her rocker; I couldn't hear little boys laughing as they played; I didn't detect women's voices coming from the back of the house—no Mamma, no Mother. The house smelled odd, a mixture of odors that I couldn't identify. My legs were shaking, but I managed to stumble through the house to the back porch. I sat down on the steps. The warmth of the sun caressed my body. With the stimulation of its penetrating rays, I started breathing deeply.

Soon, things became clearer. Finally, I knew where I was, why I was there, and where everyone else had gone. In a short while, I realized I had probably experienced expectations that weren't realistic. When I opened the front door and didn't see or hear any of the family as my mind had somehow tricked me into expecting, I was shocked into thinking this was not home anymore. And in a way, it wasn't. Family makes a home, and for various reasons, members of mine were gone. I remained seated on the step thinking, *What a strange experience that was; sort of like when I feel sad for no reason. I must never tell anyone about this. I can't imagine what they'd think of me.*

When Jim arrived an hour later, around 11:30 A.M., I had recovered from that bizarre episode and had gone through the house opening windows and doors. It was good to see my big brother. He drove into the backyard. I ran to him as he was getting out of the car.

He said, "Hi, Sis."

I responded, "Hi. So glad you're here."

We hugged and shed a few tears. He asked how I was doing, to which I responded, "As well as can be expected under the circumstances." I told him what I knew about Aunt Clara's death.

Around 12:30, we drove to Mr. Brown's Funeral Home. We had left the windows in the house open but closed and locked the doors. It was a rather quiet, sad trip to Mt. Olive. At the location, Mr. Brown was waiting in the lobby. He invited us back to his office. We went through the usual ritual of discussing plans and making decisions. We told him that we wanted to have the ceremony on Thursday at 2:00 P.M. if possible. He said there shouldn't be a problem. He'd get in touch with the minister and they would work out the details. We tried to be as thoughtful in making arrangements for Aunt Clara's funeral as the family had been in planning Momma's and Mother's. Following our discussion, the three of us went to the showrooms and made selections.

I asked Mr. Brown if I could use his phone for a brief long-distance call. Telephone calls were expensive back then—so much per minute. He said, "Yes, of course." I thanked him and went back into his office to call Verable. He was near his phone waiting for my call. I told him the funeral would be on Thursday afternoon. He said he had checked bus schedules for the week, so he knew that he could leave the next morning at 9:00 A.M. He also told me what time the bus was due to arrive in Dudley. I said Jim and I would meet him at the store—the bus stop. He asked how I was doing; I said fine. He told me he loved me and we said goodbye. I went back and joined the men. We thanked Mr. Brown for his kindness, shook hands with him, and left.

Jim drove us back to Dudley in about 40 minutes. He wanted to see Cousin Georgia to thank her for helping Aunt Clara. He was also going to tell her about the funeral arrangements. Our house needed to be closed, so he dropped me there and drove on to Cousin Georgia's house. He assured me he wouldn't be gone long.

I entered the house with no trepidation this time. The sun hadn't set, plus electricity was still connected, so I knew I would have enough light to begin my tasks. First, I checked the kitchen to see if there was any food for us. The icebox was empty but there were eggs and other foods in the kitchen which didn't need ice—enough for us to have breakfast in the morning. We could decide about other meals when Jim returned. Next, I dust-mopped the lanolin-covered floors in the two bedrooms then changed linen on the three beds: one in Aunt Clara's room where I would sleep and two in the back bedroom where Jim and Verable would slumber. Finally, I dusted and polished the furniture. I would do the same in the rest of the house the next day.

It was well past nightfall. I had been so engrossed in my cleaning that I didn't realize Jim hadn't returned. About the time I was wondering about him, I heard his car drive into the backyard. He entered the kitchen and began apologizing.

"Cousin Georgia said the dinner she was cooking was nearly done and she insisted that I stay and eat with them. She even wanted me to come back to the house and get you to join us. I thanked her and said you were so intent on getting the two bedrooms cleaned so we could sleep at home tonight, that I didn't think you would want to be disturbed. (I thought: *He was right about that.*) Cousin Georgia said, 'Well, she's got to eat! I'll fix a plate for you to take to her.'" He smiled and handed me the plate.

I said, "Thank you."

Jim added, "She wants you, Verable, and me to have dinner with her after the funeral on Thursday. I told her I didn't think we had any plans, but I'd check with you."

As I unwrapped the plate, I said, "That's very thoughtful of her. Yes, we'd love to."

Jim said, "I told her we'd let her know in the morning."

I went to the porch and washed my hands. He followed me with the foot tub (small washtub) to get water for bathing. After he put the container on the electric stove to heat and left the room, I sat in the kitchen alone eating and reminiscing.

The next morning, Wednesday, Jim made breakfast while I started cleaning the living and dining rooms. After breakfast and washing the dishes, we left to meet Verable. On our way out of the neighborhood, we stopped by Cousin Georgia's to tell her we were happy to accept her invitation to dinner on Thursday.

When we arrived at the Smith Brothers' store, we had a few minutes before Verable's bus was due, so we made a quick trip into the store to purchase the ingredients for sandwiches for lunch or snacking later and steaks, salad, vegetables, etc. to be prepared for dinner. We walked out of the store just as the bus was arriving. Verable was the only Dudley passenger disembarking. As soon as he was out of the bus, I ran over, hugged, and kissed him. Jim came to us after putting the groceries in the car. I introduced them. After the formalities, I walked between the two, holding the hand of each as we went to the car. I felt so fortunate to have those two men in my life. I smiled to myself and was thankful. Home was our next destination. Instead of taking the passenger seat in front, I suggested that Verable sit there so he and Jim could hear each other better. I climbed into the back.

The three of us hadn't eaten since breakfast. When we got home, the men brought the few groceries in; I put the food away and started making sandwiches. Jim and Verable kept a conversation going while we ate. Afterward, I cleaned up the kitchen, and Jim showed Verable their room for the night. When Verable and I visited Aunt Clara in the early summer, she had given up her bedroom for our guest. She and I slept in the back bedroom. The arrangement had to be different now.

Verable changed into more comfortable clothes and the two fellows went for a walk. I was sure my brother was giving him the history and idiosyncrasies of rural Dudley. Fortunately, Verable had experienced farm life and was familiar with all its particular necessities—like the outdoor toilet.

That evening after I had prepared and served dinner, I cleaned up the kitchen and joined the men on the front porch. It was a beautiful evening. It seemed like we were seeing millions of stars from where we were sitting. Sometimes, a single streak of light would start from an indiscernible point and move swiftly across the sky disappearing as quickly as it had come into view. Verable and Jim started a competition on who could name the most star formations. They seemed to like each other a lot and this meant more to me than I could describe. Bedtime came and each of us took turns in heating water and getting ready for bed. Then I hugged and kissed each of my beloved men goodnight.

It had been a difficult day for me. While I had enjoyed being with Jim and Verable, I couldn't help thinking about *why* we were in Simmons Town. Tomorrow, we would bury the last of our family whose surname was Simmons at birth. Aunt Clara had been a dear person, except when she had her hateful spells. Later in my adulthood, I would learn what had caused her fits of anger and that she hadn't had much if any control over them.

Mother nature was very kind to us that week. The day of the funeral was sunny and mild, again. Aunt Clara's body had lain in state in the church that morning, starting at 11:00. We didn't have the body taken home the afternoon before, as we had done with Momma. Many relatives and friends had arrived early that day to view and spend time with the body. Jim, Verable, and I were the only family members seated in the Funeral Director's Limousine as it followed the hearse to the Congregational Church.

The funeral service went well. Our Aunt's ceremony had every frill that her mother and sister had, including flower girls and male relatives for pallbearers. There was quiet grieving and some words to God uttered by members of the congregation, but no one required help from the nurse who was present.

After the service was over, we followed the hearse to the cemetery where Aunt Clara was laid to rest next to her father—a daughter on each side of the parents. The small family was together again. I prayed at her graveside that she was resting in peace and free of pain. Before leaving, I knelt beside Mother's grave and quietly said how much I loved and missed her.

I was drained of energy as we left the cemetery. I asked Jim if we would have time to stop at home for a little while before going to Cousin Georgia's. He agreed.

Chapter 16

I had about 45 minutes of rest before we left for dinner. So, I felt less tired and melancholic. There were just the five of us: Cousin Georgia and Mr. Fred, Jim, Verable, and me. The evening was very pleasant. We sat around a mahogany, lace-covered table and enjoyed a delicious meal of baked, stuffed chicken with gravy, cranberry sauce, home-canned corn and green beans, and candied sweet potatoes, all from their farm. Salad and hot homemade rolls, apple pie, and ice cream topped off the meal. The dining room was lovely, the atmosphere warm and comforting.

Our hosts brought us up to date on what was going on in Simmons town, the Congregational church, and Dudley in general. They said the only thing changing was the younger generations leaving Dudley. They said, "The college graduates are beginning to settle where they go to college or some other locations. Even some of the young adults who aren't in college are gradually leaving. Our church is feeling the effects of this youth migration."

My mind began to wander. A year earlier, Mr. Powell had commented to Verable that he "looked like one of us" referring to his light complexion. It seemed that the mindset of the older ones in the community had not changed—white was still right. Remember the little rhyme I mentioned earlier? It appears the older members of the community continued to believe the closer a Negro was to being white, the more acceptable he/she was in society. My guess was that some of the younger adults did not want to live in that kind of environment anymore. As an adult, from time to time, I met spouses of the children with fair skin and long silky hair with whom I had grown up. Interestingly, nearly all of them had married dark African Americans. The adult child's choice had at times caused friction with the parents. I wondered if the choice of a dark spouse was, without realizing it, the young adult's way of defying the old "caste" system among blacks. With Verable, my fiancé, having a light complexion, one could say that I believed light-skinned African Americans were better than others. That *could* be said, but it wasn't true of me at that time. Life was teaching me just how erroneous that assumption was; I had come to realize through observations and education that all humans were the same regardless of color, race, nationality, lifestyle, and religion. The problem with growing up in Dudley was the lack of positive reinforcement. The African-American children could look around them and not detect anything *positive* about the African culture—our culture. In future professional roles, I would have opportunities to demonstrate my feelings about equality. Meanwhile, I believed those with whom I had grown up were also beginning to realize the damaging effect of discrimination and the flawed belief that whites were better than blacks.

At dinner, when the discussion about Dudley and migration abated, Cousin Georgia suggested we continue our conversation in the living room. After we had settled in the front room, Cousin Georgia questioned Verable about A&T and his being in the ROTC. Mr. Fred asked Jim about life in New York and his family.

The three of us were leaving the next morning. We explained our travel plans and I asked Cousin Georgia if she would be willing to have the few foods we had left—they would only spoil otherwise. She said sure. We thanked them for dinner, which we had enjoyed tremendously. There were hugs all around, then we said goodnight.

We were up early and anxious to leave on Saturday morning. We skipped making breakfast at home, planning to get food later. I had packed most of my things the night before, so I made the beds while the men packed. Then I made one last inspection of the house—not knowing I would never see it again. Jim put the few bags and Cousin Georgia's food in the car. Afterward, he locked the house and we drove away. We stopped to leave the food at our cousin's. Verable and I said goodbye to Jim at the Smith Brother's store. He was driving on to New York by himself. The bus would stop at the store for Verable and me as we headed back to Greensboro and our last year in college.

Chapter 17

My senior year in college was possibly the busiest and happiest I had ever experienced. I had coursework, student employment, extracurricular activities, and planning a wedding, all requiring attention—plus seeing Verable as often as possible. My curriculum included student teaching, so 14 semester hours of my courses were for education. These included two courses on The Pupil and School: the theory of education, and Teaching and Practicum. The latter was the six weeks' student teaching component. Although I was majoring in Home Economics, I had become more interested in Sociology. Therefore, I asked to do my practicum in Family Life Education one of the areas in home economics that I considered close in content to sociology. I was assigned the course I had requested at a Negro High School not far from the College. There were approximately 30 junior and senior students and I developed a good rapport. I enjoyed making lesson plans, teaching the class, and interacting with the students. I did evaluations and kept records. I was very pleased when I received an "A" from the practice teacher supervisor and my professor. My other two courses that semester were Religion and Modern Living, and Theater Guild Workshop. I passed those with good grades as well.

    I worked in the registrar's office a few hours per week. Among other duties, I sat on the balcony and recorded absentees during required chapel services. What I earned was applied to miscellaneous school expenses, which had been covered by the small individual scholarships I had received during high school commencement. Some of those were awarded for only one or two years. My Picket and Hatcher Fund was still available for tuition. Finally, my biggest extra curriculum activity was being the Sunday school superintendent, a position to which I had been elected by the student body the previous spring.

During the second semester, I enrolled in Art for Teachers, Bacteriology, Household Physics, and Advance Clothing. This included Fitting and Pattern Design, which required designing and making an outfit. As I mentioned earlier, the Clothing instructor, Dr. Bullock, had taught me a course in clothing nearly every semester and I considered her my mentor—everything about her seemed perfect. During my senior year, she became not only a mentor but also a strong supporter. Once she knew I was getting married and planning a June wedding, she suggested that I design and make my wedding gown for the class project. I knew it would be less expensive than purchasing one. And I had confidence in my ability to do the project, so I determined that *I would*. I would design and make the most important gown of my life!

The process included having my measurements taken and recorded by one of my classmates, making a drawing of the style of gown I wanted, which included a moderate length train, determining the size and shape of pattern pieces, testing how well the pieces would fit together, then drawing the pattern pieces on tan tissue paper and cutting them out. That would be the pattern. There were many other steps involved before and during the actual construction of the gown. Could I complete this project by my wedding? Verable and I had decided that day would be June first, but we hadn't divulged this to anyone.

Verable's family invited me to spend the Christmas Holidays with them. We would have about two weeks off. We spent the first few days at his home in Mt. Airy. On our second day there, we walked in the woods behind his house looking for a suitable Christmas tree. He told me some stories about adventures he had in those woods when he was growing up. We selected a tree for the living room, went home, and decorated it. All of us were pleased with the results. I slipped away and went to my room. For the first time since Aunt Clara's funeral, I sobbed quietly to myself. Decorating that tree had brought back many memories. I didn't mention my melancholy mood to anyone.

Early Christmas Eve morning, Verable, his mother, father, and I joined his brother-in-law, James, in the latter's car. We were going to Washington D.C. James' wife had gone up earlier. Verable had two sisters who lived there: Margaret and Naomi. The family was gathering to share the joy of the season. I had no idea then, but Christmas Eve of 1958 is a date I will always remember in my memory with ecstasy.

We arrived at Naomi and her husband, John's, house around mid-afternoon. Naomi was a public-school teacher. The parents and their three teenage children greeted us as soon as we rang the doorbell. They invited us in.

No one in Naomi's family had met me before, so I felt uncomfortable like the star of the show, for a little while. Verable was admired and loved by everyone related to him, so meeting his girlfriend for the first time was special for them and for me. Jesse, who had been busy making a salad, came out to speak to everyone. Eventually, we sat down on the enclosed back porch, which was behind the dining room and kitchen. There was a small heater on the porch causing the room to be very comfortable. While chatting, we smelled delicious aromas coming from the kitchen. The children had scattered to other parts of the house. Once or twice, Naomi got up and went to check on the food. Soon, Margaret and her husband, Hood, arrived. We went through introductions again. Everyone was amicable and Verable was very loving to me, so I began feeling more relaxed.

    Naomi called us to dinner. Verable and I were the first ones to wash up and go to the dining room. We stood behind two dining chairs looking at the table. It was beautiful, covered with a white linen tablecloth and a centerpiece of three tall, red candles surrounded by green holly with red balls. The China glasses and silver shone as if they were new. She was also using colorful, Christmas napkins. In a few minutes, everyone else came pouring into the room and we sat down. John said a prayer, giving thanks to the Lord for enabling us to see another Christmas and for having dear ones together. When he finished, Naomi began bringing in the platters of food. She told us to serve ourselves. There was some murmuring as people began to talk again. Naomi had brought in a steaming platter of spaghetti, sauce, and meatballs, then salad, three dishes of vegetables, and garlic bread. Everyone was engaged in conversation, laughing and generally having a good time. I couldn't resist thinking about George and John, wondering what kind of holiday they were having.

    Verable, who was seated beside me, noticed how quiet I had become and asked, "Are you alright?" I said, "Yes, just listening." I smiled at him. When dinner was over, we complimented and thanked Naomi. Everyone was so stuffed that no one wanted dessert. One of the men said, "We'll catch up with that tomorrow, it won't go to waste!" Everyone laughed.

    It had been a rather long day for all of us. About an hour after dinner, someone suggested we should call it a night and at least let the travelers get to bed. All agreed. Verable's parents, his sister, Jesse, and her husband, James, were staying with Naomi, her husband, and her children. Verable and I were to stay with Margaret and Hood. We said good night to everyone and left. It didn't take long for Hood to drive to their apartment building. As we went through the neighborhood, I could tell it was one of the better areas in the city. I wasn't surprised because both had government positions. Also, I was not surprised at how lovely, comfortable, and inviting her living room looked. We entered it from the front hallway. It was decorated in muted tones of gray and blue, with pink accents in the framed pictures and flowers on one of the end tables. She turned on the lamp on the other end table and it provided a soft light. Margaret removed her hat, coat, and gloves. She stored them in the closet in the front hall and asked if we were warm enough to remove our coats. Verable helped me with mine then removed his and handed both to her. Hood had said good night and gone to their bedroom almost as soon as we entered the apartment. Margaret said, "I know you two are tired. I'll show you where your bedrooms are and you can go to bed whenever you'd like." She showed us where everything was, and then as if she had a second thought, said, "You may stay up as late as you like. You won't disturb us. Good night." We told her goodnight and thanked her for everything.

    I sat down on the sofa and sighed. Verable joined me and asked if I were tired. I replied, "Not really, just needing to unwind a little, I guess. It's been an exciting day. I like your family, by the way. They seem to be genuinely nice folks."

    Holding my chin, he gently turned my face toward him and gave me a long kiss. "They like you, too," he said. He stood and said, "Excuse me, I'll be right back." He came back quickly with one hand hiding something.

    I smilingly said, "What are you up to?"

    He returned to his seat next to me and said, "Close your eyes," which I did. I could feel movement as he tried to get off the sofa quietly and put something on my lap. "You may open your eyes now," he said. When I opened them, he was kneeling, and a small black velvet box was in my lap. I opened the box as he grasped my hands and said, "Anece Faison, I love you more than anything in the world. Will you marry me?" He released my hands, took the diamond ring out of its box, and slipped it on the third finger of my left hand.

    There were tears in my eyes when I said, "I love you, too. Yes, I will be honored to marry you." He sat back down on the sofa beside me. We kissed and cuddled for a while. When we moved apart, I looked at the ring. It was a plain white gold band with a square diamond of about two karats set in a delicate floral design. It was beautiful and I told him so. He gave me a brief statement on what marriage meant to him. I agreed while admiring my ring. It was getting late and we would have a busy day tomorrow. So, we kissed once more and said good night.

Christmas Day was cloudy and cold. The four of us in Margaret and Hoods household were up, showered, and dressed by 9:00 A.M. We wished each other a Merry Christmas and left shortly to go to Naomi's. The same family members from the day before were present. Everyone was cheerful and the words "Merry Christmas" resounded throughout the house as we greeted each other. One of the greeters noticed my engagement ring, not that I was trying to hide it.

Cindy, one of Naomi's daughters standing nearby, said, "Does that mean what I think it does?"

I laughed and called out, "Verable, I need your help!"

Several of us were in the living room where beautifully wrapped gifts encircled the lovely Christmas tree. Verable walked in from the back porch. He said, "Yes, dear, what's up?"

I held out my left hand and wiggled my fingers as the diamond sparkled like one of the night's biggest, brightest stars.

He chuckled and said, "O.K. Everybody, come to the living room, please." When everyone was present, he put an arm around my shoulders and said, "Last night, I asked this young lady to be my wife and to my good fortune, she said yes."

We hugged and kissed lightly while everyone clapped. Some said congratulations; some asked each other: "Did you know this was going to happen?"

"No" was the response. Even his parents looked surprised. Others wanted to know if we had set the date. Verable and I said in unison, "June first." The comments continued. His sisters and two nieces hugged both of us. The men shook Verable's hand and hugged me. All the men present, except Naomi's teenage son, were married. One asked, "Verable, do you know what you're getting yourself into?" Everyone laughed.

Verable was enlisted in the Air Force and had gotten permission for an early discharge to attend college. Additionally, he had nearly completed four years in the University and hadn't shown any real interest in a woman until his junior year when we met. He was 27, six years older than I, and he once told me that his family had pretty much given up on his getting married—thus, their reactions.

Finally, everyone settled down and found comfortable places to sit and talk. Naomi was busy finishing dinner. Jesse was helping her and every once in a while, Margaret went in to see if she could do anything. I also offered to help but was quickly told, "No, you're a guest. We want you to sit down, relax, and enjoy yourself." The ladies finished dinner by 3:00 that afternoon and had everything on the table when they invited us to be seated. All of us gathered around the bountiful feast. Roasted turkey with trimmings was the preeminent dish, among several delicious competitors. John said the blessing and after that, everyone lifted their iced tea glasses to toast Verable and me. All of us ate with gusto and still managed to carry on interesting and sometimes humorous bits of conversation. When everyone had finished the main course, we agreed we were, again, too full to have dessert right then. We decided to open gifts and have dessert afterward.

We moved to the living room. John playing Santa (without the red suit) found the name on each package and handed out gifts from under the tree. There were oohs and aahs as the recipients opened their presents. I had slipped a wrapped gift for Verable under the tree when we first arrived. However, I didn't expect one from him because of receiving the ring. John finally came to Verable's name and handed him a package. He opened it and seemed pleased with the male's jewelry box I was giving him. It had his initials engraved in silver on the black leather box and was rather handsome. He came over, kissed me, and said, "Thank you, sweetheart. I love it."

Before I could acknowledge his gratitude, he reached in his pants pocket, took out a small, square, wrapped box, and handed it to me. I looked up at him and said, "What is this?"

He was smiling and said, "It's your Christmas present." I started to say, "But the ring . . ."

He cut me off and said, "An engagement ring isn't a Christmas gift. It has a completely different purpose and meaning. Now, open your *present*." By then, everyone was looking at us expectantly. I unwrapped the package and opened the small box.

I said, "Oh, how lovely!" Then I took out the gold cross with pearls inset along each extension of it. I held it up by the delicate gold chain for everyone to see. I looked up at him again and said in a very low voice, "Thank you, Dear. I love it *and* you!"

That evening after having a dessert of coconut cake and/or blueberry pie a la mode, those of us staying at Margaret's left Naomi's house around 8:00. We were in bed by 10:00 P. M. because we were to leave for Mt. Airy with Jesse and James at 9:30 the next morning. Mr. and Mrs. McCloud, Verable's parents, were going to stay in D.C. until after New Year's Day. Jesse and James stayed with Verable and me at his parents' home each night for the remainder of our Christmas break. Our days in that mountainous area of North Carolina were mostly sunny but crispy cold. The weather was the same in Greensboro when we returned to campus a week and a half later.

Chapter 18

January 1959! We were back on campus: Verable at A&T and me at Bennett. My first priority was to do well in my classes, and a close second was my determination to design and make my wedding gown. The third was to plan the wedding for June first at 8:00 P. M. in the Bennett College Chapel. We had gotten permission to use it. That would be an extremely busy day for us because of the two commencements—mine in the morning and his in the afternoon. We didn't know then that he would be the salutatorian, meaning he would have the second-highest academic rating in his class. Also, he was to receive his lieutenant's bars. He wanted me to pin them on during the graduation ceremony. I felt highly honored! Obviously, I would have to take care of most of my priorities during the interim five and a half months, culminating on June first.

Within a few days of our return to the campuses, most of our friends and acquaintances knew Verable had given me an engagement ring and that we were getting married in June. The girls, of course, wanted to see the ring. Everyone thought it was exquisite.

During the months of planning, I worked on my gown as frequently as possible. The teacher of the Advanced Clothing class, Dr. Bullard, not only supervised my work on the gown but also advised me in planning the wedding. I wanted it to be an impressive affair—at least as far as the planning was concerned. The other factor that would determine its grandiosity would be attendance and the only part we could play in that was to send out lots of invitations, which we did. We wanted to have as many of our college friends, staff, and administrators present as possible. Therefore, all those groups, plus family and friends from outside the academic arena were included on the invitation list.

The attendants to the bride and groom could be as few or as many as we wanted: I selected six of my girlfriends from Bennett for bridesmaids. They seemed pleased to be included, even to the extent of each accepting the pattern number for her gown and assumed the responsibility of having it made. The color I had chosen was true pink. I asked Verable's youngest sister to be my maid of honor. Although we had not met before, it was my way of paying tribute to Verable, his family, and my anticipated relationship with them. Her gown was to be a slightly darker shade of pink—almost violet. Verable had contacted six of his friends to be ushers.

It seemed many on the campus loved weddings and were willing to get involved. The university organist was going to provide the music. When the college nurse learned about the wedding, she suggested the bridesmaids should carry bouquets of white magnolia blossoms from the many trees on campus. I liked the idea. She volunteered to go out during the early morning on the day of the wedding and pick the best-looking flowers to prepare for the evening ceremony. For the bride's bouquet, Verable was giving me a small bible with an orchard, baby's breath, small ribbon bows, and streamers attached.

When the professional photographer came to take individual pictures of members of the senior class, he overheard some of my classmates discussing the wedding. He used that opportunity to sell me on the idea of his taking our wedding pictures. The campus publicity director sent announcements about the wedding to the Greensboro newspapers, as well as to our hometown papers. One reporter obtained additional information on Verable and wrote an article entitled, "McCloud's Big day." In it, he mentioned all three ceremonies McCloud would have on June first: graduating with honors, receiving the bars of an Air Force officer, and getting married. It was the end of May. All preparations for the wedding were completed—even my wedding gown, which was beautiful. Mrs. Bullard was satisfied and complimented the finished product. I received an A in the advanced sewing and design class.

All my grades for the last semester were good. Yea, I had done it! I had completed the requirements for graduation from Bennett College in three and a half years. I would walk through the front gate with my original classmates on our way to the chapel to receive our diplomas. I thought of Mother and the first day we were on campus. I hoped she, my, grandmother and aunt were looking down on me and knew what was happening in my life. If so, I knew they were happy.

Seeking Personal Validation

June first was on Monday in 1959. Parents, other relatives, and friends of graduates on both campuses began arriving in Greensboro during the last weekend in May. My older brother, Jim, who was to give me away during the wedding, his wife, Josephine, and their younger daughter were the first of my family to arrive. One of my cousins and her family lived in Greensboro. They owned and ran a restaurant in which they planned to have a wedding reception for us. Several cousins and their spouses came in later from Dudley and one, my godmother, arrived from Atlantic City. Mrs. Baumgartner and her younger daughter, Mrs. Kruger—whom I had worked for in Atlantic City—came from Philadelphia, specifically for the wedding. My high school Home Economics teacher was there from Goldsboro. Verable's family arrived early. They included his parents, two of his sisters, and one of their husbands. There were so many people present for one, both, or all three of the celebrations involving Verable and me, and so many details to try to keep compartmentalized in my brain that it felt like I was in a whirlwind but a pleasant whirlwind. I felt beyond happy if that's possible. I felt lighthearted; everything and everyone were beautiful, even me. Had I developed self-esteem? If so, was it going to be a permanent characteristic for me?

The Bennett College Graduation, as I remember, began around 10:00 Monday morning. The sun was high in the sky and promised a glorious day. All graduates, wearing our caps and gowns, followed the faculty marshal through the Iron Gate at the front of the campus down a long walk into the chapel. We took our seats on the first several rows and listened, perhaps somewhat impatiently, to the speaker and other activities during the ceremony. Finally, we were called on stage one by one to receive our diplomas. During a ceremony like this, there are strong feelings of pride and accomplishment. We returned to our seats and remained standing until the last recipient joined the class. We sat while the last remarks were made and the benediction was given. Then we followed protocol in exiting the chapel. The audience began flowing out the front doors as soon as the academics were out of the building. There was a lot of hugging, kissing, and congratulating among the graduates and their supporters. I was delighted to see my family looking very proud. After the celebrating began to die down and folks started to disperse, my brother, Jim, his wife, daughter, and I went to lunch.

The format of the graduation ceremony at A&T, which started around 2:00, was not very different from ours. Of course, being a state institution, there were many more graduates and a much larger audience. I looked for

Verable as the graduates marched into the auditorium. Our eyes met and we smiled at each other. It turned out to be a very long ceremony because of the number of schools represented in the university and the multitude of students receiving diplomas. Near the end of the program, cadets of the ROTC (Reserve Officers Training Corp) were called to the stage with their selected person to receive their new insignias and have them pinned on their uniform jackets. This was a very blithe moment for Verable and me. After the program, when we left the auditorium, people lingered on the campus for a while expressing greetings and felicitations. I joined Verable and his relatives. We had a short kiss and congratulated each other. He thanked me for pinning on his military ribbon. The weather wasn't keeping its promise—it was getting cloudy and looked like it would rain. James, Verable's brother-in-law, took me to my dorm and the others to where they were staying. We would see everyone again at 8:00 P. M. in the chapel.

It did rain the night of our wedding, literally poured. The bridesmaids and I used plastic bags to cover the gowns we were carrying to the chapel by hand. We also hand-carried our makeup and other necessities. We dressed in the chapel balcony. One of the ladies said, "I didn't expect to be getting dressed with the bride tonight." Ha, ha. I hadn't expected that either, but nature had ruled. We were dressed before the guests began to arrive. Everyone looked fantastic. The nurse, who had picked the magnolia blossoms for the bridesmaids' bouquets, came to the balcony and handed them out. Verable had sent the bridal bouquet up to me by his sister, the maid of honor. Male attendants were seating guests when we went downstairs to form the procession.

The interior of the chapel was beautiful, as always. It had white walls and pews. The pews were trimmed along the top edges with dark brown wood. The floor was carpeted in a maroon color, which continued up the steps and into the pulpit area. Two large green plants stood inside the right and left railings in front of each speaker stand. The Congregational minister, Reverend P.O. Alston, stood on the second of three steps. He was in full academic attire. Verable, who had changed from military dress to a tuxedo, was standing to the left, one step down from Rev. Alston. Both were looking in anticipation toward the entrance. The organist started playing and the bridesmaids preceded me to the front of the chapel and took their places, three on each side of the steps. Each male attendant moved in line beside a bridesmaid. The maid of honor stood slightly behind me and spread out the train to my gown. Verable moved off the bottom step and stood beside me. Rev. Alston began the ceremony.

The service was numinous, elegant, and perfectly timed. The most momentous part was exchanging vows, which are paraphrased here: Verable and I promised to be lawfully wedded . . . to live together after God's ordinance in the Holy Estate of Matrimony . . . to love, comfort, honor each other and to keep one another in sickness and in health, forsaking all others . . . as long as we both shall live. Each of us answered "yes" when presented individually with the challenge. After the minister pronounced us Man and Wife and made a few other statements, Verable and I walked down the chapel aisle together, into our future *life*.

The reception at my cousin Mae and her husband's, John, restaurant was very decorous. It was held in the banquet room. All the tables had been removed, except a long one on which sat plates of refreshments, a tall wedding cake with white frosting, and the figure of a couple on top. Chairs were in a semicircle against the wall facing the table. When we arrived, guests were either seated or standing in small groups conversing. Everyone applauded when we entered. The hostess and her attendants began passing out glasses of champagne. Verable and I moved to the table and stood behind the cake. Three of the male guests made toasts; after each, everyone clapped. The photographer took pictures of various groups with us. We cut the cake and fed a piece to each other. Then, as soon as it was possible, we thanked Mae and John and left quietly while everyone was eating.

Verable had made arrangements for his best man, Franklin, and his wife to take us from the reception to each of our dorms to change clothes and get our luggage. Then Franklin drove us to South Carolina where Verable had made a honeymoon reservation at a motel. The sign out front gave the name of the motel and underneath were the words "for Colored." Despite the colored designation, it was a very clean and nice place located right on the beach. We had brought our swimsuits. It was early in the season so we had the hotel and beach to ourselves—the manager and staff were the only others present. There was a restaurant across the road, where we found the food was very good. Everything was perfect! We spent an enjoyable, romantic week before taking a bus back to Mt. Airy.

Many times after those momentous occasions, I have thought about how fortunate I was—a poor black female from the segregated south who had almost serendipitously and with much assistance (1) obtained tuition to attend and complete one of the most renowned and elite Negro colleges in the United States, (2) met and married a fine gentleman who loved me, and (3) had a beautiful wedding that fulfilled my most fervent dreams. The part I had played personally in these recent accomplishments did not elude me. I had worked hard to be a good student, a trustworthy employee, and a caring person. Should or would these characteristics meet my criteria for being a worthy member of society? I had doubts, because some of those negative profiles of me in my childhood often rose, like ghosts from a grave, and haunted my thoughts—making me feel unsure of myself.

Chapter 19

Verable and I spent the summer in Mt. Airy with his parents. I began searching the want ads for a teaching position to begin in the fall. Verable had received orders to report to Woodbridge Air Force Base, England in September. I wasn't going with him overseas because he needed to get settled into his new position and arrange housing for us. He would stay in the bachelor officer's quarters until the spring.

The opportunity to teach came unexpectedly. Mr. Chavis, the principal of a black, junior high school in Greensboro, N.C., needed a second Home Economics teacher for his eighth-grade class. He contacted Bennett College and asked if there was a recent graduate in that field they could recommend.

The registrar gave him my name, address, and an excellent recommendation. Surprisingly, the principal drove to Mt. Airy and met with me at my in-laws' home. Verable was present when Mr. Chavis and I discussed all aspects of the job. I asked questions and told him that if I took the position, I could only promise one year because I planned to join my husband in England in the spring. He assured us that would not be a problem because the year would give him time to recruit someone else. Apparently, the teacher I was to replace had given him very little notice about leaving. I accepted the position and by the end of August, I had moved to Greensboro into a rented room which included the use of the kitchen.

The house was home to a minister and his wife. He had once served our church—the First Congregational Church in Dudley—but had relocated to Greensboro many years earlier. There was one other renter, an older woman whose room was across the hall from mine. The occupants of the house were all very congenial, but when I wasn't at the school or church, I mostly stayed in my room. I was pleased to have the job because as newlyweds, we needed

Verable's *and* my salary. I recall that in 1959-1960, I received only $3,000.00 for the nine months of teaching.

I had a homeroom of approximately 30 eighth graders and taught several sewing classes each day. My most prominent memory is having to counsel a girl in the homeroom class about hygiene. Several of her female teachers mentioned to me how dirty her clothes were and how odorous she was. Of course, I had noticed these things about her, too. I also knew that she was from a very poor family in which there were several other children. I can't recall now if there was a father residing with the mother and children or not. Anyway, one day, I asked the young lady to stay after school. I said we needed to talk. Her name was Penny. She was a very slender, average height, dark-brown-skinned girl with short crinkly hair. She spoke softly and seemed somewhat timid. It was difficult discussing such a personal topic with her. I didn't want to make her feel bad about herself.

I started the chat by mentioning some positive things: "I'm really enjoying having you in my homeroom. I think you are one of the best-behaved students in the class and I appreciate that. A few others could take some lessons from you on how one should act." She dropped her head and gave a shy smile. I asked if she was enjoying school.

She said, "Yes, ma'am. I just wish I could do better in math." "Who teaches you math?" I asked.

"Mr. Brooken," she said.

"Have you talked to Mr. Brooken about your concern?" "No ma'ma, I didn't think I should bother him."

"Well," I said, "Let's make an appointment with him. I'll go with you, and we'll see what suggestions he may have for helping you." She nodded her head enthusiastically. "I'll get the meeting set up as soon as possible and will let you know the time."

"Penny, the reason I asked you to remain after school to talk is that I wanted to discuss hygiene with you. I like you very much and not a thing I'm going to say will change that." She lifted her head and looked me straight in the eyes, totally absorbed in my words. "I just want you to be the best person you can be in all aspects of your life. Do you agree?"

She said, "Yes, ma'ma."

I was happy to see that she didn't look perturbed or that her feelings were hurt. We discussed who washed the clothes at her house, how often she took a bath or washed herself. She answered my questions candidly. I made suggestions for improvement. For example, I told her that she definitely needed to wash herself every day, and sometimes, if she realized she didn't have clean underwear or some other piece of clothing for the next day, she could wash the item by hand the night before, then hang it to dry for the next morning. I talked about oral hygiene. We concluded our discussion with her thanking me and saying she would use my suggestions. Her hygiene seemed to have improved the next day and was good throughout the year.

At the end of the school year when I was getting ready to leave for England, Penny came to the house where I lived. When I opened the door, she handed me a neatly wrapped small package.

She said, "This is for you."

I was shocked and eagerly replied, "Thank you so much. I will always cherish whatever this is." She gave me a warm smile, turned, and left. I opened the wrapping and found a lovely, new, floral handkerchief. Tears came to my eyes because I knew she really didn't have the money to buy me a gift.

During my last day on campus, the faculty gathered in one of the classrooms after the last period, called me in, and presented me with a gift. It was a brilliant white leather purse with gold-colored trim. All wished me a safe, pleasant trip and much happiness in the future. I cried. I was astonished that my colleagues, whom I had known for only a short time, thought enough of me to be so kind and generous.

Many of the students gave me greeting cards. One purchased a scrapbook and asked all my homeroom students to sign the first page before she presented it to me.

Dr. Bullock, my sewing instructor, invited me to have lunch with her. We talked mainly about how beautiful my wedding had been, the trip to England, and marriage in general. Before we left the restaurant, she handed me a wrapped package and said, "Open it." I did and found a pair of bright red panties in a thin, white box. I looked at her in surprise. She said, "Those should get your husband's attention." We both laughed—that joke was so out of character for her! I thanked her for lunch and the gift—and promised to use the latter sensuously.

Grandmother whom we called Momma

Seeking Personal Validation

Anece, Mother, Jim, Aunt Clara

Cotton Pickers

Seeking Personal Validation

Anece picking cotton

Brother Jim

Seeking Personal Validation

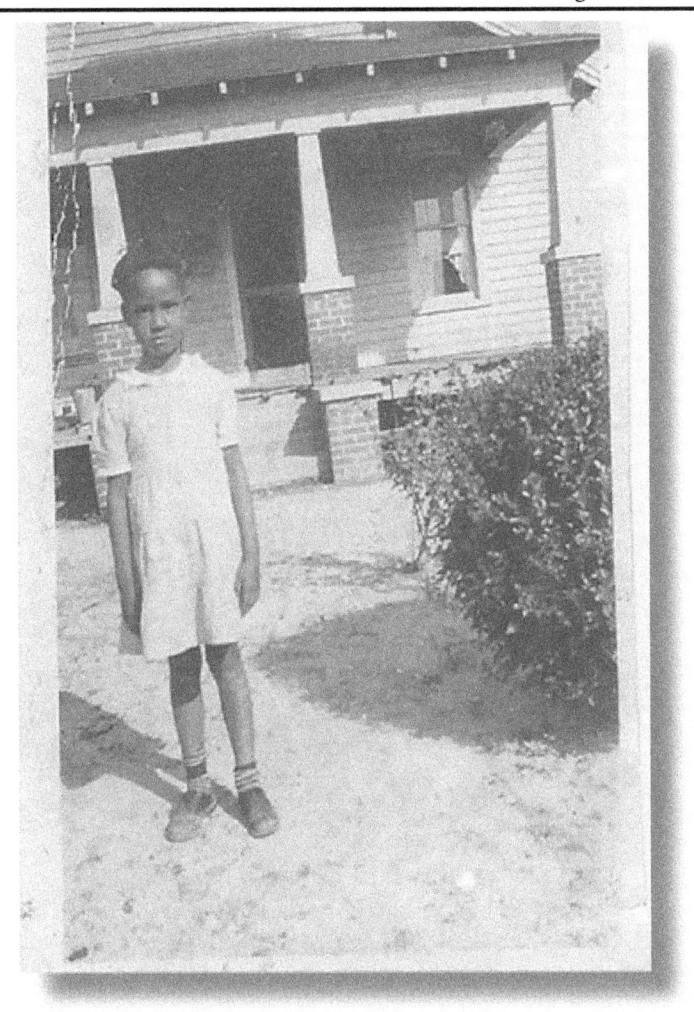

Anece

Anece and Dad

Seeking Personal Validation

Dad's Mother

Anece F. McCloud

Younger Brothers

Seeking Personal Validation

Moving in Dorm at Bennett College

Bennett College Bell Tower

Seeking Personal Validation

Isabel, my best friend in college

May Day Celebration at Bennett College

Seeking Personal Validation

Students wrapping May pole

Boyfriend: Verable McCloud

Seeking Personal Validation

Verable and Anece on Bennett Campus

Summer job: Anece and Debbie

Seeking Personal Validation

Anece on Graduation Day at Bennett

Anece F. McCloud

Bride and groom

Seeking Personal Validation

Relatives at Wedding Reception

Anece and Verable with Lynn, first born

Seeking Personal Validation

Baby Dannell and older sister, Lynn

Christmas 1965

Seeking Personal Validation

Cowgirl Dannette

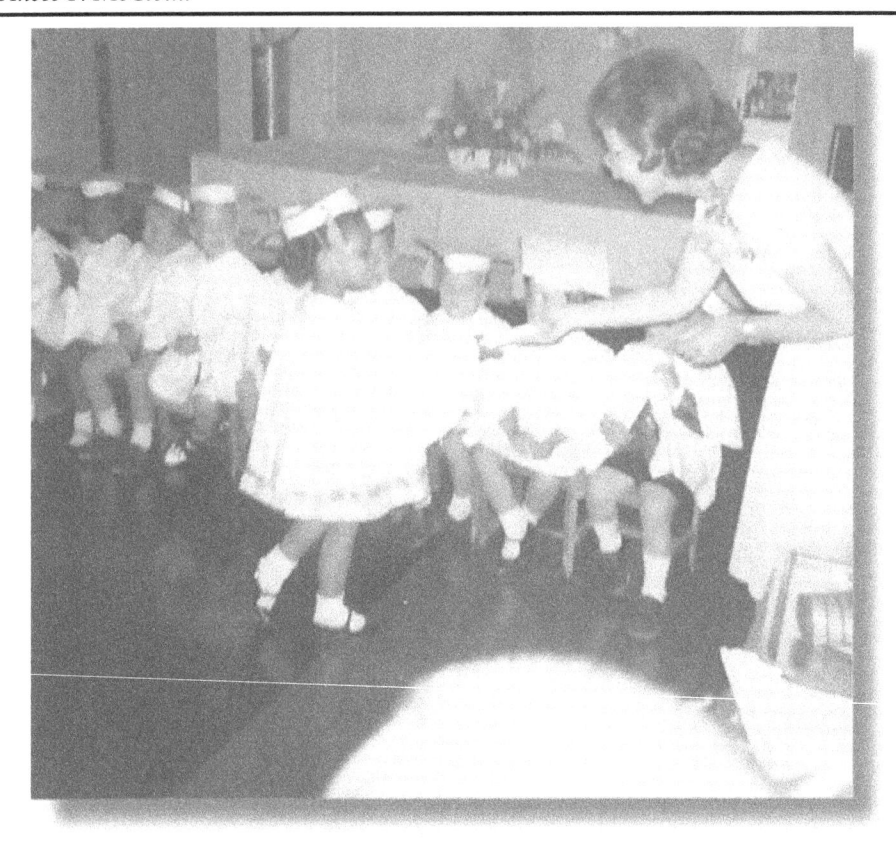

Lynn graduating from Dodo Birds

Seeking Personal Validation

Lynn and Mrs. Lockett at the duck pond

Verable at Offutt AFB, receiving a Military Award

Seeking Personal Validation

Verable receiving a golf award

Daddy opening a Father's Day present

Chapter 20

On June third, 1960, three friends from the Congregational Church I had attended in Greensboro drove me to the train station. Before I boarded the train to New Jersey, they gave me a bunch of long-stemmed flowers, mostly gladiolas. I was to take a flight from McGuire Air Force Base to Europe. The flowers were comforting to me when I thought about how far from home I was going to be. Yet, I could hardly wait to see my husband. As I left the train in New Jersey, I gave the flowers to one of the porters.

My brothers, Jim, George, John, my sister-in-law, Josephine, her sister, and my two nieces were at McGuire AFB to see me off. My going to England was very significant to me and my family because none of us had ever been out of the United States. We didn't have to wait long in the airport before boarding was called. The family and I took turns hugging, kissing, promising to see each other in three years, and finally saying goodbye. Then I boarded an airplane for the first time in my life.

It was an Air Force carrier; I don't remember the kind of plane or number, but it seemed big to me on the outside and was very spacious inside. There was a row of seats on each side of the aisle, as in civilian planes. There were other dependents as well as a few military service members on board, but the aircraft was not overcrowded. I was pleased to have a window seat and on the side where I saw my family. I waved goodbye to them one last time.

I have taken many flights since that first one. The take-off was then, and continues to be, the most exciting and enjoyable part of each flight to me. I love the weightless feeling I experience when the plane begins its gradual, gentle incline toward the sky then watch the objects below getting smaller as the plane goes higher and higher until it levels off and eventually meets the clouds. I usually feel safe, but every time, I think about the number of people the pilot is responsible for at one time. All of us are in his hands, so to speak, not just one at a time as with doctors. Although I do acknowledge that doctors have tremendous responsibilities, too.

Our flight took off from New Jersey at 3:30 p.m. Eastern Standard Time (EST). We made two one-hour stops en route: one at Harmon Air Force Base in Newfoundland, around 9:30 p.m. EST., and the other at Prestwick Air Force Base in Scotland at 5:00 in the morning EST. During both stops, we passengers were confined to the terminal. Fortunately, we were served good meals while on flight. It was night and pitch black in Newfoundland; however, light from the airport and the plane illuminated some of the views. In contrast, the awaking sun gave the mountains of Scotland a welcoming glow. We arrived at Mildenhall AFB in England around 10:00 a.m. EST in the USA, which was 3:00 p.m. British time. I saw my husband waiting at a distance, as we disembarked.

Before going to each other, I had to complete formalities for entering the country. As soon as I was free, we ran to each other and embraced. We were overjoyed to be together again. There were so many things we wanted to say, but first, we had to retrieve my luggage. Afterward, we talked and laughed a lot as we took my bags to the new, light blue Volkswagen (bug).

"Oh, this is cute," I said when I saw the car.

"It's a little small," Verable responded. "But it should satisfy our needs and it's economical on gas. I missed you so much!" he added and gave me a big kiss.

"I missed you, too," I replied, "It's so good to be here with you." I held him close and looked into his dark eyes. We got in the car and started our 70-mile drive to east Anglia.

Verable had planned for us to live in different English hotels for four weeks while we waited for base housing that had been assigned to us. The objective of this plan was for me to become familiar with various parts of the area. As he drove, he pointed out differences in England and the USA: driving on the left-hand side of the road; roundabouts—circles placed in the middle of what could be called an intersection with four roads individually going north, south, east, and west from the circle. Some may have had less than four roads extending from them. The driver would go around the circle to the road of choice and turn there, rather than turning a corner. Many colorful flowers filled the roundabouts. However, those planted in private yards were surrounded by fences. Verable said every home he had visited off base had lovely flower gardens in their front yards, but one couldn't see them from the street because of the fences. He added that some Americans had commented on how the British seemed to love beautiful flowers but kept them hidden. Everything was so new and different to me. I continued glancing out the window as we talked, bringing each other up to date on the nine months we were apart.

Later that afternoon, we checked into the Orwell Hotel, a large typically British building with three floors. (We have to remember that everything described here is how it appeared in 1960.) The first two floors were for guests primarily. The roof was slanted, with three dormers on the third-floor front and a tall chimney standing as straight as a soldier at each end of the roof. Our room was on the first floor. It was furnished modestly with dark furniture of an earlier period but looked very comfortable, was highly polished, and exceptionally clean. The dining room and all amenities were located on the first floor, also. After unpacking, Verable and I went to dinner. In this formal dining room, there were numerous linen-covered tables for four. On each, there was a dimly lit candle and a single flower in a vase. The atmosphere was perfect for the beginning of our reunion celebration. There were many dishes on the menu: Yorkshire pudding, steak and kidney pudding, Shepherd's pie, etc. But Verable and I chose what was most familiar to us: soup, roast beef, baked white potato, various vegetables, and a dessert. Verable ordered wine for each of us. We enjoyed our meal as well as the rest of the evening. Of course, the best part of the night was finally having the chance to make love again after nine months.

Verable was stationed at Woodbridge Air Force Base. It was approximately seven miles from Bentwaters AFB where the main commissary and different services, as well as military units, were located. All three hotels where we stayed were fairly close to the bases, so we had breakfast at one of the Officers Clubs most mornings. Verable had accumulated some leave time for when I arrived. We spent most of the days visiting Woodbridge, Ipswich—both nearby towns—and other places of historic and scenic interest. Framlingham Castle is an example of some of the ancient and unusual structures we explored. The history of this castle is varied, based on accounts from different sources, and therefore, confusing. Many royals and high-ranking officials had owned and lived there at various times since the mid-tenth century when it was thought to have been built. Military wars and/or scrimmages, as well as some owner disputes, had occurred throughout the history of Framlingham. Most walls and upper-level walkways were still standing when we visited in 1960. Some historians have written that the main building and living quarters were destroyed by the royal edict of a former king. We walked up several flights of stairs to reach the top of the high walls of the structure. There was a walkway that allowed us to go all around the top of the building where we could see distant fields in which there were some scattered buildings. Being that high up gave us a view of the whole courtyard. Every scene— the far away fields, the mound upon which the structure was set, and the courtyard—was covered with a carpet of flawless green grass. During our days of sightseeing, we saw too many magnificent places to list and describe here. Suffice it to say, the parts of England we visited were historic, intriguing, and beautiful.

Verable's father passed away during the fourth week following my arrival in England. We had not moved on base. Rather than leave me in a hotel alone, Verable asked one of the two black officer's families, whom I had met, if I could stay with them while he went back home to attend the funeral. Being so few, we black Americans felt as if we were family. I stayed with the Swayzes, who were very welcoming. Their family of four lived in an English house they were renting in Ipswich. It was nice and fairly modern; however, most English homes did not have central heat at that time. Unfortunately, theirs didn't. Swayze was a dentist who worked on Bentwaters base and was one of two black officers. The other, Dr. Croons, a dentist, was also assigned to Bentwaters. They had two young children and rented a British house in a nearby city. A black gynecologist, Dr. Arnold, was assigned to Bentwaters AFB. He and his family arrived a year or so after I had. Since he was a physician, they were able to move into Bentwaters housing upon arrival. His presence brought the total number of black officers to four on the two bases. Verable was the only non-medical officer of color. His position was in an area I wasn't privileged to know much about—Intelligence. I think it involved national and international security.

Within four days, Verable returned from Mt. Airy. He was sad but managed his feelings well. Staying with the Swayzes had been pleasant; however, it was wonderful being able to welcome my husband home—to me, to England, and, finally, to our new living quarters on Woodbridge AFB. We moved into Quarters 1414B on July 1, 1960. It was our *first* home!

All the houses on base were of identical design and had gable roofs. They were single-story and semidetached; therefore, another officer and his family shared half of our building. Each half had a small front lawn and a concrete walk up to the front step. The officers and enlisted personnel lived in separate sections of the base and each of the two groups had its own club. Under normal circumstances, they did not visit each other's club. All other facilities on base, such as the commissary, movie theater, chapel, etc. were open to all personal and their dependents. Black officers and enlisted personal were not discriminated against—not openly, anyway.

Now, back to the description of our new home. It had a large, open living room and dining area. There wasn't a formal entrance, so you walked directly into the living room when you came through the front door. A large window filled most of the front living room wall. Toward the back of the house, on one side, the dining room shared a wall with the kitchen and had a pass-through opening in the center. A hallway started at the end of the living room, went past the kitchen door, and continued to the back of the house. There, doorways to a large bedroom, one small bedroom, and the bathroom opened to the hall. The house was furnished sufficiently and a couple needed only linens to start home life. There was a sofa, a large dining table with six chairs, a China cabinet, all kitchen appliances, a washing machine, and a double bed. These belonged to the base. We had a few things of our own the movers were to deliver. At the end of three years when we were to return home, I was sure we would have increased our belongings.

We met our neighbors who shared the other half of our building the day we moved in. They were the parents of a young son and daughter. The father was a pilot. In the house to the left of us were the base Chaplain and his wife. An American Officer and his British wife lived across the street. They all seemed very nice and welcomed us to the neighborhood. They told us about the many activities and clubs on base and encouraged us to get involved.

Chapter 21

Verable worked Mondays through Fridays. And sometimes, the alarm sounded in the house during the wee morning hours, summoning him and others to check in at headquarters for additional duties. The alarm made such a loud, ferocious noise that I joked to myself it was enough to make the fiercest animals in Africa tremble with fear. Since Verable was busy, I decided to become active on the social scene, which officers' wives were expected to do. I had received a pamphlet entitled, "The Air Force Officer's WIFE." It was published by the USAF Personnel Retention Program. It seemed the main purpose was to make us feel welcomed as supporters of and incentives to our officer husbands. While the pamphlet contained pertinent and helpful information, emphasis on the male as the only member of the couple who was the officer would be considered chauvinistic today.

My husband was in the 79th Technical Fighters Squadron (T.F.S) on base. I was a member of that wives' group by affiliation with him. Squadron wives were also members of the base-wide (including Offutt) Officer's Wives Club (OWC). Both the 79th T.F.S. Officers' wives' group and the OWC sponsored small and large social functions, as well as participated in volunteer projects, such as the Red Cross and family services. I was in both organizations and served for six months as a reporter for the 79th squadron wives. My job consisted mainly of editing social news from the families in our squadron and sending an article to the OWC for the monthly newsletter. This helped me get to know several of the wives quickly. I also played bridge (or tried to) with the OWC once a month. Several of us were just learning, so the more experienced players were patient with us.

Verable and I went to church in the base chapel on Sundays. Some of the women had formed a group called Protestant Women of the Chapel (PWOC).

I was invited by one of the members, so I joined. As one would expect, the organization's activities centered on religion. We met every Wednesday afternoon. Programs were planned by a member or group of members for the entertainment and knowledge of the group. When it was my time to plan the program, I decided to be different. I had just read <u>Dear and Glorious Physician</u> by Taylor Caldwell. It's the story of the life of St. Luke, the physician. It was released in 1959 and was an inspiring story. I selected a few of the most poignant parts, developed scenes for them, and recruited a few members to assist me by acting out the scenes while I read about them from the book. The program was very well accepted by our members.

One cloudy morning, I was at home alone, lining shelves in the kitchen cabinets. It was grey and rainy outside, the kind of setting and mood that encouraged random thoughts. My mind drifted to memories of the various interactions we'd had with fellow club members, neighbors, and guests at social gatherings. It dawned on me that Verable and I, black Americans, were living in a white society. Wasn't that what I had wanted—to be a member of the white middle class? Hadn't that been my dream, my goal? I remembered thoughts and feelings from my formative years. Back then, I had hated myself because I wasn't white. I wasn't even as light in color as the relatives living in our community in Dudley, nor did I have beautiful hair like theirs. I didn't have a father when I was growing up to reassure me that a male could love me for myself, who could have thought I was special, who may have, even, thought I was pretty. We were very poor, and some sociologists back then would have classified our family as dysfunctional. But to be fair, there were white Americans who were as poor and having hard times.

On second thought, how could I evaluate us as being on par with our white neighbors? We were not white middle class. I didn't know if we were even black middle class. Most, if not all, of the white people whom I consider peers *were* middle class. In my mind, they had come from more privileged backgrounds than we had. If nothing else, the fact that they had grown up as Caucasians gave them an advantage, plus being from families who had not been poor, whose lineage probably consisted of earlier generations and/or grandparents who were able to provide for their families. In some instances, older great-grandparents who were able to leave inheritances that were passed from one generation to another— old money. A professor once told me that being in a family with "old money"—I guess he meant inheritances—was one of the characteristics that distinguished the white upper class from others. African Americans, he said, are gradually developing a black middle and upper class, but their advances are based in some instances on their color (light vs dark skin), the source of their wealth, and how many generations had not been poverty-stricken before them.

By that time, I had stopped working on the cabinets, was standing with my back against the counter, and my right hand supporting my bowed head. I questioned previous thoughts. Why was I thinking so much about class, equality, etc. at that time? There was no question that our lifestyle then was no different from others living in our community. But it would change when we returned to the States. I resumed my chore and pushed those thoughts out of my mind.

Verable and I settled into married life and our new home; at least, it would be our home for the next three years. We went to the commissary to shop for food and to the base exchange to equip the kitchen with things such as cooking utensils, dishes, and tableware. Later, Verable bought a T.V., and some months afterward, he splurged on a large floor model record player and speakers. I worked on making drapes for the living/dining area and the larger bedroom. I was very pleased when I found material for kitchen curtains that had a grey and bright yellow design on a white background. The early morning sun came through that window and made it very bright and cheerful for us during breakfast. The place began to look like a real home with our own personal touches. Sometimes, I'd go shopping in the nearby villages with one of the wives and would purchase a novelty item or a small antique for the house. We were invited to dinners and parties; likewise, we had friends and neighbors over for meals, parties, or to play bridge.

We were careful with spending and kept a diligent eye on our budget. Food and other things were cheaper on base than off. There were only the two of us. However, I wasn't working and Verable didn't earn very much as a First Lieutenant. I had paid some on my Pickett and Hatcher educational loan while I was teaching, and then we prorated the balance making it a part of our monthly bills. We had little savings and a lot of confidence that we would be okay—as long as we had each other.

The protestant Chaplin who, as I said before, lived next door to us, was in charge of the base kindergarten. Parents paid monthly tuition, but I'm sure it was sponsored mostly by the US Government. It was for military dependents of preschool age. The Chaplin said he needed someone with US teaching credentials to manage the school and conduct classes. Knowing that I had taught in Greensboro, N.C. the previous year, he wondered if I would be willing to accept the job. I reminded him that my certification was for secondary education. He said that didn't present a problem. So, I accepted his offer and started to work during the first part of September.

My hours were for half days—8:00 a.m. until 12:00 noon, Monday through Friday. My primary responsibilities were to teach students the alphabet, numbers, how to print, as well as other skills that would help prepare them for first grade, and we had some fun activities. The classroom was in a military hut, which also housed the base post office. The building had two spacious rooms, with ample windows in each. Our room had everything we needed, including small desks, a good size chalkboard, bookcases with books, games, crayons, and other equipment.

There were 20 children in my class. They were well-behaved except for some small disagreements from time to time. There was one boy in the class who was biracial but of a light complexion. Some of the other kids picked on him more than anyone else. I would break up whatever squabbles occurred between any students, redirect them to the activity they were supposed to be doing, and I'd remind them that it wasn't nice to be rude or tease others. They were good children, very respectful of me, and I soon loved every one of them.

Verable and I were ready to add a little person to our family. We had been together five months since my arrival in England. It seemed like that was time enough for me to get pregnant. What was the problem? I was beginning to be somewhat frantic about the situation. Verable remained calm and suggested that I make an appointment with the base doctor. I called and was scheduled for a few days later.

After the doctor had examined me, he said, "You are fine. I see no reason why you can't get pregnant. You know, five months is not long for a couple to try to conceive. Sometimes, it takes longer than nine months or a year. I think you are overly anxious and need to calm down." He added, "I'll give you a prescription to help you relax. And come back to see me if you have any additional problems." I thanked him, picked up my prescription, and went home feeling a little better. When Verable got home, I gave him the doctor's report.

"That's not bad news," he said. "You do tend to get upset over little things. Maybe you should try to take life easier." He saw by my facial expression that my feelings were hurt. He smiled and hugged me tightly. I was okay and after that, I started dinner.

I tried to relax as the doctor and my husband wanted. They were proven right. About two months later, I began to have morning sickness. It was December 1960. I didn't eat before going out in the mornings; thus, I avoided being sick in the classroom. I'd have a snack as soon as I got home. Many times, I became sick afterward. I went back to the doctor to make sure I wasn't experiencing an upset stomach for some other reason. He confirmed I was pregnant and told me the morning sickness should begin to diminish. He advised me to check in with the gynecologist at Bentwaters AFB, who would schedule me for regular office visits to monitor the pregnancy.

We had two notable events to celebrate: First, our initial Christmas together as a married couple, and second, expecting our first little McCloud. We didn't tell anyone that we were expecting. We wanted to enjoy the anticipated event privately for a while. The baby was due in August of 1961. We had lots of time before spreading the good news. My morning sickness was less severe than it had been. The kindergarten would be closed for about two and a half weeks during the holidays. I'd appreciate the rest but intended to complete the year after Christmas.

Verable and I couldn't have been happier. Our families and friends from the States sent cards and letters. Everyone was doing well. We were invited and attended Christmas parties neighbors and others had during the holidays. Verable used snow spray and painted beautiful scenes on our living room window. We bought a tree, Christmas ornaments, and other things to make our home look festive. We put the tree up in the living room and decorated it. Some new friends we had gotten to know well stopped by to wish us happy holidays and had cocktails with us. Verable knew that most military families kept a well-stocked bar. So, he was prepared for unexpected guests.

A couple of days before Christmas, I baked a cake and a pie. Afterward, I checked a cookbook to refresh my memory on how to prepare baked turkey with stuffing and to make a few special side dishes. We had invited Pat and Colin, a British couple about our ages, to have Christmas dinner with us. We'd met them through some American friends who lived in Ipswich. I was feeling unnaturally energetic, capable of taking on the world. I had completed all the preparations for our special dinner, so on Christmas Eve night, Verable and I sat on the sofa in the living room with the lights low. This allowed us to see Verable's artwork on the windows. The manger scene he had done seemed to come to life. We snuggled together admiring his work and the Christmas tree. We listened to Christmas music and before going to bed, we enjoyed a glass of wine. Life had never been better!

(Years later when we were celebrating by ourselves one Christmas Eve night and were sitting close, Verable said to me, "Christmas Eve will always be *our* special night. That's when I asked you to marry me and you said yes." His simple statement was so sincere and sweet. I would remember it for the rest of my life—and sometimes, remembering would add to my sadness.)

The holidays passed. School reopened and the children were glad to be back to share with everyone what Santa had brought them. Therefore, the first activity of the day was for each student to stand and say whatever they wished to tell us about the holidays at their house. I heard some interesting and cute stories. The rest of the year went by quickly. By the end, some of the children had learned much more than I'd expected. They knew, also, that I was going to have a baby and had told their parents. A few of their parents sent cards of congratulations and one, Mrs. Stuyvesant, sent a gift (a silver dollar) when our baby was born in August. Peter Stuyvesant was her son's name. I remember him as being an intelligent, energetic, and pleasant little boy. I often wondered if his father, a high-ranking officer, whose name was Peter also, was a descendant of the Dutch leader with the same name who lived during the 17th century. 'Guess I'll never know.

As soon as school was out at the end of May, I started making plans for our baby. August was approaching fast. I shopped and found the ideal material to use in making curtains for the baby's room. The fabric had a light blue background with lots of small white bunnies wearing pink ribbons around their necks. I thought that selection would be appropriate for a little boy or girl's room. I wasn't the only proud parent around—Verable went to the commissary shopping for groceries and came home with bags of food.

I asked, "Why did you buy so much?"

He replied, "I'm feeding my wife and baby."

How could I argue with that? Even though I knew he would empty the bags and put the meats away, I would have to find space and store the rest of the food.

Our baby arrived! And I slept through the whole delivery process. It's difficult to believe but once I had gone into delivery, during preparation, the nurse gave me sedation known as Twilight Sleep. I don't know what strength it was but being sensitive to it, I went into a deep sleep and didn't know anything else until I awoke the next morning.

Friday morning, August 26, 1960, I woke up in a hospital ward lined with beds that had a female patient in nearly each one. The sun was shining brightly through the row of windows facing me. Suddenly, experiencing a shock, I tried to sit up and immediately felt my stomach. It was flat! Then, I remembered where I was and what I was doing there.

I called out, "My baby! Where is my baby!"

A patient called back, "I don't know, but you certainly had it!"

The ward nurse heard us and came in to check. She said, "Oh, you're awake, Mrs. McCloud."

I asked somewhat agitated, "Where is my baby?"

The nurse smiled and said, "Everything went very well. We'll bring your baby in to you right away." A few minutes later, a tall, handsome, Hispanic doctor walked in carrying a little bundle.

It seemed even smaller in his hands. I reached for it.

He placed it gently in my arms and said, "You have a beautiful baby girl. She weighs seven pounds and six ounces. She seems very healthy. And you are doing well, too, I see."

I had been looking down at our precious little girl and acknowledged him for the first time. I said, "Oh, Doctor, she's perfectly beautiful. Has my husband seen her yet?"

"Just briefly," the Doctor said. "He wanted to share the first moments of seeing the baby together with you. He was very proud! Right now, he's gone over to the canteen to get a cup of coffee. He's probably a little tired. He was with us most of the night and watched the birth." I thought, *A precious baby girl—a life we created together!* The doctor turned to leave and said, "Congratulations. I'll drop by to see you a little later." I thanked him for everything. He smiled and nodded his head in response.

Shortly after the doctor left, Verable came in wearing a big grin and carrying a dozen red roses. He gave me a coffee breath kiss on my lips and baby Lynn a kiss on the forehead. We had decided months earlier that we would name a daughter Vicky Lynn, so she'd have her dad's initials. He was hovering over both of us. "She is such a beautiful baby," Verable said. She cracked her eyes open as if she knows we were talking about her.

"She has your coloring," I said looking at her head of shiny, black curls and creamy complexion. She was trying to look around but remained quiet. "And she has my facial features," I added. I called attention to her short pug nose and round face.

"She resembles both of us," he said, laughing.

Lynn started to whimper. I rocked her side to side, saying loving words to her softly. She stopped the noise and looked at me. "I'm your mother," I said. At some point, Verable had brought a chair over and was sitting beside the bed. I pointed to him and said, "That's Daddy. We're happy to welcome you." I loosened her blanket so we were able to see her plump little arms and a leg. At seven pounds and six ounces, she was a perfect size. I put her blanket back in place and hugged her gently. Verable had been looking at us. I asked if he wanted to hold Lynn. He said, no, that he would wait until she was a little bigger. I said in a loud whisper, "Chicken!" We both laughed. The nurse came in. "I'm sorry to disturb the three of you," she said, "but it's time for baby to be changed and fed."

I said we understood, but please bring her back as soon as possible. The nurse smiled and said she would. After they left, I thanked Verable for the roses and invited him closer so that I could hug him.

A few days later, "Daddy" took baby and me home in our blue bug. We had everything ready for her in the smaller bedroom. The curtains I made for her room were completed and had been hung. We had purchased a crib, a bathinette, and a baby carriage, or pram, as the British called it. There seemed to be competition among new British mothers to own the most august pram, similar to automobile owners appreciating the most expensive cars. A few American parents had joined the contest. We didn't. We had gone to the Base Exchange and purchased a green and navy-blue plaid, American-styled, waterproof-baby carriage with a comfortable interior. I'd bought some appropriate baby pictures for the nursery walls. And of course, we had gotten baby clothes, cloth diapers, and other necessary products to use in caring for Lynn. When she was three months old, she was christened in our living room by the Chaplin from next door.

Lynn grew fast and was an ambitious little person. By nine months, she was able to pull herself up and walk around in the playpen by holding on to the top. She was learning some words and could crawl very fast—for that reason, she didn't have any interest in learning how to walk. After she passed her first birthday, Verable, in true military fashion, stood Lynn in a corner and said, "Young lady, you are going to learn to walk."

She said, "Dada," then started to sit down to get in her crawling position.

He stood her up again and held his hands out to her, which she ignored and tried to sit back down. He stood her up once more. With patience, he worked with her until she finally took a step. We cheered; he picked her up, kissed her on the cheek, and told her what a good girl she was. He stood her up again and she took a few more steps. By Christmas, Lynn was walking as if she had forgotten how to crawl.

It was important for Lynn to make the progress she had because we had another baby on the way. Apparently, I had gotten pregnant in July, but without the morning sickness, I didn't know until I missed a period. We were pleased because we had planned to have a second child but not quite that close in age to the first one. Later, I was glad they were only 18 months apart because they were such good friends and played so well together.

Christmas was very exciting that year. Our decorations were the same. Verable used canned snow to paint scenes on the front windows again. The one big difference was playing Santa Claus for the first time. Lynn had helped decorate the tree by handing ornaments to her dad as he'd point to one and ask her for it. We had told her the meaning of Christmas and took her to service at the Chapel on Christmas Eve. As soon as she woke up on Christmas morning, we took her to the living room to see what Santa had brought. The first thing she picked from under the tree was a doll—white, of course, none of color were available from Santa. Lynn had a wonderful first Christmas and seeing her so happily engaged in the festivities enraptured Verable and me.

After Christmas, the baby I was carrying had caused me to become mostly stomach and to lose weight in my arms and the rest of my body. When I'd go to the clinic for checkups, some of the medical staff would comment: "To look at you from the back, you don't even look pregnant, but when you turn around, you look like you are all stomach." We prepared for the second baby by buying a smaller crib and adding it to the nursery. Lynn was nearing 18 months, so I told her she was going to get a new sister or brother soon. I also let her feel my stomach when the baby moved.

The Arnolds had arrived on base by that time, and we had become friends with them. He was the gynecologist who treated me. He was concerned about how big the baby was getting, so he told Verable and me if I didn't deliver by the due date, he would have to do a C-Section (Cesarean Section). The due date was Sunday, March 5, 1961.

On Friday night, the third, Verable and I had dinner consisting of steak and complimentary side dishes—no wine. Late Saturday afternoon, I started having labor pains and by night, my water broke. We called the neighbor who had promised to take care of Lynn when I was ready to deliver. She came right away and Verable rushed me to the Bentwaters AFB hospital. Dr. Arnold had been notified and was waiting for us. The medical staff took me right in and began preparations. I don't remember anything after that specifically, except a lot of pain and discomfort.

I guess I was tired because I went into a deep sleep after the birth. I can't remember being moved to the ward with the other mothers. I can't remember waking up or wondering about my baby. I remained in a fog for some time. Verable and the doctor filled me in on all the details later: The baby, a girl, was in the wrong position to be delivered normally, meaning her legs and buttocks instead of the head were in the position to exit first; it would be a breech birth. The doctor decided not to do a cesarean section. So, having the baby normally caused much difficulty and pain. Another problem was that the baby weighed 10 lbs. and eight ounces. At that time, I weighed only 120 pounds. The poor baby probably did not have sufficient room to turn around. I had experienced lots of pain. Verable said that I cursed him a lot during the birth and exclaimed, "I'll never have another baby for you!" The doctor assured him that my reaction was normal due to the pain and my discomfort. I didn't remember making that statement. Neither do I remember when she was born during the wee hours of that Sunday morning.

Verable and I had decided to name the baby Carol Dannette if it was a girl. When I finally woke up, he and Dr. Arnold came to my bed with Dannette. The doctor handed her to me and said, "Congratulations. You have a healthy baby girl. I'm sorry you had such a difficult time during the birth. She is not only big but long." He and Verable shook hands. Verable said, "Thank you, doctor." And Arnold left.

I was busy examining our new baby when the doctor left. She was perfectly formed, except her legs were a little thin for her body. I mentioned this to Verable. He said, "She's fine. I'm sure her legs will grow and catch up with the rest of her. She didn't have room for them to develop fully."

"You're probably right," I said. "She is another pretty baby, though," I said as I looked at her peaceful little face. He agreed. She had straight brownish-black hair. Her complexion was a light reddish tan—a shade between her dad's and mine. I looked at him and said, "You look so tired. Dannette and I are fine and in good hands here. Why don't you go home, check on Lynn, take a nap, and come back later?"

He thought that was a good idea. He kissed both of us and left.

After Dannette was born, I had lots of time to spend with the two babies. We were fortunate to find an English woman who did house cleaning for us once a week. Her older sister, who was much more congenial, babysat with the two children when Verable and I went out locally and even sometimes when we took brief trips on the continent, like to Scotland and Italy. We trusted her implicitly. We wouldn't have been able to get that kind of help in the States for the minimal prices we paid.

Spring arrived. It was warmer but we had to contend with rain. We had Dannette christened on a beautiful May morning in an English Congregational Church. We had made arrangements some days earlier with the minister. It was a lovely ceremony and Dannette was very well-behaved.

I took the girls to the Base Exchange sometimes. Lynn would tell me the book or toy she wanted and we would select for Dannette, with a little help from her by pointing and mumbling. We also went to the base playground. Most Sundays we went to the chapel. There was a class for toddlers that Lynn attended while Dannette played in the nursery and Verable and I attended the church services. On some weekends, Verable took us to one of the beaches. All were covered with small pebbles rather than sand. At other times, we'd go to one of the city playgrounds. We did as many fun things as possible because our time in England was coming to an end.

In the fall, Verable received orders for his next assignment—McClellan AFB in Sacramento California. Farewell parties were given for him by various friends and a prodigious one by the 79th squadron at the Officer's Club. Around the middle of November 1963, movers provided by the military packed all of our belongings and readied them for shipment to California. Meanwhile, Verable had made arrangements for our little Volkswagen bug to be shipped to New Jersey, where we would arrive. All of us were excited on the day we left Woodbridge, AFB to go to Mildenhall. From there, we would fly to McGuire AFB in New Jersey. A major adventure in our lives was coming to an end.

Chapter 22

The trip back to the United States seemed much faster than I remembered the time spent traveling to England. I guess it was because Verable and I were trying to keep Lynn, who was 21 months old, and Dannette, who was nine months old, entertained, although they did sleep some. The frustrating time occurred when we arrived at McGuire. Once the plane landed and we were given the all-clear sign, I buttoned the babies' winter clothes while Verable gathered the toys and other things and put them in the carry-on bag. There was a crowd rushing to get off the plane. Verable carried Lynn and the small bag and I carried Dannette, but we took our time getting to the exit.

When we walked into the airport, we were taken to a nursery in the building and told to leave our children with the attendants. I told the two girls that Daddy and Mommy had to go check-in but that we would be back to get them soon. As two attendants took them and started to walk away from us, both babies started crying. I was sad about their not being able to go with us. However, once we were shown to another room to go through the entrance procedure, I knew it was best they had been left behind. The paperwork, etc. for reentering the USA was much more involved and time-consuming than when I was entering England. Probably because there were four of us and the two younger ones were born in England.

Finally, we were finished. Verable asked where he could pick up the car he had sent over earlier. He was given directions. He said to me, "I'll go and get it and pick up our luggage. You get Lynn and Dannette from the nursery and the three of you wait for me in the front of the waiting room. I'll come in to get you."

I went for my two babies. They had stopped crying but still weren't very happy. One of the attendants who had taken them in helped me bundle them up again.

She said, "They're spoiled, you know."

I didn't respond, except to thank her for her help. Lynn held my hand and walked beside me, and I carried Dannette while we went slowly to the designated place to meet Daddy.

It didn't take Verable long and we were ready when he came for us. It was late afternoon and very cold. The little "bug" had been transported from England with no problems. In anticipation of the trip across country, we had bought a car bed for Dannette and a car seat for Lynn. Both items fitted snuggly but very well on the back seat. The children seemed happy with the seating arrangements. We were going to visit relatives in the east before traveling to California. However, we would stay only one or two nights at each of the places before getting to Mt. Airy. Since Verable's mother and his sister, Jesse, lived there, we planned to stay a few weeks.

Our first visit was with my brother, Jim, and his family in Brooklyn, N. Y. My younger brothers, George and John, came to Jim's apartment to see us. I thought momentarily about when my mother died and how I nearly had to become the guardian and supporter for those two boys. Now they were grown and looked like they had been well-cared for by their dad and the woman with whom he lived. My oldest brother, Jim, had done the right thing when he took Mr. Winters down home to get his two children. Back in the present, everyone wanted to talk and play with Lynn and Dannette. The girls responded very well to all the attention. Plus, Jim's family had a medium-size, mixed breed, black dog who was very friendly with strangers. The girls were intrigued by him and played okay at first but then they wanted to pull his tail. I broke up their game at that point.

It was getting late and both of the girls were tired. They said, "goodnight." I took both of them into the bathroom, ran water, and put them in the tub together. What fun, for them! Lynn wanted her bath cloth and the soap. I gave her the bath cloth, not the soap, to keep her occupied while I bathed her sister. Dannette was very busy splashing water—both arms and hands going up and down as fast as she could move them. Verable was right; her legs had filled out and were perfect for her body. Although she had been large at birth, she was now the right size for her age. She was crawling and would be walking by the time she was a year old. She tried to do everything her big sister did. I held her little plump hands and told her to stop splashing, that Mommy was going to make pretty bubbles with the soap and wash her. Both babies watched me as I rubbed the soap and started bathing Dannette. Once I had finished with her, I called Verable to take her to the other room and put her nightclothes on. He had gotten accustomed to holding and doing things for her soon after we took her home from the hospital. The same was true with Lynn—no more of those "she's too small for me to hold" comments. I finished Lynn's bath, dressed her for bed, and kissed both of them goodnight. They smelled so good and were asleep before I left the room.

It was very good seeing my relatives and finding everyone well. We sat in the living room and talked for a while. My brother Jim's daughters were away. I looked at my watch and realized it was nearing twelve midnight.

I said, "I'm sorry to interrupt, but Verable and I need to go to bed. It's been a long, tiring day and we have to do more traveling tomorrow."

George and John said it was time for them to go back to New York City. So, the party broke up. Josephine showed Verable and me where we would sleep, near the children. She and Jim were ready to retire, also. All of us got a good night's rest and awoke in the morning later than Verable and I had intended.

It was a sunny but very cold day. After feeding the girls, having the breakfast Josephine had prepared for us, Verable and I bundled up ourselves and the children. We put the few things we had taken out for the night back in the car and the girls in their bed and chair. We said goodbye and that we would stay in contact. "Come out to California to see us." I called out the window as Verable drove off.

We spent the next two nights in Washington, D.C where we visited with Verable's two sisters, Naomi and Margaret. Activities and reactions by the relatives were much the same as they had been in Brooklyn: Verable and I were welcomed, told how well we looked, and then, with the exception of preparing and serving meals, Naomi and her family paid most of their attention to our children. We slept at Naomi's and visited Margaret in her apartment the next day. On the third morning, we left Naomi's right after breakfast and started the drive to Mt. Airy. The weather continued to be sunny, but every place we went was much colder than we were accustomed to in England. However, we stayed warm in the little Volkswagen. We arrived in Mt. Airy, N. C. just as it was getting dark. Verable's mother, his sister, Jesse, and her husband, James, were at Mrs. McCloud's house when we arrived.

It was a tender moment for me seeing Verable and his mother embrace. I imagined both were remembering his father who had passed away. But, in the next few minutes, their grandmother turned her attention to the new grandbabies. I recalled that Verable was the son she had thought would never marry, so, of course, his offspring were very special to her. All of us exchanged hugs and expressed how good it was to see each other.

Although we had nearly a month in Mt. Airy, the time passed quickly. There was much sharing of news about the family members we wouldn't get to see, stories about our life in England, much joking, laughing, and eating during our stay. Our fourth day, there was Thanksgiving. Jesse prepared a large, traditional Thanksgiving dinner for us, so we spent most of the day at her house. On other days, when the weather allowed, Jessie and James took us to places where the children could see the mountains up close. We also visited some of their friends—mainly to show off the kids, I think.

On December fourth, we got ready for the trip to California. Verable had suggested that he drive there alone; the girls and I could stay with his mother and fly out to California later. He was concerned that the seven- or eight-day trip in a small car would be too tiring for us. I didn't like that idea—we wanted to travel with him. The time we were apart our first year of marriage was enough. So, we packed the car with toys and necessary things for the children on the back floor with some around my feet in the front. During the ride, I would do a lot of reaching into the back to give toys to the children and take care of their needs. The trunk, which was in the front of the Volkswagen, was packed with everything else. Verable had the engine checked and filled the car with gas.

Chapter 23

At eight o'clock on the morning of December fifth, we left Mt. Airy N. C. for Sacramento, California. It was cloudy and cold. We planned to stop each night in whatever city we were near. The route Verable had selected would take us through some parts of Georgia, Alabama, Texas, Arizona, and on into Bernadine, CA. In some of the states, we had to look for the "Negro" section of town to find a motel that would accept us. Sometimes, it was difficult finding a bathroom for Verable or me. This was not different from what we had expected.

Nevertheless, we enjoyed the trip. I was very sore from reaching back to the children after the first day, but by the third, my body was accustomed to stretching and the soreness diminished. Verable stopped the car and pulled off the road when the children got grumpy or needed special attention. He'd do the same when there was a roadside scene that was especially interesting. Sometimes, he would take photos. Each time we would get out of the car, everyone walked around briefly. Verable designated our sixth day on the road as a time for resting. We stayed in a motel in El Paso, Texas. The next day was fair and very warm. The people seemed friendly, so I thought it was an ideal place to restock our food, especially goodies for the children and to wash a few clothes. Verable took the car to be serviced and then he rested. We stayed overnight in the same motel, had breakfast there the next morning, and left around ten o'clock.

Not long after leaving the motel, we saw the Running Indian Trading Post and couldn't resist stopping to look around. We bought a few souvenirs. Back on the road, we traveled to Mesa California, and spent the night in a motel there. We were in California! The next day while traveling, the girls and I were wide-eyed and exuberant while looking at the roadside scenes. By five P.M., we were in Sacramento. It was easy to find McClellan AFB. Once there, we were directed to the visiting officers' quarters, where we would be allowed to live for a limited period. Expectations were that a family would be able to find permanent housing by the end of the allotted time. The date was December 13. Verable checked in for his new assignment the next morning, the day before his orders dictated he was due. He had made good time in driving.

The apartment we were in was roomy, but it didn't have a kitchen, so we went to the Officers' Club for our meals. Otherwise, there was a large bed for Verable and me and a fold-away sofa bed on which the children would sleep. The room had two bedside tables, a bureau, and a couple of cushioned chairs. There wasn't a T.V. Also, Christmas was only two weeks away so we needed to make the place look a bit more festive.

As always, "Daddy" saved the day. I gave him a list of some things the children might enjoy getting from Santa Claus. He went shopping and bought what I had suggested, plus some gifts he selected. He also bought an 18-inch black and white television. When he came home, he brought in a small decorated Christmas tree, and the television. He left the gifts in the car, so that, *"you know who"* wouldn't see them. I took the tree and placed it on a table, and said, "Oh, look at what Daddy bought!" Lynn, who was very capable on her feet, jumped up and down, clapping her little hands while saying her toddler version of "a Christmas Tree, a Christmas Tree." Dannette, sitting on the floor, wasn't walking yet but could crawl, clapped her hands too, and made sounds. We laughed. I picked her up, hugged her, and repeated "Chris-mas-Tree." She watched my mouth and tried to mimic me.

Verable put the T.V. on one end of the bureau; it was in front of our bed. Some evenings during the holidays, all four of us would sit or lie on the bed and watch Christmas specials. Well, I should say, Verable and I watched. The two girls played around us with small toys or a game of peek-a-boo with the sheet. It was a treat for them to be on the big bed for a while with Mommy and Daddy.

I was enjoying being a mother. Our little girls were so cute (no doubt all parents think that) and bright. A lot of time, effort, and patience were required in carrying for them, but I had a good helpmate in my husband. I was looking forward to our finding a house where I could create a real home for us.

We contacted a black realtor in downtown Sacramento. We told him that we wanted to live as close to the base as possible, so that's where he concentrated our search. He showed us a couple of houses we didn't like, but the third one we really loved. It was like a small cottage, with an eat-in kitchen, a living room, three bedrooms, and a bathroom. Plus, it had a lovely rose garden along the backyard fence *and* it was in our price range. Upon checking, the realtor found someone else had placed a bid on it. All the neighborhoods near the base were predominately white. After the experiences we had traveling through the southern states, I thought the owners didn't want to sell to us because we were Negroes. I didn't and still don't know what the housing laws were in California in 1963. We went back to the base with our feet dragging and our heads hanging low.

The realtor called us a few days later to inform us that he had another house he wanted us to see. We took the children and met him at the address he had given us. In driving through the neighborhood, we noticed it was nicer than the one where the house we had tried to buy was located. We arrived at about the same time as the realtor. The house was grey, ranch-style with an attached two-car garage. There was a small lawn and a tree out front and we soon saw the much larger lawn in the back.

The realtor unlocked the front door and escorted us in, then stepped aside so that we could see the interior. He followed us and answered questions. The house was larger than the one we had expected to buy. There was a short entrance hall and to the left of it a small kitchen, fully equipped with conveniently arranged appliances and pine cabinets. Going through the kitchen, past the garage entrance, we walked into a large open room, a dining area that extended to the end of that side of the house, with sliding glass doors opening onto a patio. There was a large fenced-in backyard with shrubbery along the back section. As we reentered through the glass doors and looked to the left, there was a wide opening in the wall through which we could enter the living room. It had a brick fireplace. A hallway to the left of the living room led to four bedrooms. The master bedroom was last on the left side. It contained a small bathroom. A larger bathroom was at the end of the hall. The house was cooled by central air conditioning and was comfortable.

Our faces gleamed with delight as we walked through the house. The rooms looked like they had been freshly painted. We saw nothing that needed repair. We thought it would fit our needs perfectly. Of course, the cost was more than we had planned to spend at that time, but in talking with Verable, we decided a comfortable, ideal home was worth the sacrifice. We would delay buying any unnecessary furnishings and other things we might want but not need. With savings we had for a down payment and the possibility of a V.A. loan, we would be able to buy that house. We went to the realtor's office and filled out the paperwork.

All the papers went through channels with no difficulty. Within the next two weeks, the house became ours. The little we owned was delivered by the movers. We put the girls' cribs in the room just before ours on the left side of the hall. Since we didn't have furniture yet for the room across the hall from theirs, we called it their playroom and put their small table and little chairs in it as well as toys. It was necessary for us to buy a bed for Verable and me. So, we also selected a brown and black pinstriped sofa for the living room. We decided the bedroom across the hall from ours would be the T.V. room. We purchased a television stand and a sofa for it. We would buy other furnishings when money was available.

We got to know most of our neighbors. There were several families who had children about the ages of ours or a little older. They came over to meet Lynn. Dannette was walking then and would soon join the others outside. It was a well-established, quiet neighborhood, so I watched our children when they were playing out front but didn't worry about them. We soon learned that an older Negro couple and their teenage daughter lived in the neighborhood on the corner of the street behind ours. It didn't take us long to get to know each other. Mrs. Lockett, the neighbor, or her daughter would babysit for us at times. We became very close, like family. Verable was doing well in his new location. I think his responsibilities were similar to those he had in England—confidential. He played golf in a military league and won several prizes. We were invited to military functions where I met various ones with whom he worked and their wives. We also met the other four black officers who were there but were not in the same unit as Verable. All of them lived on base. Infrequently, members of the black group would invite the rest of us over to have dinner or to play bridge. When a couple in this group had a party, white and black friends were invited. There was an Officer's Wives Club, which I joined but did not become very active in. When we went to church, we attended services at the base chapel. We also took our children there to participate in some of the youngsters' activities. Even with what I've described, social life on our new base was not as active as it had been overseas. I guess the difference was being in the United States rather than in a foreign country. While we were in England, everyone was away from home and felt the need to cling together and support each other.

Once, Verable had to go for a week of temporary duty to a base in San Diego and invited me to go along. I accompanied him and went sightseeing during the day while he was on base. We planned special activities for the evenings. We didn't know then that it would be the last trip we'd take together for a long while.

At age three, Lynn was old enough to enroll in the base preschool, DoDo Birds. This school was similar to the one in which I had taught on the base in England, except this one was more firmly established. It had been in existence longer and had a teacher who returned every year. The curriculum consisted of academic and physical activities as well as unusual visits and experiences. For example, the local fire department sent a fireman and fire engine to the school. Students were allowed to get in the truck and the fireman explained the different gadgets. The teacher planned other unusual experiences for the class. Of course, tuition was charged. I enrolled Lynn. She would be able to complete two years before entering kindergarten. The public school she and Dannette would attend later was only a few blocks from our neighborhood. Dannette, who was growing and developing very fast, would start DoDo Birds in about two years.

On the first of December 1965, our happiness disintegrated as if a bomb had been dropped in the center of our lives. A few days before Christmas, Verable received orders to report to an assignment in Viet Nam for a year. The children were in bed and we were sitting on the sofa in the T.V. room when he told me about this new assignment. He had just received orders that day. I became so distraught, I wanted to put my hands over my ears and not listen as he expressed dismay over this new development. He was worried about our daughters and me during the year he would be gone. I thought about the possible danger for him that loomed ahead. We sat with our arms around each other and tried to be consoling. Then we knew we couldn't brood any longer. There were plans to be made, things that had to be done. We decided to discuss plans in the morning. We got ready for bed and went to sleep, cuddled together like two spoons.

The next day was Saturday. Verable cooked pancakes for breakfast—something he loved to do. I dressed the girls. They wanted to rush to the kitchen as soon as they learned what Dad was doing. He hugged and kissed them, then hoisted each onto a dining room chair. (By then, we had bought more furniture for the house.) I joined them at the table. Verable served us his pancakes and sat down. I had put bacon, butter, orange juice, and everything else we needed on the table while he was finishing the pancakes. We enjoyed our breakfast, but we were quieter than usual. When the girls were ready to be excused, Verable told them that we needed to talk with them about something first. My head drooped and they glared at their father.

Verable began by saying, "You girls know Daddy's in the Air Force, right?"

"Yes," Lynn said, "to keep bad people away."

He answered, "You're exactly right, Baby. Well sometimes, in order to protect the United States, where we live, daddies have to go to places overseas where the bad people are, and their families can't go with them."

Dannette thought for a moment. "You go bye-bye?" she asked, with tears forming in her eyes.

"Yes," he said, "but not for long."

Lynn became teary, too, and I could see sadness spread over Verable's face like a dark cloud. I spoke up, "Your daddy and others have to go to Viet Nam for a year, but he'll be back before we know it. Then he'll stay with us just as he is now." Both girls started crying. I said as cheerfully as possible, "But you know what?" Both looked at me wide-eyed. "Since Daddy won't be here for Jesus' birthday on the 25th, we're going to celebrate it—Christmas, that is—early. How would you like that?"

The tears and sniffles ceased. "Will Santa come early?" Lynn asked.

Daddy said, "Sure he will! I promised Dannette that he'd bring the large bouncing horse she wants. Santa has to come before I leave so I'll know he kept his word about bringing it."

"And my Negro doll," Lynn said. Their dad answered, "Right."

"Do you two feel better now that you know Daddy will celebrate Christmas with us this year and will be back home soon?"

Dannette responded, "Yes."

Lynn said, "I guess so." Verable had about one and a half weeks left with us. From time to time, I'd sneak away to a private place and let my tears flow.

We celebrated Christmas a week before Verable left. I cooked a big dinner, consisting of the foods he liked. The previous night, Santa Claus had brought gifts the girls wanted. In the morning, they were happy. The Negro doll Lynn received was about three feet tall, a chocolate brown, with long, silky black, braided hair. She wore a deep pink dress. Lynn treated the doll as if she were another sister. Dannette's horse was large, gray, and attached to springs that made it bounce rather than rock. She'd climb up on it wearing a cowboy hat and pretend she was riding the range like she'd seen on T.V. Of course, there were other gifts. Dannette hadn't asked for it but she also received a doll like Lynn's.

On the day Verable left, we rode with him to Travis AFB from where he was scheduled to depart. We had timed the drive so that he arrived just a little before his plane was scheduled to leave. In doing so, the girls and I didn't have to spend a long time at the airport feeling sad. We couldn't hold back our tears as we said "goodbye." He told the girls to be good and me not to worry, that he would be fine. I drove us back to Sacramento and home.

Chapter 24

Lynn continued in DoDo Birds. Dannette and I took care of chores at home and went shopping sometimes during the mornings when Lynn was in school. School was over at twelve, so we'd pick her up and occasionally have lunch out. Home did not seem the same with Verable gone. I could only pray that he would be safe and make it back to us. The girls said a prayer each night, too, so I told them to ask God to bring their daddy back home safely. Verable had all our business matters and other things in good order for me to do the tasks that he had done. These included paying the monthly bills and taking charge of the budget. He had even talked with the manager at the gas station where our car was serviced and asked him to assist me if there were any problems with it.

Lynn, Dannette, and I tried to carry on normally. But the girls missed Daddy, just as much as I did. However, they displayed their missing him by misbehaving. For example, Lynn, who seemed to be the most disheartened, took a book of unused stamps off my desk and, without my knowing, she stuck them on the bedroom doors. Another time, she took her daddy's phonograph records out of their jackets and stood the records in the fireplace. There wasn't a fire going, but I tried to impress upon her how they could be scratched. Dannette didn't perform any untoward stunts, but she cried more than ever before, at the least provocation. Sometimes when crying, she'd say, "I want Daddy." I'd try to explain why he couldn't be there. It was difficult trying to keep the children pacified. I have to admit that things bothered me to the extreme sometimes. It wasn't because of the children necessarily. It was life in general. I was very angry at times with myself, my life, and often felt depressed but tried to hide my emotions when I was around the children. I didn't tell Verable about those episodes because I didn't want to worry him. Everything else was going well.

Verable and I contacted each other nearly every day—by letters and/ or small recorded audiotapes. He said it was rough in Viet Nam, but he was O.K. He always wanted to know how and what we were doing. Bits of news and words of affection going back and forth helped each of us persevere as the months dragged by.

Verable's sister, Elizabeth, and her husband, June, visited us in California during the early spring. They drove down from Aurora, Colorado. It was their first time meeting our children. The couple brought a respite to our daily routines. They talked, played games, and teased the kids. We went to some places the children liked to visit—especially a farm, open to the public, that had a large pond with ducks. We were allowed to feed them. During that visit when Dannette was feeding one, its beak closed on her fingertip. It didn't hurt enough for her to cry or tell anyone, but it did leave her with a negative impression of ducks. Our relatives left at the end of the week. Some days after they left, Dannette was drinking milk with her lunch. She took a swallow and said, "Yuck! This milk tastes like duck milk."

I laughed and asked, "What?" She didn't answer but made that comment a few other times while she was young. She never told us why she said that until she was an adult. We were teasing her about that expression and she explained what had happened at the farm.

Dannette was born with an umbilical hernia that seemed to be getting larger. At times, it became strangulated and looked painful. Her pediatrician said it did not hurt, but I disagreed with him and wanted it to be repaired. Since her father was overseas, I got permission for the surgery to be done in the base hospital at no cost. She would be admitted one day, have the surgery the next morning, and go home in the afternoon. I stayed with her overnight and until her surgery was completed the next day. The doctor said she was fine. Although when he brought her out of surgery, she was so pale and looked so lifeless that I worried. After the sedative wore off, she looked and seemed to be better.

One of the parents from Lynn's DoDo Birds class, who also lived in our neighborhood had volunteered to keep Lynn while Dannette was in the hospital. She had two daughters. The younger one had been in DoDo Birds with Lynn, the other was a little older. As soon as I was assured Dannette was okay, I drove over to see how Lynn was doing. Then I stopped by home to get a fresh set of P.J.s for Dannette. She was awake and bright when I got back to the hospital, anxious to go home. I changed her clothes and took her with me to get Lynn. Finally, all three of us were safely at home. I was so stressed and tired from activities of the past thirty-six hours but relieved. As soon as we walked through the door, I hugged both girls tightly and started crying like a hurt child. When I let them go, they stared at me with stunned expressions. I explained, "Mommy's just so happy that the three of us are together."

At the end of May, Lynn completed her second year in DoDo Birds. The teacher held a graduation ceremony for the students who would go to kindergarten in the fall. Of course, parents and some special guests were invited. It was such a cute affair. The students wore little white academic robes and square, white mortarboard caps with royal blue tassels. They looked like miniature high school or college graduates. The teacher opened the program and made some remarks including words of congratulations. Then she called each student by name, one at a time, and they walked upfront to receive a certificate. Upon returning home, I hugged and kissed Lynn and tried to explain what an achievement she had made—how proud Daddy and I were of her. This was an important point in her life he had to miss due to his career. I gave her a gift from the two of us. It was a necklace with a small golden cross. She was so tired, she nearly dozed off while I was talking to her.

On the first of June, Jesse and James, Verable's sister and brother-in-law from Mt. Airy, N.C., came to spend two weeks with us. They are the couple with whom we had Thanksgiving dinner when we returned from England. The girls remembered them very well and were delighted to see them. So was I. The things we did while they were there was a replay of what we had done when Elizabeth and her husband visited. Of course, it was much hotter, so more time was spent outside, with the girls playing in their kiddy pool and the adults sitting on the patio out back talking. They left around the middle of June.

We had approximately seven weeks before both girls would go to school—Lynn to the public elementary school and Dannette to DoDo Birds. During the latter part of August, we went shopping for school clothes. By the second week in September, both girls were successfully enrolled and seemed to enjoy their new schools. Each class only lasted half a day. "Daddy" would be home in three and a half months—in three months—in two months—We were getting very anxious. Our neighbors, the Locketts, invited the three of us to have Thanksgiving dinner with them. The girls enjoyed going to their house because they could play with their little brown Dachshund. Dinner was delicious and I always enjoyed visiting with them.

Finally, it was December 15. Verable had written to me concerning his expected arrival at Travis AFB on the twentieth at two o'clock in the afternoon.

We made a large sign using white paper and bright colors, which read, "WELCOME HOME, DADDY." We hung it above the fireplace so that he would see it upon entering the house. I cleaned until the house was spotless and had planned the menu for that evening's dinner. The morning of December 20th arrived. The girls were jumping up and down, clapping their hands. They asked what seemed like a hundred times that morning, "When are we going to get Daddy?" My response was always, "Soon."

We left the house around 12:30 P.M. and made good time in going to the base—I didn't make a wrong turn even once. We were a little early for the arrival of the plane, so we sat in the waiting room and watched people and traffic. The girls were very fidgety. One minute they were sitting in seats next to me, the next they were running to the front window to see if any more planes had arrived. I knew they were excited. At last, the plane Verable was coming on eased into its slot. I took Lynn and Dannette each by a hand. We waited until we saw him coming down the steps, then we made our way through the door and ran to him. What a reunion! The girls were first to get to him. They were too large for him to pick them up together, so he picked up Dannette first, hugged, and kissed her. As he put her down, he told her she had really grown. He pick up Lynn, went through the same ritual, and congratulated her for being in first grade. I was last, but I got the biggest hug and kiss. We lingered telling each other how good it was to be back together.

Verable had so much luggage that he wanted to get the car first, then pick up his bags. In addition to his belongings, he had brought numerous gifts for us. With some struggling and by using the floor in the back, we were able to secure everything. Verable wanted to drive us home, so I agreed. I didn't like to drive anyway, especially when he was a passenger, because he was a very annoying back seat driver. I remembered that from the time before he went to Viet Nam. He told us about his trip, asked the girls about school, and reiterated how much he had missed all of us. He and I exchanged comments about our taped messages to each other. Before we realized it, we were at home. When Verable walked in the front door, he saw the welcome home sign. With teary eyes, he complimented the artwork on it and thanked us. He also commented on how good the house looked. Again, he hugged each of us and told us how happy he was to be home.

※

A look into our future beyond the scope of this memoir reveals that my dear husband developed PTSD as a result of being in Viet Nam and it became more evident as he aged. Also, his exposure to deadly chemicals there caused him to have Parkinson's and probably contributed to his having cancer of the kidneys in his late seventies. At that time, he had one and two-thirds of his kidneys removed, which eventually required his having dialysis three times a week for approximately the last five years of his life.

He arrived home from Viet Nam on December 20, 1966, just 5 days before Christmas. That evening after dinner, Lynn, Dannette, and I tried to bring him up to date on everything that had happened while he was away. Afterward, he opened his bags and gave us the gifts he had brought: several pieces of jewelry, two Viet Nam-style dresses with pants, and a pair of silk P.J.s from Hong Kong for me. He explained that he had gone to Hong Kong while he was on R&R (rest and relaxation)—a brief vacation.

He brought the girls silk P.J.s, a silk kimono each, Japanese dolls, and origami books. And he brought various decorative items for the house. The girls and I modeled the pajamas for him before going to bed. We kissed his cheeks to thank him. He seemed very proud. It's no surprise that our Christmas celebration that year was extra special. Verable's next assignment was Offutt AFB in Omaha, Nebraska.

Chapter 25

Captain Verable McCloud was scheduled to report for his new assignment in Nebraska not later than January 30, 1967. In preparation for leaving Sacramento by January 15, we made arrangements for a realtor to sell the house, although we knew that wouldn't happen before we left. We contacted movers to pack our belongings and move them to Nebraska in time for our arrival. I withdrew our two daughters from their respective schools. Verable had purchased a larger car—Mercury Cougar—before leaving Viet Nam and had been assured it would be delivered to Sacramento in time for him to drive to Nebraska. Unfortunately, it didn't arrive as expected, so Verable had the delivery rerouted to Omaha. We packed the Volkswagen with things we would need on the road and Verable drove it.

The route from Sacramento to Nebraska was long and treacherous with snow-covered roads through mountainous areas—but it seemed there weren't many bad spots of hard ice. We seldom saw other vehicles on the road, so the falling snow had not had a chance to become packed and slippery. To stop every night, sometimes, we had to travel after dark to get to the next motel. One morning after leaving the motel, we stopped to have breakfast in a restaurant at the top of a mountain. The view was breathtakingly beautiful. And the food was good.

Surprisingly, we reached Omaha two days early on a Saturday afternoon. The rooms we had reserved at the guest quarters on base wouldn't be available until Monday. We could only stay there three nights, because of the number of military families traveling to and from the base. We checked into a motel for the weekend. Since the real estate offices were closed by that time, we planned to start looking for permanent housing the next day. There weren't any vacancies in the officers' housing on base. Sunday morning, we checked the local paper and base newspapers for private listings. When we investigated the rentals, we found most were too small, too expensive, or already rented. The last homeowner who showed us a rental suggested that we look at houses in a neighboring town which was about a 20-minute drive from the base. He said that where we had been looking and where he lived was Bellevue, a town that surrounded the base, and "Therefore," he said, "the rent is probably higher here." We took his advice, searched the newspapers for a house in the town he had mentioned, and found a realtor there who advertised he was available on Sundays. In thumbing through the materials, Verable had received from his sponsor. I noticed the same realtor was recommended in materials from the base Family Service. We called him. He was a very pleasant-sounding man who assured us that he had at least three rentals available.

With a little optimism and lots of hope, we drove to his office. It was in the basement of his home. He invited us in, but the pleasantness I had detected in his voice on the phone had been replaced by nervous anxiety. When we sat down in his office to talk, the three houses he assured us he had for rent were decreased to two—possibly. However, he said, "Come with me and I'll show them to you."

On the way over to the houses, we realized he was asking us a lot of questions: "How long have you people been here?" "Where were you before?" "Where are you from originally?" "You're both college graduates, aren't you?" When we replied "yes," he said, "I thought you sounded like it. What do you do in the Air Force, Cap'n?" When Verable said he was in intelligence, the realtor asked, "What exactly do you do?" The realtor didn't get any additional information on that subject.

We finally arrived at the houses and had a look at them. They were both ideal so we indicated the one we preferred and rode with the realtor back to his office to draw up the lease. He was so pensive on the return trip that we should have known what to expect. We followed him into his office. After asking us to be seated, he said, "You know you folks are the first ones that have been to me and I'm going to have to get the owner's permission before I can rent to you."

I said, "The first ones?" But then answered my own question, "You mean the first Negroes." "Yes," he replied. "You are apparently very clean, intelligent people, but even if the owner does agree, I don't know how the neighbors will take my renting to you. We just don't have any Negroes living in this community."

It's difficult to describe how we felt at that moment—angry, subhuman, hurt. We had not gone to that realtor wanting to be first nor the last Negro family to move into his community. It really hadn't crossed our minds. We were not "blockbusters"—a term that was used back then. We were simply an American family trying to find suitable living quarters. And we were being told "no" not because my husband wasn't employed or for other rationalizations that were usually given. We were being denied the privilege to rent a house because of who we were, *Negroes!*

In reply to his comments, my first thought was of our children, especially the five-year-old who would be attending kindergarten in the neighborhood. I told him if there was a chance we'd be harassed, we would rather not rent that house.

"Well, suppose I just call around and get the feelings of some of the neighbors about this."

We knew that we no longer wanted to live in that neighborhood, but we wanted to see how far he would go in making a fool of himself.

He proceeded to dial a number and after exchanging greetings with the person on the line, he explained: "I have a nice Negro couple here (He sounded much like I imagined a slave auctioneer had sounded) who wants to rent the Jones house next door to you. I wonder how you think the people on your street will take it." He went on to give what he considered our qualifications: "educated, clean—the husband is a capt'n over at the base." After a few "un-huh's" and "is that right?" He hung up the phone, turned to us, and said, "He doesn't want to commit himself. He said he just doesn't know." He reflected a moment, then the realtor said, "I'd really rather not to rent to you people because I don't want the town to 'black ball' me. I've been in this neighborhood too long to have to move somewhere else and start over again. I'm sorry." He concluded.

My husband said, "We're sorry, too, but if your neighbors feel that way, we'd rather *not* live here."

I said, "But your agency is on the list Family Services supplied to us. In order to be on that list, you are supposed to be willing to rent to any military family."

"Yes," he said, "I remember they called me about that and I told them they could include me. Come back tomorrow morning and I'll be happy to show you houses in the northern part of town. It's a new development and I know there are Negroes living there. It's probably just what you want and I'll be happy to sell you one of those."

Verable said, "No thank you. That's farther from the base than we want to live."

Night had fallen when we drove away from that little town. It was moonless and dark, a description that described our feelings. The thing that hurt me most was the thought that Verable had risked his life to help preserve freedom for people like that realtor and his neighbors. One consolation I held on to was the fact that Negroes and whites could live together as neighbors because we had participated in examples of that on the base in England and in civilian housing in California.

The next morning was Monday. We packed our bags and moved out of the motel by 10:30. Check-in at the base guest house was not until 2:30 that afternoon. Soon, snow began to fall and I thought of just how homeless we were. Verable remained calm, as usual, and tried to reassure me. But I continued to worry about where we would live after our three-day stay in the guest house. (The motel was too expensive.)

We went to the Officer's Club and had lunch. Afterward, we used a phone to call real estate offices that were listed in Bellevue. To avoid any other disappointments, I explained to each one I called, "We are a Negro family, if you have any reservations about renting to us, please tell me now so we won't waste each other's time." I felt as if I were apologizing for our heritage. Several said they would have to check the owner's contract to make sure they hadn't included a written objection. In most instances, the number of houses they had available decreased after they checked. Others said they would be willing to rent to us, but they didn't have any homes available at that time. There were two who said they had rentals available and it didn't matter to them that we were Negroes.

With the aid of one of the latter agencies, we found a new house that was listed for rent with an option to buy. We liked the house and thought the agreement was a good one. We found out later it would be to our advantage economically to buy the house after renting it for two months. All our neighbors, except one, were Caucasian. The one other Negro was a single, female Air Force Major who lived a block from us. She and my husband were the only military members in the community. However, our neighbors were very friendly and did not show us any animosity. In fact, there were lots of children with whom our girls became good friends and playmates. Some of the parents and I exchanged visits at times. Our little family was comfortable and usually happy.

It is with a heavy heart and feelings of deep remorse that I admit most of the times my family, especially my husband, didn't feel happy was due to my actions and words. I can remember, even as a child, having very great feelings of melancholy, when I was sad and would privately cry over nothing I could identify. Up until my late teens, these symptoms only included depression. As I entered my early twenties, my moods started to include anger. At other times, I would feel just the opposite: happy, cheerful, and empowering, as if nothing was beyond my ability. By the time I was married and had children, my mood swings became impossible for me to hide from my husband. He was the target of all my fury, perhaps because he was the closest person to me—the one I loved most. I thought about my Aunt Clara, who had acted the same way toward her mother and sister when she experienced angry moods. I was afraid I was becoming like her.

Was I experiencing a breakdown of values and morals? Where I had always been a quiet, easy-going, friendly person, I began to find fault mainly with my husband and I verbalized these feelings by criticizing, calling him names, and cursing at him. Those behaviors were shown only toward him at home. At the same time, I began to crave the attention of other men. I developed a greater taste for alcoholic drinks. Finally, I was very jealous and possessive of my husband. Still, these diatribes did not last forever. Within a few days or a week or two, I was back to being calm and loving to Verable. I would feel more energetic and capable. I was not self-loathing anymore. In fact, I had an exaggerated opinion of myself and my abilities. Sometimes, those feelings of grandeur stayed with me even when the dark mood returned. It always returned, but later when I was employed, the dark periods never interfered with my performance on the job. In fact, periods of mania made me more creative and energetic.

The mood swings continued. I realized I was hurting my husband. One day when I was in an especially choleric mood and was raving about something to Verable, he started crying and said, "Anece, I just can't take it anymore!" I left the room with no further comment. I realized then I had to try to gain control of my actions and words. But how could I when control seemed out of my hands?

I went to a psychiatrist. He listened to my problem but did not tell me why I was experiencing such behavior. I don't think he knew. He gave me a prescription for Valium and told me to return in two weeks. The medicine made only a slight difference; I became calmer generally and slept better. However, I still had mood swings and my anger subsided only a little.

My husband continued to show love for me but couldn't understand why

I acted the way I did at times. He thought I could stop the periods of anger and outrage if I wanted to do so. Because of that assumption, at times, he was unpleasant to me. It's regrettable that we didn't converse more with each other about my health problem rather than writing about our feelings in notes to ourselves: I wrote in the mornings expressing my deep, dark feelings about myself. I learned later that all through the time we were having problems, Verable couldn't sleep and would get up in the middle of the night, go to another room, and pour his grief into writing poems. I found them while cleaning the house one day and read them. Afterward, I felt sad and guilty for making his life so terribly miserable. I sat down and cried, my tears flowing like a slow waterfall. I tore up most of his writings but saved the less depressing ones to always remember the hurt I had caused this wonderful person. Three of his writings I saved are included below:

I

> I watched you sleeping
> this morning
> The beauty of your sleep
> runs deep and quiet
>
> Like a banked fire, all your
> emotions are stilled.
> Only your breathing belies
> what lies beneath:
> The warmth and need for
> love,
> The acid thrown by your
> words.
> If I should touch you now
> Which would it be?

II

> I walked into loneliness
> when I married you.
> I walked into loneliness,
> hidden from my view
> I walked into a world that
> fools dare not tread
> I walked in, my darling,
> full speed ahead
> I walked into the darkness
> of a world apart

I walked into emptiness
now within my heart.
Your world was filled with
wonderful things
When I first walked in
I wish there was a way for me to
crawl out and walk back in again.

III

Dearest:
For the words I never say
and the prayers I never pray
the wrongs I always make
never realizing my mistake
the deeds I never do
Please forgive me—but I
still love you.

The following is a copy of one of the messages I wrote to myself during a depressing morning.

"Dear God, where are you? Why can't I enjoy peace of mind? I feel so boxed in. It seems everything I'm doing is required of me and I hate all of it. I wish I could go someplace else. My life has become so humdrum! I can't settle down and concentrate on anything; I'm like a worm in hot ashes. Oh, God, if I could die right now, I wouldn't mind. My thoughts, my hopes, my dreams are all in turmoil. I am not satisfied with anything in my life at this moment and it's all my fault. I have every right to be happy. But I can't. I desire, I crave, I want—and even when I get what I thought I wanted, I'm not satisfied. There is no peace. I hate myself. I want to leave but I can't get away from me."

While we were trying to learn more about my mood swings, the doctors found I had sarcoidosis, an inflammatory disease that can affect any part of the body. It had selected my lungs. I'm not sure if there was any connection to the sarcoid, but later, I was diagnosed with hyperthyroidism. I was given a radioactive iodine treatment and oral medications. I was to take that medicine until the hyperthyroidism ceased and became hy**po**thyroidism, predictably some years in the future. At that time, I would be prescribed a different medicine. But nothing else was done about the mood swings.

These health problems occurred at various times in the early years of our life together. Verable and I learned to live with the good and bad times—more good than bad. We were happy with each other most of the time and our love stayed strong.

I have noted the discovery of my illnesses occurred during the early years of our marriage because the problems continued in the future when I was employed. However, my health never interfered with my productivity.

Chapter 26

By the late 1960s, I realized I needed to get involved in an activity outside of the home. The girls were in school most of the day. Lynn, the oldest, had joined a local Brownie Girl Scout Troop. One of the mothers in the neighborhood led the group and announced she could use help. I volunteered for that year. We had fun thinking up projects and helping the girl scouts work on them.

When the year of volunteering ended, I decided I wanted and needed to have a salaried position. I went to an employment agency in Omaha and applied for a job. The person who interviewed me was impressed with my resume and assured me she would be able to find a position to match my qualifications. She said she would get back to me. She called me in three days and said a home for unwed mothers, Child Saving Institute (CSI), had an opening for a resident advisor. She gave me some information about the job and asked if I would like her to make an appointment for me with the supervisor. I said yes and thanked her for her assistance.

I had the interview with a Mrs. Moss, the supervisor, on a Wednesday the following week. She was a very pleasant, medium height, slender, blond woman, who looked to be in her early thirties. She greeted me at the front door of the brick building that reminded me of a large house from the early twentieth century. The interior of the building was very spacious and homey. Mrs. Moss invited me into her office and offered me a seat. We had a conversation about my past, including where I was from originally, my family, and some details about my work experiences.

Then she told me about the home and the agency. They accepted girls at three or four months of gestation and at various ages. The youngest at that time was 15. These were women who for various reasons did not want people in their communities to know they were pregnant out of wedlock. There were approximately 20 residents at that time. They were from different locations, but mostly from the Midwest and the Western United States. They were all Caucasian except two, who were of ethnic backgrounds. The women were provided with medical care throughout their pregnancy and were escorted to the University of Nebraska Medical Center when they were ready to deliver. The Medical Center was right across the street from the home. After giving birth, most women used the adoption services provided by the institute.

Child Saving Institute was a Red Feather Organization and agency of the National Benevolent Association of the Christian Church. It was well-organized and managed. The staff consisted of an administrator, a treasurer, a minister, several caseworkers, the supervisor (who was also a caseworker), and five (RAs) resident advisors. While the RAs worked with all clients, each had a main interest and, in some instances, special training that became part of her position. For example, one was a registered nurse, one a cosmetic/beauty consultant, another taught art and pottery; I was an educational coordinator for administering tests from some of the clients' schools, plus I taught sewing and cooking. The fifth person was a sociologist; she planned activities for girls in the home and at places in the city. With the RAs having a variety of abilities, we conducted a plethora of programs for the women. The staff members and the young women with whom I worked were very friendly and pleasant to be around. Although I was receiving a salary, I couldn't help but think I was doing a good deed by being there and trying my best to help make our young clients' lives happier.

The Resident Advisors worked in shifts—no less than two at a time. I chose the period of 3:00 pm to 11:00 pm. This allowed me to be available during the school day if one of our daughters needed a parent. We paid a teenage neighbor to make sure our girls arrived home safely from school. She gave them a snack and stayed with them until their father returned from work, which was usually at 5:30. He'd eat dinner with them and later in the evening supervised their getting ready for bed. I'd get home around 11:30 pm. Although our daughters were supposed to be in bed and asleep then, the younger one, Dannette, was usually awake. Rubbing her sleepy eyes, she would come to the living room where her dad and I were talking. She would climb up on my lap and lay her head against my chest, listening to my breathing and heartbeat. She told me this when she was a teenager and remembered these were special moments.

I worked at CSI from 1969 to 1971. I missed having evenings with my family. First, I asked to have my hours changed to part time—5:00 to 11:00 pm—so that I could see my children more. Then when I realized we needed those evening hours together as a family including my husband, I resigned.

A year later, in 1972, a new position led to others and a series of experiences that assisted in my efforts to become a better and different person. In explaining how this happened, I will have to give detailed descriptions of the times and my professional roles.

First Professional Role

The University of Nebraska Medical (UNMC) was advertising for an Assistant Registrar in academic records. The position would have regular hours, 8:00 a.m. to 4:30 p.m., five days a week. I applied, was interviewed by the Registrar, Mrs. Rosewater, and was hired. My physician was on the medical staff there and spoke to Mrs. Rosewater on my behalf—I had told him about my plans to apply. During the interview, she mentioned he had spoken with her about me. The question I recall most vividly from our meeting was her last one. "What would you like to be doing in five years?" I answered, "I would like to be in a position similar to yours." She smiled. The Registrar was professional in her demeanor and friendly. She was around five feet tall and very thin. She looked to be in her early sixties. An Assistant Registrar for admissions, Maude, worked with her. Maude was around 35, a woman of medium height, a creamy complexion, long silky black hair, and a bubbly personality. She had worked with Mrs. Rosewater for several years.

Much of the University Medical Center campus consisted of large buildings and driveways as one would expect. I had been able to find the Registrar's Department very easily. It was on the first floor of a building located across a driveway from the hospital. The entrance to the building was separated by a foyer with stairs leading to the second floor. From the foyer, a hallway on the right ran past the two doors of the Registrar's department. The first door entered the main part of the Registrar's area and a secretary was located there. It was the only entrance to the registrar's section. Inside, to the right of the door, was a wall opening into Maude's office, a glass enclosure with a sliding glass front where Maude provided various services to students and managed admissions. On the opposite side in the secretary's office, an interior door opened into Mrs. Rosewater's office. The second office door to the right of the hall opened into the area where an assistant and I would do all student record-keeping duties. Adjoining it, a room was being remodeled for the vault, where the student files would be stored. The door that normally opened into the vault room from the hall had been sealed off and the whole room fireproofed.

The UNMC student records had been stored at the University of Nebraska in Lincoln, Nebraska since 1913. The registrar's office there had also sent out transcripts when requested. Both university campuses were growing so the administration determined all past, present, and future Medical Center student records would be housed and transcripts issued by the UNMC Registrar. That's how the position for which I was hired came about.

As the first Assistant Registrar for Academic Records at the Medical Center, I had the privilege of learning firsthand about collecting records, arranging them to be moved in the order of time needed by colleges and programs. I learned, also, how to arrange and file them in the UNMC vault for efficient retrieval. Mrs. Rosewater and I went to the Lincoln campus. There we met with their director and staff of registration and records. Mrs. Rosewater knew everyone, so after she introduced me, the Lincoln Registrar escorted us into their vault to have a look at the Medical Center records. During a brief meeting, the group agreed that the records should be moved on six dates, about three months apart, between November 1973 and August 1974. There were 10,663 records to be moved and filed in the UNMC vault. That would be my primary responsibility.

At that time, there were three colleges: Medicine, Nursing, the Graduate College, and four Allied Health Programs for which we had student records, plus all of those for past attendees. The campus news reported that the oldest record among those moved was for a student who matriculated in 1902. The College of Dentistry was located on the Lincoln Campus; their records would remain there. When the College of Pharmacy building was completed at UNMC, their student records would be filed on our campus.

Even before I was hired, the administration decided that a secretary/records clerk would be needed to assist with the many responsibilities of the office. Since this was a new section of the Registrar's office, I decided to prepare a general statement that defined the relationship between the Registrar's and Assistant Registrar's offices. I hoped the statement would serve as a guide for the present and the future.

Statement: "While the Academic Records office is a part of the Registrar's Department, and we feel confident that we can call upon the Registrar and members of her staff in emergency situations, we will be autonomous in handling the duties of this office. Therefore, the Assistant Registrar and the Records Clerk will have the full responsibility for this office, including but

Seeking Personal Validation

not limited to receiving and cataloging records from the Lincoln campus, of establishing permanent records for each person new to the University Medical Center Colleges and Programs, of posting grades for each student at the end of every quarter, semester and/or trimester, of making authorized grade changes, of issuing transcripts, answering correspondence, receiving and checking degree applications and recording degrees." This list was based on the position description the Registrar had prepared and given to me when I was hired. Using this statement for reference, I prepared a position description for the records clerk.

Within two weeks of posting the ad for a Records Clerk, we received several applications. We finally selected whom we considered the best candidate—Carol. She was a 22-year-old, tall, slender woman with short dark hair. She was energetic and easy to work with. As I learned the job, I taught her. Everything went smoothly. The Academic Records office experienced continual growth as exemplified by the increase in the number of official transcripts issued in a sixth-month period, from 598 at the beginning of the year to 837 by the end of six months. Within approximately three years, I would be promoted.

In American society in general and education in particular, race relations were changing. This led to my becoming involved with students in a very special way. Some might ask why was there a change in black and white interactions? The answer requires a brief reference to mid-twentieth century history.

As most Americans know, the 1950s and 60s were tumultuous years in race relations. Negroes began to become more and more agitated and aggressive about the way we were being treated. There were increasingly physical and vocal uprisings. Some were helpful. We cannot forget "The Little Rock Nine" in 1957 who, only with the presence of armed soldiers, were able to enroll at Central High School in Little Rock, Arkansas. Remember? The Greensboro Lunch Counter Sit-In in 1960, opening the way for Negros and other people of color to sit at counters in various places. Remember? The Student Nonviolent Coordinating Committee, whose members worked hard in the decade of the 60s to register Negroes in the South to vote. This action opened many political doorways for Negroes.

Other acts only helped to fan the flames of anger. This was true with riots that took place in the 50s and 60s. There were many uprisings due to inappropriate actions by police and other whites. The news reported that during a 1963 civil rights demonstration in Birmingham, Ala., the leaders, including Martin Luther King, were beaten by police and other whites. Dr. King was arrested. President Kennedy called out 3,000 troops to bring order.

The aforementioned demonstrations are just a small example of what fed the civil rights movement. Many churches, organizations, including student groups and individuals, worked together to bring about change. Of course, Dr. Martin Luther King was the leader and at the forefront. I think it was in the 1970s when Black Pride became prominent and Negroes dropped the third designation we had been given by whites— Negro—after being called slaves and colored. We recognized ourselves as African Americans and blacks and those two names became the standard references.

The social actions mentioned here helped to turn the tide in a lot of things, but especially in educational institutions. In the professional schools, specifically in medical education, some school administrators acknowledged that blacks and other ethnic Americans were grossly underrepresented in their schools and, therefore, among practicing professionals. The University of Nebraska Medical Center was one institution where the administers knew the school had a problem with minority enrollments and were ready to try to remedy the situation.

There were only a few African American professionals at UNMC. Not one was a Medical Doctor, and only three, as I recall, were nurses. The others were in technical fields and the Medical School library. However, the ones there were interested in seeing more black students in programs on campus. This small group of black professionals, interested black students, and some caring white professionals formed a committee in 1970 (two years before I arrived). One report says the group was named the Minority Student Recruitment Program (MSRP). In 1973, it was changed to the Minority Student Recruitment Committee (MSRC). The main objectives of MSRC were creating awareness among minority students of programs available at UNMC, aspiring them to pursue a health career, motivating within them the desire to take the appropriate courses in high school and college, and encouraging them to maintain good grades. Minorities in Nebraska included African Americans, Mexican Americans, Native Americans, and Mainland Porto Ricans. These groups are often referred to as "under-represented" minorities because their percentage representation in various professions, such as medicine, is much less than their percentage in the population. In some locations, disadvantaged whites were also included. The voluntary MSRC did not have its own budget, but the Chancellor had granted the Assistant to the Chancellor for Student Affairs, Mr. Gibson, permission to use a portion of his budget for committee publications and other small expenses. The committee was performing a great service to the Medical Center and the administration realized this. I was impressed by their efforts and joined the organization.

The members worked to become a viable committee on campus. In doing so, we elected an executive committee that consisted of the MSRC officers and chairmen of the sub-committees on Communications, Tours, Recruitment, and Retention. The MSRC's activities involved visiting high schools in Omaha and on the Winnebago Indian reservation, talking with students about opportunities and the need for them in health professions, preparing pamphlets to hand out, making and showing movies and slideshows about healthcare needs, encouraging assistance of and support from the members' departments, and many other actions on behalf of minority students. Creighton University had an Office of Minority Affairs for Health Sciences. The UNMC committee of volunteers often joined Creighton's personnel in hosting programs at the local schools. Together, we presented programs to approximately 2,200 ninth-graders at eight Omaha Public Schools in the fall of 1974.

The Creighton Minority Affairs Director and an MSRC member prepared a questionnaire for the students to serve as a follow-up to the programs and to furnish information for the second-semester health careers activities. The questionnaire asked each student if he/she was interested in a career in health; if yes, which one of the programs? It continued: Are you a member of a health club? Would you like to attend a summer health career program? And other similar questions. Counselors from the Career Education Office of the Omaha Schools distributed the questionnaires in December and collected them in January 1975. Upon their return, I tallied the number of students who were interested in each *area* of study and prepared a report which showed, among other data, the Caucasian, and ethnic minority breakdown of the participants. Copies of the report were distributed to personnel at UNMC, Creighton, and the Omaha public-school Counselors. The entire report is too long to include here; however, numbers of minorities interested in three areas are included as a sample: Medicine-30 minorities, Denistry-11, Pharmacy-5, and Nursing-51. The questionnaires would be given to new ninth graders each year. The calculated numbers from the answers would serve as a pool from which to recruit students for health career programs in the future.

Another source for identifying minority students who might become interested in health careers was through CETA. We worked with the UNMC Human Resources Department in conducting activities for participants in the CETA Summer Youth Employment Program. CETA stood for Comprehensive

Employment and Training Agency for teenagers. It was based on a U.S. Federal law enacted by Congress and signed by President Nixon in 1973. Resources, such as the internet, show that the goals and, in some instances, the names of similar programs were developed later for adult populations. The goal of the CETA program at that time and in that place was to provide summer employment for teenagers while giving them the chance to learn about professions in various fields. During the summer of 1975, 31 youths participated in the program at the University of Nebraska Medical Center. Six of the 31 transitioned from summer employment to permanent part-time jobs on campus in the fall. The MSRC assisted with this program by participating in an orientation session, doing educational counseling, and maintaining contact with supervisors of the student employees. The CETA program was held each summer throughout the seventies and into the eighties.

The MSRC membership elected me chairperson for the academic year 1975-76. In addition to serving as leader of the group, the position included being the program coordinator. I had nine comprehensive duties as coordinator which required the help of various members and others on campus. Our programs for the schools and other community projects were increasing in number and in the degree of planning. Again, it is important to remember that all of us were working on the minority project as volunteers, while still performing the duties of our regular positions.

The MSRC was fortunate in having the support and interest of the head administrator, Chancellor David Randolph, M.D. He liked to receive reports on the Committee's activities. He assisted us in developing a more formal association with the Omaha Public School System by meeting with a counselor and talking with the Omaha superintendent of schools. He held a luncheon meeting with the Committee Officers and heads of departments in the Medical Center to discuss minority recruitment/ retention problems as well as the status of enrolled minority students. A goal of the committee was to encourage the University Medical Center administration to appoint an Office of Minority Student Affairs, with its own budget, office space, staff, equipment, and supplies. This could be accomplished only with the interest, commitment, and backing of the administration. Dr. Randolph worked on behalf of the committee to achieve this objective. It was not an easy undertaking.

The Chancellor began the process in May 1974 when he discussed with the Board of Regents the possible addition of a "minority recruitment and retention officer to UNMC." In a meeting with the Chancellor on May 13, the MRSC Chairman learned that the recommendations of the Committee were being "responded to, but there [were] no funds in the 1974-75 budget for the addition of a recruitment-retention officer." This may, however, be under consideration for 1975-76. The Student Affairs department was directed to expand its services in minority affairs and the financial aids officer was told to investigate additional sources of funding for supporting minority students. The Committee continued its usual school visits throughout the spring.

A member and professor in the College of Nursing reported during a June 1975 meeting that the College of Nursing Recruitment and Retention committee had established the Elizah Mahoney Memorial Fund to provide emergency grant money to minority nursing students for needs not covered by scholarships or loans. Elizah Mahony, for whom the fund was named, was the first black graduate nurse in the United States. The desire to increase and maintain the enrollment of minority students was gradually spreading throughout the UNMC Campus.

On June 25, 1975, the Chancellor shared additional information about establishing an office of minority affairs on the Medial Center Campus. During the MSRC meeting, he reported, "The Legislature rejected plans for a Compliance Officer on any of the three University of Nebraska campuses." There was a line item cut in the state's budget, resulting in the deletion of the Chancellor's discretionary funds.

The Chancellor added, "Despite financial problems, [he was] continuing plans to select and implement the Coordinator of Minority Student Affairs and the resulting program."

Questions about the position and office ensued from the members. The main point of contention was the title for the position. Some members thought the person should be called Officer rather than Coordinator. Thus, the title, Minority Student Affairs Officer, was approved.

My Second Professional Role

I started my term as MSRC Chairperson in 1975. As Assistant Registrar, I was also a member of the Assistant to the Chancellor, Gibson's staff. My supervisor, Mrs. Rosewater, reported to him. Because of this affiliation, I felt even more responsible for helping with the minority affairs project. In January, five months before the Chancellor's budget announcement that is mentioned above, the Financial Aids Director informed us of a grant proposal for minority health career programs he had received. I decided to ask a group of co-workers to assist me in writing a detailed proposal for the grant. The well-qualified small group included a professor from the College of Pharmacy, the Director of Financial Aid, and Mr. Gibson. My husband Verable, who was retired from the military and working then at Mutual of Omaha, helped with the statistics for the proposal. In our next MSRC meeting, I reported on the project to the membership. I had undertaken writing the grant because I knew whoever was appointed Minority Student Affairs Officer would need financial assistance beyond what the University could supply.

I was the primary author of the proposed program and the main person in drawing the grant application together, but I did not have an official title related to minority student affairs. Therefore, Mr. Gibson wrote the cover letter and signed the application. We had received the grant application materials rather late. By the time it was completed, the deadline for submission was upon us. On February 5, the last day it was due, I took a flight to Kansas City and hand-carried the application to the Region VII Department of Health, Education and Welfare (DHEW). I met with a representative by the name of Wolf Bedenfield. He received our application. Afterward, we discussed the DHEW, how the grant process worked, and additional helpful information. I returned to the campus the next day feeling very pleased about the visit.

Mr.Gibson received a letter from the Assistant Director for Project Review (Health Planning Council of the Midlands) in March 1976, announcing, "Approval of the application as submitted." What a wonderful surprise! Mr.Gibson sent copies of the letter to the Chancellor and grants office director. He identified me as the one who prepared the grant and included more kudos than I felt I deserved.

Plans were underway for recruiting and appointing the UNMC Minority Student Affairs Officer. The Chancellor, with suggestions from the MSRC, had approved a position description, appointed a selection committee, and started receiving applications. I had applied for the position and, therefore, I was not privy to the progression of the selection process. I continued assisting the MSRC with the school programs and doing my regular job, managing the records office.

The one thing that worried me was the day of meetings with individual committee members and the group dinner. The worry resulted from my having developed an uncomfortable condition that had started several months earlier. I woke up one morning and my neck was hurting. After getting out of bed, my head involuntarily twisted to the right and then returned to its center position.

After the condition continued for several days, I went to a doctor. He said I had adult-onset Torticollis or Spasmodic Dystonia. It's a condition that affects the right or left side neck muscle. The doctor said there wasn't a cure for it. He gave me some pills to help the neck muscles relax. These helped only a little and very temporarily. I hoped no one would notice my head jerks because it would be embarrassing. So, I developed the habit of keeping my neck as rigid as possible and would take the medicine just prior to participating in a meeting or public affair. The head jerks occurred without warning, so I didn't want to take any chances. Sometimes, when I was with someone and my head jerked, I'd shift my body in some way to make the movement seem like it had been intentional. I continued the application process for Minority Student Affairs Officer. I had made it that far with numerous health problems and I wouldn't let the new one-stop me.

Chapter 27

I learned much later, that after carefully scrutinizing over 20 applications selected for consideration, and conducting some interviews, the search committee recommended five names to the Chancellor. Based on the consensus of the search committee, the Chancellor made a selection from the five recommended nominees. I received a letter from Chancellor Randolph around April 26, 1976, appointing me the *First* Minority Student Affairs officer for the University of Nebraska Medical Center. I was pleased but also a little terrified. The role of Minority Student Affairs Officer, director, coordinator, or whatever title a school elected to use was a *new* position on campuses where such offices had been installed. Therefore, there were no guidelines for program design nor any proven methodologies for achieving the goal of increasing minority student enrollment and retention. I had to devise my own approach to the situation.

  I resigned from the position of Assistant Registrar for Academic Records and began my duties as Minority Student Affairs Officer (MSAO) on June one of 1976. My salary, which had increased some because of the new appointment, was still being paid from State funds. Within six to eight months, we added a secretary, Sara, and an Activities Coordinator, Mary Anne, for the office using grant funds. The budget and everything concerned with Minority Student Affairs had been turned over to our office. Mr. Gibson was my new supervisor, and I was on the same management level as my former supervisor, Mrs. Rosewater. I remembered the final question she asked during my interview with her:

  "Where would you like to be in five years?"

  My response was, "In a position similar to yours."

  While the five-year comparison had not been a defined goal of mine, and

I applied for the new position mainly due to interest, I had been promoted to a managerial position on a level comparable to hers. When I thought about that, the accomplishment aided in building my self-esteem.

I moved into our new offices, two rooms located in the same building as the Registrar's, on the same hall, next door to the vault room. The Activities Coordinator and secretary shared the first office and I had the second. Within a few years, after our program had grown, the salaries of the Activities Coordinator and secretary were switched to the State budget. We added a fourth position to the staff, a recruitment counselor, and his salary was paid with grant funds. At that future time, the secretary's desk would be moved into an office with another secretary located just across the hall and the activities coordinator would remain alone in the office they had shared. I would give the recruitment counselor my office and would be moved next door, into the last office on the hall.

The first thing I did in the new position of Minority Student Affairs Officer was to assess what was being done for minority recruitment and retention on campus by different colleges, programs, and departments. Then I began to develop a formal program. I made appointments to discuss with each entity how the minority students were doing in their courses on campus. When a few were identified as having trouble, I asked the professor leading the class to make arrangements for the student to be tutored and that the MSAO would pay for the assistance. I designed timesheets for the participants and tutors to sign each session and I asked to receive periodical reports on each student's progress. These ideas were well accepted.

With the assistance of the public affairs office, we had announcements about the MSAO and our activities included in the campus newsletters. And when the items were of interest to the public, the news staff sent articles to the local newspapers. In a short time, various enrolled minority students were stopping by at first to just chat, and later because they had problems or concerns.

One counseling session I remember most vividly occurred early in my first year as director. A neatly dressed, young black man was directed to me by our secretary. After introducing ourselves and sitting, he began to tell me about himself. He was a junior at the University of Nebraska at Omaha (UNO), our sister campus. He was majoring in chemistry and expected to graduate on time in a year. At that point in his life, he was thinking about his future and wanted very much to go to the College of Pharmacy after completing undergraduate school. We talked about the application process, which he would begin during his senior year. In comparing his college courses and grades for entering the program with those required, he looked like a strong candidate. He asked other questions and I was answering them when I noticed tears forming in his eyes.

I said, "What's wrong? Have I mentioned something that is problematic? Are you feeling okay?

All the while, he was shaking his head. He responded, "No, ma'am, I'm alright. I apologize for breaking down in your office."

I couldn't help being puzzled and I'm sure it showed by the wrinkles on my forehead. He took a clean folded white handkerchief from his pocket and wiped his face. At that time, I noticed how tidy and appropriately dressed he was, wearing a navy jacket, white shirt, and creased gray pants. Again, he said, "I'm very sorry, but as you talked, I started thinking about my mom. You see, there are only the two of us. I don't have any brothers or sisters and my father passed away two years ago. Mom is in fairly good health and she has a little money from my father's insurance to provide for herself, but she doesn't want me to go to school beyond finishing college!"

I was shocked and asked, "Why not? She should be very proud of you!"

He said, "She hasn't gotten over Dad's death. She's lonely and she'd like for me to spend more time with her, going grocery shopping and helping her around the house. I love my mom, but I really want to be a pharmacist."

"Listen, Joseph," I said. "Of course, you love your mother, but try thinking of the situation another way: You are a young man who is going to have to make a living for yourself and maybe one day for your own family. While you would be able to get some type of employment based on your undergraduate degree, being a pharmacist would give you a stable profession for all your life. You would even be in a better position to help your mother. Explain this to her as I have to you. Reassure her that you do love her and would do anything for her, but you have to consider what will be best for both of you. If you go to pharmacy school here, which I hope you will, you will still be in the same city with her and can help her when she needs you. I think she will understand this reasoning. But, remember you must think about yourself, your future."

Joseph listened and seem to agree with what I was saying. He shook my hand, thanked me, and promised to stay in touch. As he left my office, he stood tall and looked as if a weight had been lifted from his shoulders. He did enter the pharmacy program two years later and was a good student.

On another occasion, a tall muscular African American fellow who had played football in undergraduate school stopped by my office. He was very polite and friendly. He wanted my opinion about him quitting medical school. He was in his third year and had good grades. I reminded him of how far along he was in medicine and that I knew his grades were okay.

I asked, "Why in the world would you want to withdraw now?" He said, "I don't know, I'm just tired of it."

I asked about his family situation.

He said, "Everything is fine. I'm not married. My parents are doing well."

"Then why do you want to withdraw from school?" I asked again. "Are you having financial difficulties?"

"No," he responded. "Sometimes, I just get tired and want to do something different."

I said, "Do you miss football?" "No," he said, "not really."

I began my little sermon, "You are an intelligent person. Think about what you're saying. You have put a lot of time, effort, and just plain hard work into reaching the point where you are in life—four years of undergraduate education, taking and passing the MCATs (Medical College Admissions Test), going through the anxiety-ridden process of applying to medical school, wondering if you would be accepted, and most of all, having nearly completed three years of medical school. How can you throw all of that effort away?"

He thought for a few seconds while I stared at him questioningly.

Finally, he smiled and looked directly at me.

He said, "Well, I guess I can't." Both of us laughed. He said, "You've given me a lot to think about."

I said, "Good. And recall the things we've discussed here if you think about leaving school again." He thanked me and left. However, he came back to talk with me every month or so. I surmised that when he came, he was feeling discontented and perhaps a little lonely in classes with only white students. At graduation the following year, he thanked me for being patient in listening and talking with him so often. I congratulated him and said I was glad to have been there for him.

At the UNMC Medical College, students were allowed by professors to keep their written tests after they were graded and would store them for future students to use when studying for exams. The white student population had done this for some time. I don't know if any students of color had ever tried to borrow from their collection or not. The African American students asked me if they could use some space in one of the MSAO's file cabinets to start such a collection for any student to use. I said "sure" and showed them a suitable area for them to use. Several students brought in old tests and stored them. I showed our secretary, Sarah, where the tests were and told her if a student wanted access to them, she could take the student to the files and let the person select whatever he or she wanted to borrow, then make a note of the student's name and what the person had borrowed.

One day, a white male went to our secretary and said, "I understand the minority students keep a collection of old test files in this office. Is that true?"

Sarah said, "Yes."

Then he asked, "Can I use them?"

Later, Sarah told me, "I smiled and then responded, 'Yes, I'll be happy to take you to them.'"

As she was getting up from her desk, the student said, "That's okay, I'll come back later after I check on the subjects I need to study most. I just wanted to make sure they are here and that I can use them."

He thanked Sarah and left. Sarah and I knew that had been a test— and our office passed. There didn't seem to be any blatant animosity between blacks and whites on campus. However, I only saw the groups at school. I didn't know if they socialized together or not.

I went to meetings of faculty members in Medicine, the other Colleges, and Allied Health Programs to ask for volunteers to be matched with a local minority student interested in their field, to form a big brother/big sister type relationship. In doing so, they would try to spend some quality time with the student every two weeks. We called this the Protege Program. Responses were slowly coming in but eventually, the number of volunteers increased and relationships proved to be rewarding.

We continued to visit local high schools and speak with ninth graders. This was named the High School Visitation Program. Sometimes, the Activities Coordinator or I responded to the school's request for a speaker. By then, with the office in full operation, the school visits were mainly scheduled by our office, but the MSRC committee volunteers gave many of the presentations in partnership with Minority Affairs from Creighton University.

We set up Project Network, communications with high schools in other parts of the state where there were some minorities living. We invited the schools in those areas to share minority students' contact information with us. We also encouraged them to organize minority health career clubs in their schools. We visited each of these schools every year. This assisted us in getting to know minority youths in parts of Nebraska outside of Omaha. Also, through my membership in NAMME, the National Association of Medical Minority Educators, a group of African Americans with jobs similar to mine, I learned about their programs for minority students. We contacted the directors of these programs and sent them announcements about our summer programs.

I submitted a renewal application to DHEW for the second year. It was funded for the amount we requested, whereas the first one had been for half of the requested amount. Additionally, the announcement came early enough in the new year for us to plan the second phase of the UNMC minority student program. (The first phase, for currently enrolled students, was described above.) Using the grant title, we called the collection of activities at the Medical Center The Minority Health Career Opportunity Program (MHCOP). When fully established, I planned for the MHCO Program to have activities for several different levels of students: (1) The Academic Support Program: Counseling, tutorials, and special workshops for enrolled health professional students; (2) Recruitment: Visiting schools, identifying and counseling undergraduate students; (3) Summer Enrichment Program (residential): Planning and conducting a six-week academic summer program at UNMC for high school seniors and recent high school graduates. This happened in 1977 and 1978. Funds were not available for high school programs in 1979; (4) Baccalaureate Level Summer Program: An eight-week residential program at UNMC for minority college students who planned to apply to a health professional school. The curriculum for this program included academic enrichment in undergraduate basic sciences, an introduction to health professional school basic sciences, research experiences, and skills enhancement. All the courses were taught by professors and certified teachers. I asked the associate Dean of the College of Medicine to be co-director with me for the Baccalaureate Level Summer Programs. I wanted him to oversee the medical school's basic sciences and research. He graciously agreed.

The University administration was very anxious for our programs to serve mainly residents of Nebraska. I could understand their reasoning because it was (and is) a state school. However, to have a summer program for the number projected in the grant applications, it was necessary to accept some students from out of state.

The Minority Student Affairs Officer's position was one of multiple responsibilities and tasks, both on campus and off. I learned that I liked having many and various challenges. Here are some examples:

In 1975, The Association of American Colleges (AAMC), a very important organization in medical education, appointed a committee to devise a method of evaluating the medical school applications of minorities. This group included blacks, Mexican Americans, American Indians, and Mainland Puerto Ricans. By reviewing the histories of a variety of medical students and graduates, the committee learned that individuals with lower academic credentials could succeed in medical school. They identified eight variables that were more predictive of the minority students' ability to succeed than the traditional criteria: MCAT (Medical College Admissions Test) scores, grade point averages, letter of reference, and interview reports. These eight variables are: 1) positive self-concept, 2) ability to deal with racism, 3) realistic self-appraisal, 4) preference for long range-goals, 5) availability of a strong support person, 6) leadership experience, 7) demonstrated Community service, and 8) demonstrated medical interest.

The AAMC committee devised a workshop called Simulated Minority Admissions Exercise. This was based on the eight identified variables. They invited a select group of medical educators, admissions committee members, and others of interest, and they taught us how to use the eight non-cognitive variables in evaluating medical school applications of underrepresented minority students. In addition to training, we were given a handbook with instructions. Participants were to take knowledge back to our campuses to use this new method of evaluating minority applicants. Back at UNMC, I conducted several of these "Variable Evaluation Workshops" for faculty groups. I also talked with the Chancellor about my getting permission from Deans and Directors to review the applications for minorities each college and program received. While I expected their admissions committees to try to discern proof of these eight variables, I was offering to review the folders, without letters of references, if the committee preferred, to give them my written assessment. I believed that being a minority myself, I might be able to detect indications of the variables when the all-White committees could not. The Chancellor agreed and had no problems with me contacting the committee chairpersons about this idea.

When I met with the Nebraska College of Medicine admissions committee in trying to help them understand how black and other minorities might feel when that student is the only one in a class with all white students, I asked if any of them (they were all White doctors) had been the only white person in a group consisting only of blacks. One person said he had.

I asked, "How did you feel at that time?"

He answered rather emphatically, "Very uncomfortable!"

He had confirmed the point I was making. All the colleges and every allied health program, except one, accepted my offer to review applicants' folders.

Another of my duties was assisting a dean or program director when there was a conflict involving a minority student, usually a grade dispute. Once in a while, the hearing involved a lawyer. My role was to serve as a neutral participant, to offer clarification or another point of view when needed. However, I had hopes that my being there—another face of color—would help the student feel less anxious.

In keeping with the emphasis on affirmative action in most of higher education at that time, the Chancellor appointed three of us from different employment categories to serve on the Medical Center's Equal Employment Opportunity Grievance Committee. Three members were elected by the UNMC community at large and the six of us selected three more, making a committee of nine who would serve for eighteen months. Our primary responsibilities were to educate people on campus about their rights and responsibilities as employees and/or supervisors, receive complaints, investigate, and try to reach a just conclusion to the matter. Then, we prepared and presented our conclusions to the Chancellor. The composition of the committee was more varied in terms of job categories than in the racial or ethnic background. However, all nine people seemed to be caring, fair, and intent upon doing what was right. The group elected me chairperson. We requested booklets and whatever information was available from the government on Affirmative Action policies and procedures. We were well-prepared and had several complaints to resolve during our tenure.

The committee of volunteers, MSRC, continued to assist with minority student programs. However, with the office now being in charge of the committee's previous activities, the group decided that the committee needed to rethink its objectives and decide on some new projects of its own. The first recommendation was to write a new constitution, defining the relationship between MSAO and the Committee. After which, they would identify projects, such as minority employment on campus, which they could work on improving. In the Committee's next meeting, the officers submitted newly proposed articles for the constitution. One read, "the Minority Affairs officer or her representative will be an ex officio non-voting member." I thought the new relationship would work well and was stated as it should be.

Several appointments and opportunities came to me unexpectedly; some through acquaintances and friendships I had made with public school teachers and other contacts in the city. For example, one of the schoolteachers with whom

I had worked on CETA and the UNMC high school programs recommended me to the Mayor of Omaha for membership on The Mayor's Commission on the Status of Women. Some months later, I was elected treasurer of the Commission.

In another instance, I was asked to be a participant in the Omaha Public School Program's Positive Image Program. A white, female, senior high school student met me in my office one morning. I had planned an itinerary, so after we introduced ourselves and I described my position, we began a day of my regular activities. These included a meeting with my staff. After which, she accompanied me to an auditorium where I presented an hour's session for health professional students on test-taking skills and the formation of study groups. I took her to meet all members of the Student Affairs Division. We had lunch in the hospital cafeteria. Then, back in my office, with the permission of each student, she sat in on two individual student counseling sessions. Our last activities were taking photos, followed by a discussion between the two of us about the day.

I asked if she had any questions. She said, "No, I have enjoyed the day, and have learned a lot. Thank you very much for your time and for sharing your experiences with me." She was a very pleasant, intelligent young person and I had enjoyed having her with me.

We gave each minority group special recognition by having a separate Minority Health Emphasis Program devoted to them. Accordingly, a health issue most prominent among Indian Americans would be discussed by an expert in that area. A health problem prominent among African Americans would be addressed on another day by a specialist in that area. Then another expert would speak on a Hispanic health issue. These programs were highly publicized because speakers were often paid to come from Washington, D. C or some other cities. But the attendance was never as good as I thought it should be.

I was employed at the University Medical Center for twelve years: three in the registrar's office and nine as the *first* Minority Student Affairs officer. The latter was, at times, a very stressful job, not because of the whites, except in one instance, but rather because of some of my comrades in the MSRC. Several of the black men decided that the office wasn't being run the way it should be, so they planned to have me meet with them. I was at home on vacation at that time. A male Hispanic member of the committee knew about the plan and called to warn me. Sure enough, as soon as we hung up from our call, one of the planners called to say that several of the MSRC members wanted me to come in to meet with them that afternoon. I calmly said I would be there.

I knew my rights and if something was wrong in the way I managed the office, my supervisor would have let me know. It was *not* their place to critique my management style. So, I called the Equal Employment Opportunity Officer (EEO Officer), a Black man, and explained the situation. I gave him the time and location of the meeting. He confirmed that management of the office was not their concern and said he would meet me there. Once in the meeting, it took only a few minutes for the men—none of the female members were present—to start asking questions about my office and employees. The EEO officer stopped them. He said, "Those topics are none of your business and it's inappropriate for you to ask them." I asked if there was anything on a different topic they wanted to discuss. They said, "No." We remained friendly to each other and I never again had complaints from them.

The other instance made me feel I was being treated as if I were inferior to the white male who took a very minor complaint to my supervisor. The man and I were on the same employee level. He told my supervisor that I had failed to sign one of the grant budget forms that I had sent to him. My supervisor told me about his call but wasn't upset about it at all. I called the complainer and asked why he had not contacted me directly about his concern. He said he thought my supervisor should know about it.

I said, "Once you told him, my supervisor knew my not signing the form was unintentional. It seems to me that you took the opportunity to report me to my superior because I am a woman and you wanted" —he started to say something, but I interrupted him—"wanted to label me as an irresponsible female. Don't go over my head again with a complaint as insignificant as that one. Bring it directly to me and if you aren't satisfied with my solution, then take it higher. Return the form to me and I will sign it," then I hung up.

Although I was working in a very male environment, those were the only two times I felt I experienced chauvinism.

The Federal grants we received were awarded in three-year cycles, with a progress report required at the end of the first and second years. A grant renewal application could be submitted at the end of the third year. The UNMC was funded for three complete cycles. I wrote an application for a third cycle and was still at the Medical Center to supervise activities for the first year and a half: 1983-84 and part of 1984-85. Grants were reviewed and evaluated by a board of previous grant directors who were appointed by the Director of the Division of Disadvantaged assistance, Bureau of Health Professions. I was appointed a peer reviewer twice. During my final year at UNMC, the Health Resources and Services Administration, Division of Disadvantaged Assistance on behalf of the Assistant Surgeon General, invited approximately 40 health education personnel members to participate in a three-day Forum on Health Professions Education for Disadvantaged Individuals. Our task was to evaluate past efforts and to determine a course for helping minorities in health professions school in the future. We worked in groups and were assigned three issues to study. In the end, we prepared a comprehensive report.

The minority affairs programs were going smoothly. I had begun to feel that my position in academia was greater than my level of education, although I hadn't had any responsibilities that I was incapable of doing. However, in academia, those who are not familiar with your abilities make judgments based on the letters following your name that indicate the degree(s) you've earned. I decided to study for a Master's in Sociology. That hadn't been my undergraduate major, so I had to take a few undergraduate sociology courses to meet the requirements for entering the master's degree program. I registered at UNO in 1980 and was able to take most of the undergrad courses I needed at night. After completing those, I got permission from my supervisor to take time away from the office when I needed to take a class scheduled during work hours. He approved. I had completed all but one course by the spring of 1985. But I still had to do research and write my thesis.

Administrators, such as the chancellors and the deans of the college, changed institutions rather frequently. In 1980, a fairly new Dean of Medicine, with whom I had attended meetings concerning students, said he was considering appointing me an Assistant Instructor in the Department of Medical Jurisprudence and Humanities. He wanted to know if I approved. I said "yes," although I knew it would involve more work, like conducting a couple of workshops each year and maybe giving a guest lecture. I thanked him for his thoughtfulness. Upon the Dean's instructions, the head of the department I was to join completed the appointment papers, and as soon as they had gone through channels, she welcomed me to her department. She and I developed rapport quickly and the appointment went well.

Expand Associates, Inc., a management consultants firm, did a complete study and evaluation of our program at the end of the first grant cycle in 1979 and again in 1985. The Health Careers Opportunity Program at UNMC had grown tremendously between the two dates. In the 1985 report, the evaluator wrote, "Based on the cursory examination of the 1979 evaluation report, the current preliminary assessment results, coupled with a review of data from other MHCO programs, the UNMC program appears to have the potential to serve as a national model for MHCO programs."

The funding of three Minority Health Career federal grants over a nine-year period, plus increasing financial support from the University via state funds, provided for an office staff of four, three of whom were paid from state funds. We had designed, implemented, and directed a program consisting of components for students from senior high through the completion of health professional school. The enrollment of underrepresented minorities in UNMC health professions programs had increased 126%, from 38 students in 1976 to 86 in 1985. Fifty-four students completed the Baccalaureate Level Summer Program between 1981 and 1985. Fifteen of those students had been accepted by health professions schools by 1984. Others were still in college completing their pre-health professional education.

While my professional life was going well, my mental and physical conditions were the same or getting worse. Daily activities coupled with the medicine the psychiatrist was giving me for the mood swings may have helped a little but made me sleepy. He tried so many different prescriptions through the years that I can't recall the names. None worked well; they were mostly anti-depressives. If I drank coffee or coke to minimize the sleepiness, either drink made me nervous and affected my involuntary head movements. As a professional constantly in the public's eye, I couldn't show that weakness. So, I asked the doctor to let me try valium again with the depression medicine. He agreed reluctantly. I took medicine for depression at night and the Valium any time during the day when I was going to be in what I considered a stressful situation. These were not the directions the doctor had given me, but it was the only way I thought I could manage. I continued my work unabated.

In the fall of 1981, approximately ten individuals participated in a dinner meeting at the Vice Chancellor's home. We discuss plans for a scholarship program for UNMC underrepresented minority students. There were three UNMC administrators among the ten, and the others were black community leaders. During the meeting, the community leaders made a list of other individuals whom they would solicit to assist with the project. These included blacks who held positions such as President of a Community Bank, Branch Manager for IBM, President of a Buick car dealership, Industrial Manager at Northwestern Bell, and Vice President of Mutual of Omaha. To have a diversified representation, leaders of other ethnic backgrounds and whites were invited to join the scholarship program. The positions members held helped in the fundraising. They not only gave personally but were instrumental in getting contributions from their places of employment and/or their organizations.

Each year at the end of the summer enrichment program, we held a recognition dinner for the students. Invited guests included parents, the summer program students, the total summer program staff including visiting teachers and UNMC professors, the Chancellor, and community leaders. The program began with the invocation, followed by a note of welcome from the Chancellor, a speech by a health professional guest, comments by a student, presentation of certificates, and the presentation of academic awards for the highest achievers in academic classes. At the end of the dinner in 1983, an officer of the Scholarship Committee presented a certificate for $1000 each to three minority undergraduate students who had been accepted in UNMC programs and were to begin their programs in the fall. Similar scholarships were given each of the next two years to three new scholars. The last recognition dinner I attended was in 1985. I had announced that I planned to leave UNMC at the end of August.

Between the evening of the MHCOP Recognition Dinner and my final day in the office, two farewell receptions were held for me: One sponsored by my colleagues in the Student Affairs Department. They invited numerous professionals and staff from other offices on campus. The second was given by the UNMC chapter of the Student National Medical Association. Each gave me gifts. To my surprise, I received lots of cards from the general campus population and letters from various administrators.

I was very pleased with my accomplishments at UNMC. While I was working in a mostly white environment with professionals who had academic credentials much higher than mine, I was accepted by most as a valued colleague and had been given important appointments on the campus and in national organizations. Plus, I was able to design and run the programs without interference from the administration. In fact, my efforts were supported and praised. I left UNMC feeling very good about myself. My self-esteem was higher than it had ever been. The question I asked myself: would this feeling of self-worth and self-validity be sustained? My next job would prove to be a test of the positive feelings I had developed.

Chapter 28

My Third Professional Role

In explaining how my next position came about, I must backtrack to the spring *before* my last MHCO Recognition dinner.

In the spring of 1985, while I was still working at UNMC, Washington and Lee (W&L) University of Lexington, Virginia ran an ad recruiting an Assistant Dean for Minority Affairs. After being employed at the University of Nebraska Medical Center for 12 years and not seeing a chance to be promoted, I decided to apply for the W&L job. I updated my resume, sent it, and a letter of application to the Dean of Students, Lawrence Jefferies, PhD.

I was familiar with W&L and its history. Apparently, there had been two attempts made at starting the college before it was built in its current location. The personnel handbook reports that "In 1749, Scotch-Irish pioneers . . . founded a small classical school called Augusta Academy, some 20 miles north of what is now Lexington. In 1776, the trustees . . . changed the name of the school to Liberty Hall . . . Four years later, the school was moved to the vicinity of Lexington, where in 1782, it was chartered as Liberty Hall Academy."

In 1796 President George Washington invested $20,000 in stock for the Academy. It had been built in 1793 but burned down in 1803. The current college was started around 1798 and because of the President's generosity, it was named Washington College. In 1865, Confederate General Robert E. Lee was asked and later with some hesitation accepted the position of President of the College. Lee died in 1870 and afterward, his name was added to the title. His philosophy, teachings, and directions formed the framework for student governance that was still in effect in 1985 when I was considering the Assistant Dean position there.

Among most black people who knew about Washington and Lee University when I was growing up, it had the reputation of being an institution for opulent white gentlemen. Two black males entered the undergraduate college in 1968 and were the first to complete degrees there. Few applied and attended in the years following. The first coeducation class entered in 1985. That's probably why the Dean of Students was hiring two female administrators. I was the black one and would have the responsibility for Minority Student Affairs. The other was Joan Montel, PhD, a white female psychologist. She would work mainly with women and any student who wanted or needed special counseling. It is only fair to acknowledge that there were some students, alumni, and perhaps a few faculty members who did not like the idea of the school admitting women. This decision was voluntarily encouraged by some of the undergraduate faculty. Due to a mandate from the government, women were first admitted to the Washington and Lee Law School in 1972.

I received a response from the Dean inviting me to visit Lexington for an interview. I went. The nearest airport to Lexington was about 50 miles away in Roanoke, VA. The Dean had sent a black student to pick me up and take me to the campus. He was very courteous and told me his impressions of W&L, which weren't bad. Although he said there were very few minority students and only one African American professor. He also said there were not many female faculty members and if hired, I would be the *first* black female administrator.

We arrived on campus in the afternoon. It was so beautiful in the late day sun and shadows. There were tall trees across the front lawn, concrete walkways, and red brick, colonial buildings. Lee Chapel, perhaps the most historically significant building, stood alone near the center front of the campus. Across from the Chapel, several buildings with tall, white columns formed a covered walkway.

After leaving the car, the student driver escorted me to double doors at the center of the colonnade. Inside, within about three feet, the entry hall was crossed by another hall where you could go to the right or left. We turned left and passed a closed door on the left. I didn't know it then but that was the office being reserved for the Assistant Dean for Minority Affairs. Just across the hall, an open door led into a somewhat long room which we started walking through to get to the Dean's office. His secretary was sitting at a desk in that room. She said "Hi, Bennie" to the student as she stood to introduce herself to me.

"I'm Dora," she said, "and you must be Mrs. McCloud."

"Yes, I am," I said as we shook hands. "It's nice to meet you. Please feel free to call me by my first name, Anece."

"Well, welcome to Washington and Lee, Anece," she said.

The dean came out of his office and joined us. Dora sat back down. "Yes, welcome, Mrs. McCloud," he said and shook my hand. "I'm Lawrence Jefferies."

"It's so nice to meet you, Dean Jefferies," I said. He was a tall, rather handsome, dark-haired man of medium build who looked to be in his fifties.

Bennie interrupted, "Excuse me, Mrs. McCloud. Dean Jefferies, here are the keys to the car."

The dean said, "Thank you, Bennie. Did you have any problems?" "None at all and you're welcome," Bennie replied. I shook his hand and thanked him also. He acknowledged my thanks and left. Dean Jefferies invited me into his office and to sit down. I sat on a tan sofa against the back wall of his office and he sat in a matching armchair perpendicular to the sofa. He said, "How was your trip?"

"Not bad," I responded. "The plane wasn't too crowded and there were no crying babies on board." I smiled as I said that and he chuckled.

"And how is your family? You have what—two daughters?"

"Yes," I said. "Everyone is fine. Our daughters are in their own apartments. I'm sure my husband will be lonely with all three of us away. On the other hand, he may enjoy having the house to himself for a couple of days. He's retired from the Air Force now and is the supervisor of Time Management Administration at Mutual of Omaha."

We continued chatting casually for a short while, then he told me about the arrangements for the night and the schedule for the next day. His secretary had reserved me a room in the campus guest house. The next day would be filled with interviews. My first one was scheduled for eight o'clock with the University President. I could tell that day was going to be similar to the day of interviews I had experienced years earlier at the Nebraska Medical Center. Except for this time, I was being interviewed for the position of Assistant *Dean* of Students, a title, and on a campus where I never would have guessed I'd be.

The next day after meeting with the president for half an hour, his secretary took me to the Dean of Admissions office and after he and I talked, the dean's secretary took me to the Financial Aids officer. A professor of sociology accompanied by a chemistry professor stopped by financial aids and when I had finished with that interview, the two professors and I used a nearby office for them to conduct their interview. Their departments were in a separate building. I learned the chemistry professor's wife was a realtor. At the conclusion of our meeting, they accompanied me to the student union where lunch was to be served in a private room. Those having lunch with me were Brian Hugely, PhD., Dean of Freshman and an English professor, Donald O'brian, Associate Dean of International Students and Director of Fraternities, Dianne Rhinhart, PhD., a professor of arts and chairman of the co-education committee; John Brown, an Associate Dean and Dean Jefferies. The associate deans and Dean Jefferies would be my colleagues in the Student Services Department if I were hired. During lunch, we talked about my work at the medical center, a little about Lexington, and the changes going on with female students being at W&L. Lunch was very good. All the people I had met that day were exceptionally friendly, including the ones who had lunch with me.

As soon as we finished lunch, I had to leave for Roanoke and my flight back home to Nebraska. The Dean of Students drove me to the airport. He seemed to be a genuinely nice person. We talked some; however, I was mostly interested in the surroundings. Lexington, where W&L was located, was a very small quaint town. It reminded me of some of the little villages in England. Although we lived in a relatively small town in Nebraska, it was near the air force base and we were only about 15 miles from the larger city of Omaha. If I were to work in Lexington, I would be living in the Southern United States again. Could I contend with that? Of course, separation of the two races wasn't as blatant as it had been when there were signs on various entrances designating "white" and "black." The 50 miles between Lexington and Roanoke had mainly scattered homes and farms. I asked Dean Jefferies about housing in Lexington. He said it was good, in addition to the older homes, there were newer communities being developed with very nice, modern models.

When we arrived at Roanoke International Airport and got out of the car, he retrieved my small suitcase from the back seat, gave it to me, and shook my hand. "It was very nice meeting you," he said. "I'll get in touch with you when the committee has made a decision."

I thanked him for their kindness and hospitality and said I would look forward to hearing from him *whatever* the committee decided. We said goodbye. I was happy to be going home.

Verable was at Omaha Airport when my flight arrived. It was good to be together again. He asked if I wanted to stop and get something to eat since it was late. I said, "No, I'll get a snack at home."

During our thirty-minute drive to Bellevue, I told him about Lexington, my interviews, and the people I'd met.

"Are you going to take the job?" Verable asked.

"I don't know. I haven't been offered the position yet. If I am, working there would mean being away from you until you have accumulated ten years at Mutual, can retire, and join me.

"Well, that will be about this time next year," he replied with a smile. "There are other things to consider," I said. "Like, how well I could adjust to the area."

Verable, always the rational one, said, "By the time you hear from him, should he offer you the job, you will have had time to think about your concerns and make a decision."

"Yeah, I guess so," I said. "Did anything happen while I was away?" "Not a thing," he replied.

About that time, we arrived home. A different house from the first one we lived in when we arrived in Nebraska. With both of us working, about five years earlier, we had moved into an area where the houses were larger and the community was a bit more upscale. The house was on a slight hill and had a steep driveway. As we entered the house, a large dining room was to the right and the living room of equal size to the left. There were no walls on the entry hall side of either room. This gave the space a comfortable openness. The master bedroom and bath were to the left up to three steps. A hallway ran from those steps and behind the dining room to three steps that went up to the second wing of the house where there were two bedrooms and a bath. There was a kitchen with a breakfast area to the right, beside the dining room. Six steps led down to a lower-level family room and fireplace. A third bathroom and a short hall separated the family room from a library/game room. Sliding glass doors in the family room opened onto a two-tiered deck. There were several trees on the property. This had been a much better home than the previous one for when our daughters were teenagers and had friends over. Now here alone, Verable and I were still enjoying the space, especially when we entertained friends or had relatives who visited. I wondered: *Will we be able to find a home comparable to this in Lexington, VA?*

Verable and I went to Canada for a week of vacation. I found it hard to enjoy myself because I kept thinking about the job. When we returned home, there was a letter waiting from Dean Jefferies congratulating me. All the interviewers were very impressed, and he was writing to invite me to accept the Position *of Associate* Dean for Minority Affairs at Washington and Lee. "That's a higher-level position than *Assistant*," I said. When we were on vacation, I decided that if they offered me the position, I would accept it but this was an unexpected surprise.

"The dean responded, "Yes, it is. With the experience you have had, I decided you deserved the upgrade."

I couldn't think of anything to say except, "Thank you. I accept the position and will send you a letter confirming my decision."

I wrote the letter of acceptance the next day. I received an answer from him the following week. He thanked me for my quick response and asked if I could begin on the first of September. He included the names and addresses of three realtors in Lexington in case we wanted to contact them about housing. Finally, he said if my husband and I could visit Lexington during the summer, they would be happy to assist us in looking for suitable housing. I thanked him for the offer and said I would begin work as he requested on the first of September and would let him know if and when we could travel back during the summer.

Our correspondence occurred around the middle of May 1985. I had six weeks before my last UNMC Summer Program would begin. Verable still had days of vacation left so we decided we could go to Lexington the second week in June for four days. I notified Dean Jefferies of when they could expect us. We planned to rent a car at the Roanoke Airport and made reservations to stay in a Lexington motel. We arrived in Roanoke in the late afternoon and drove to the motel in Lexington. It was nearly dark when we checked in. I called the dean at his home to let him know we were there. When I told him who was calling, he said, "I'm glad you're here. Come to my office at 9:30 in the morning and I'll arrange for a student to show you around campus. We can have lunch in the GHQ together at 12:00. Do you have any plans for the afternoon?"

"Not yet," I said, "But I thought I'd call Mrs. Greenley to see if she will be free to show us some properties."

He said, "Oh, Claudia, Chuck's wife. That's a good idea. Ask her to meet you at the GHQ at 1:30. By the way, my wife Helen and I would like for you and your husband to join us at our house for dinner on Thursday night, the day after tomorrow."

I thanked him and said, "It'll be nice to meet Mrs. Jefferies. I'll put the date on our calendar."

He said, "She's looking forward to meeting you and Verable, too. But you may call her by her first name. We're rather informal around here when it comes to names. All our colleagues call me Jeff. You and Verable should do the same."

After a few more exchanges, we said "goodnight."

The next day was sunny and warm with a slight breeze. A student, David, gave us a tour of the campus but we mainly stood in front of the different buildings while he gave us the name of each and its purpose. We did not enter any because he wanted to have time for us to see the part of downtown that was near the campus. There was a restaurant on a side street about a block and a half from the campus that the students and others used very frequently. I think I'm correct in remembering that it was called Spankys. We went by there first. The campus was only two blocks from Main Street where there was at least one other restaurant and a variety of little shops.

We met Jeff and had lunch. Claudia was at the GHQ for us at 1:30 as planned. She was a short, slightly plump, blond lady. Jeff introduced us to her. She seemed very friendly. She said she had three properties to show us and suggested that we leave our rental parked on campus and ride with her. We did. The three houses she showed us were well-kept, older, colonial-style homes. They were on different streets not far from the campus and in two cases, were next door to W&L faculty members. We really wanted something more modern. Claudia said that was fine, she was free the next day, and could take us out to look at other places. She set a time for picking us up at the motel.

The next morning was bright and warm again. After stopping by for us, Claudia drove us to the edge of the Lexington city limits, where we went up a very steep hill. There were four homes along the left side of the road as it curved *up* the hill. There was a well-manicured vacant lot past the last house, and then at the very top of the hill, on the left, there was a brown, shingled roof, rambling ranch-style home. It was set off pretty much by itself. The one house to the left of it was a bit lower down the hill we were on. There was a curve to the right just past the Brown house where we learned a W&L faculty member and the Hospital Administer owned homes. The brown house was wide with half glass double wooden doors at the center forming the entrance, a large picture window was in the living room to the left of the entrance and double sets of windows were on each side a distance from the center.

Claudia unlocked the front door and we entered. From the four- foot square entrance, we stepped down to the left into the living room or forward down onto a hallway. We were surprised at the size of the interior. In addition to the living room which had a fireplace, there was an open wall on the far side revealing a dining room. Behind the dining room wall was one of the five bedrooms. One of the four bathrooms was across the hall from that room. It was next to a small storage area and beside that was the kitchen. Next to the kitchen, the family room had a fireplace on one side and sliding glass doors to a large, high deck on the other side. Of the four remaining bedrooms, one and a small bath were in the third-floor attic, upstairs from the family room. A laundry room, a master bedroom, and a bath were down the hall from the family room on the right. On the left were two bedrooms separated by a double bathroom. There was a large, finished basement and a two-car garage on the lowest level. We loved the house and put a bid on it immediately. I had always been particular about where we lived and the type of home we occupied. I guess that was to make up for living conditions when I was growing up, although our situation wasn't as bad as some blacks in Dudley.

Claudia told us that the house was actually new. A contractor in the city, whom she knew, built homes frequently, lived in them for a year or so, then built a new one which he and his wife moved into, thus selling the empty house. This worked to our advantage, so did the fact that Washington and Lee would finance loans for homes being bought by their employees. Claudia called the builder; he told her the price and down payment, which we approved. He said he would be by to meet us. After meeting the builder, Claudia took us to our motel and said she would go by W&L to have the treasurer there start drawing up the papers which we could sign the next day.

We had dinner that evening with the Jefferson's. They had invited the Greenleys, also. Jeff's wife, Helen, was as friendly as we had found everyone else to be. After dinner was over, we sat in their living room having after-dinner drinks.

Jeff, with a wrinkled forehead and a very somber expression, said, "There's something we've been wondering and debating about whether we should tell you or not."

I sat forward in my seat and Verable looked puzzled.

Jeff continued, "I think you should know. A retired colonel who lives down the hill from the house you two have decided to buy saw Claudia showing it to you today. He lives only two doors from her house at the bottom of the hill. Anyway, he saw her this afternoon and asked, "Why were you showing those Negroes that house? Are you planning to sell it to them?'"

Verable and I let out deep breaths. I said, "I expected something worse than that to be said."

Verable asked, "Do you think my wife will be in any danger here?" "No, none at all!" Jeff assured us. "We've never had any racial trouble here. And there are African Americans living in Lexington, just none in that neighborhood."

I said, "I grew up in the south and I know what southern whites can be like. But I won't let a bigot like that have the satisfaction of driving me away. In being married to an Air Force Officer, we have always lived in communities that were all white or with a small number of blacks. When I first meet a white person, I never know what to expect, if they will be friendly or not, but I'm always ready to respond to them in the way they treat me."

Jeff said, "We certainly don't want you to change your mind about the position."

Claudia said, "I'm very sorry about this guy, but I don't think he'll try to do anything."

Helen jumped in, "We know the people who live on that hill and they are all nice folk. Can I get anyone another drink?" All of us declined and commented how good dinner had been.

Then Jeff asked about my moving date. We discussed that for a while. We had explained that Verable would only come back for a few days to help me get settled. Hopefully, he would have enough time at Mutual to retire in the fall of '86 and join me. I would be bringing all our furniture and household items because Verable thought I wouldn't be happy without them. Jeff told me to let him know the date of my arrival and the cost of the move and he would have a check ready for me to pay the movers. I thanked him for that. Shortly afterward, we guests felt it was time to leave. Chuck, Claudia, Verable, and I expressed our appreciation for the meal and a lovely evening. Then we said "good night" and left.

Verable and I went to the campus the next day and met with the treasurer to sign papers for the loan and to find if there was anything else we had to do. We then went to the builders' office to make his initial payment and sign papers. Afterward, we walked along Main Street and visited a few shops. The following morning, Saturday, we took a flight from Roanoke back home.

Chapter 29

By the middle of August, I had completed all my responsibilities at UNMC. Verable had made arrangements to stay with our older daughter, Lynn, in her apartment. We had contacted movers who packed our furniture, etc. the third week in August. Verable drove us to Lexington in our larger car, a Buick. Our second car now was a Cougar and would arrive with the furniture. The Volkswagen had served us well and we sold it in Nebraska. We tried to schedule our travel so that we would get to Lexington the day the movers were due but we got there a day before them. They arrived the next morning and moved everything into the house. Verable left to drive back to Nebraska on our fourth day there. I was alone and felt it.

A Jewish doctor who lived with his family in the third house down the hill came over one morning when I was in our driveway. He gave me a loaf of Challah, baked bread that has three sections that look braided. I thanked him for the welcome and the bread. He said giving a loaf of Challah bread was a welcoming tradition in his culture. We talked for a while before he left.

Another neighbor who lived around the curve in the road also visited me one day. He was a professor at W&L. He and his wife rang the front doorbell. I opened the door; we greeted each other and introduced ourselves. I invited them in and felt they were not accustomed to interacting with people of color. The wife looked up at her husband and he nodded his head slightly, showing approval. I invited them to take a seat which they did and we engaged in a comfortable conversation about what my job was going to be, the city of Lexington, and other topics of interest. We shook hands when they announced they had to go and the professor said to me, "Sometimes, I'm not aware if what I'm saying to a person of another race is incorrect. If you ever hear me say the wrong thing, please correct me." I said I will. As they left, I thought *if everyone were that caring and open-minded, race relations in the United States would never be a problem.* Those visits were on a Friday and Saturday respectively. On that Sunday around midday, a car rolled up in the front circular drive and a black couple got out. I greeted them at the door and invited them in. I introduced myself and they told me they were Mr. and Mrs. Burnard from the Baptist Church on Main Street.

I said, "Oh, yes, my husband and I saw your church when we were window shopping downtown during our first visit here together. We thought it looked very inviting."

"We're here to welcome you to Lexington and we'd love for you to come to our church," Mrs. Burnard said.

"Is your husband here?" Mr. Burnard asked enthusiastically.

"No, he had to get back to Omaha to his job. But he will have enough years there to retire next September and then he will join me here. It will be his second retirement. He retired from the Air Force several years ago."

"How nice," Mr. Burnard said.

At that point, I thanked them for stopping by and said I would love for them to stay a while so we could talk but the college was having the opening assembly to welcome the students, and I needed to attend. I promised to visit their church and said I was looking forward to it. They understood and left. I followed them off the hill on my way to W&L.

The program was held in Lee Chapel, the main auditorium on campus. It was filled on the lower level with students, faculty, and perhaps a few parents. Some people sat in the balcony. I sat downstairs surrounded by strangers, all of them white. The president was the main speaker. He welcomed the students and talked about various regulations of the college, making several reverences to General Lee's philosophy. It lasted only about an hour. On the way out of the chapel, I saw a few of the people I had met during my interview visit and several black students. I went directly home.

My first regular workday would begin on Monday, the next day. I still had lots of organizing to do in the house.

When I arrived on Monday morning, I was shown to my office by the dean. It had a temporary desk and chair in the center of the back half of the room. And there was a tall white bookcase to the left of the desk. A window on the front wall provided a close view of the colonnade and a broader view of the front lawn and Lee Chapel. Dean Jeff told me that Tom, the person in charge of inventory, would be by in a couple of days to assist me in ordering what I wanted for furnishing my office.

Later in the day, the dean held a brief meeting in his office. This gave me the chance to see the colleagues I had met during the summer and to become acquainted with my counterpart, the other new Associate Dean of Students, Joan Montel. She was a rather petite female with blond hair and a pleasant smile. She looked to be in her early forties. Her office was located through a doorway between the dean's office and the secretary's desk. There was another door on the opposite side of the desk that opened into the office of the Associate Dean for Fraternity Affairs.

Student registration was held the next day. The freshmen came into our building through the front door right next to my office. They stood in line in the hallway as they waited their turn to go into Dora's room. The dean stood near his doorway welcoming each student with pleasant greetings and a handshake. I stood at my door and spoke to the students as they paraded by on their way to Dean Jeff. Some acknowledged me with a smile and others didn't notice me. There were three, maybe four black females in that class. Additionally, there were four upper-class African American males. They had visited me in my office late on the previous afternoon.

I called Tom on Wednesday and asked, "When will you be by to help me purchase furniture for my office?"

He said in a rather jovial voice, "How about Friday morning?" "That will be fine," I said.

Dora suggested that the two of us go and have a look in a couple of furniture stores. Then, I would have some idea of what was available. We went to two stores near the campus. I liked the selections in the second better. Grand Piano, the name of the store, had a teal-colored love seat with a matching sofa chair that I thought would be perfect. Unfortunately, they didn't have much office furniture. So, we returned to the office and Dora said we could figure out what else I needed from Tim's catalogues tomorrow. If he can't find what you want locally, he will order them. I definitely wanted the love seat and sofa chair. I needed an occasional table to put in the corner between the two chairs for a lamp. I wanted a three-drawer pedestal desk with a comfortable back swivel desk chair. Of course, I would need a file cabinet, preferably a lateral one. When Tom came in Friday, I had my list ready. In addition to the list, I also wanted a pair of tie-back curtains in a heavy material of cream color and trimmed in blue. When I finished telling him about these things, he jokingly said "yes, ma'am" as if I were his boss. Both of us laughed.

The black community in Lexington was planning a reception for me to be held on a Sunday afternoon in a private home. One of the hostesses called to tell me about the reception and asked if there were any guests I would like to invite.

I said, "I haven't met anyone here except the people on campus."

She said, "Well, we can invite them. Would you please prepare a list for me?"

"Sure," I responded, "I'll be happy to."

"Good, I'll give you my telephone number. You call me when the list is ready and I'll be by to pick it up. We want to have the reception within about two weeks," she said.

I was so surprised that I was somewhat breathless when I said, "I'll have the list ready tomorrow. Thank you so much. I can't tell you how much this means to me. It is such an honor."

She said very cheerfully, "We're just glad to have you at Washington and Lee and we wish you all the best."

I felt like crying when she hung up. For the first time in my life, I was glad to be a member of the African American race. The black people of Lexington had known hardships, been treated as if they were sub-human, and had been exposed to the kind of discrimination I experienced when I was growing up. However, their mistreatments had occurred in the "shadow" of one of the wealthiest and most elite, white male universities in the United States. The African American community could not help noticing, even feel the incongruent lifestyles. The University's history does mention at least one black woman who had been a secretary at W&L. But the institution was a constant reminder that young black men were not welcomed in that school. I was there to increase the numbers of black men and women. I wondered if the community's welcoming me so heartily was because they thought the hiring of a black administrator was an indication that the institution was becoming more receptive to people of color.

I would be considered remiss if I didn't mention John Chavis, the first black man who was allowed to take courses at Liberty Hall back in the 1700s. Liberty Hall, as stated earlier, was the forerunner of Washington and Lee University. Chavis had a notable life, starting in his youth as an indentured servant for a lawyer in Halifax, Virginia. He served in the American Revolutionary War. In 1789, he was listed in the tax records of Mecklenburg, Virginia, as a free black man. He took college courses in New Jersey and at Liberty Hall Academy. After which, he served as a minister and a school teacher for white and black students but in separate groups.

Thinking about Mr. Chavis reminded me that after I had worked at W&L for a while, someone not affiliated with the university nor the Lexington community asked me how I could work for a school named for Robert E. Lee. I don't remember who the person was but I certainly recall what I told him. I said that I could work there because I held no negative feelings about Lee. That he did what he was expected to do as a confederate general. But the Civil War wasn't a one-sided affair. Fortunately for people of color, there were generals and soldiers fighting from the North and they won. After the war, when Lee was first asked to serve as the President of Washington College, he declined because he thought his past position in the confederacy would prevent students in the North from applying to the school. He is reported to have said, "It is time for the country to heal itself." This gave me hope and a belief that Lee was a person who could change with the times. Also, my work at W&L was to help the students. It wouldn't have been fair to them for me to let history prevent my participation.

I made up the guestlist for the reception including all the people I had met at W&L. It was not a long list. One of the two black law professors and his wife offered to pick me up and take me to the reception. I was very appreciative of their offer and went with them. There was a large gathering when we arrived, a mix of black and white folk. All the guests from W&L I had listed were there and a greater number than I had expected from the community. I met the primary hostess, Mrs. Palmer, and learned catering was her profession. She was also the aunt of a pharmacist who was there. Lexington had one black doctor who was present also. All the guests were very cordial to me and conversed easily with each other. The food and beverages were delicious. When Kindel and Mildred, my escorts, indicated it was time to leave, I thanked the hostess and her helpers for the lovely affair and assured them that I certainly felt welcome and like a genuine member of the community. In exchange, I received a few hugs.

On our way home, Kendel said, "Well, that was the first." I asked, "What do you mean the first, the first what?"

He said, "The first time blacks and whites socialized together in Lexington."

With surprise evident in my expression, I said, "You've got to be kidding!"

He said, "No, I'm not."

I said, "We'll change that."

Chapter 30

In January 1986, I planned a reception at my home in honor of the black students enrolled at Washington and Lee. I sent printed invitations to all administrators, faculty, and various ones from the black community. I arranged transportation to my house for the students who didn't have cars. Using money from my office budget, I hired Mrs. Palmer to cater the reception. She did all the food preparations. Her assistants delivered it and arranged everything on the table, including a beautiful centerpiece in one of her silver bowls. Nearly everyone I had invited came and seemed to enjoy themselves. Every year after that, I held a reception at my house for the students. Only I decided to have it right after the students arrived in the fall. The title was changed to honor all minority students and included invitations to their parents as well as the community people. Those were very memorable occasions. The reception grew in size each year as other groups of students, such as the international ones, were added to my responsibilities.

By January 1986, I had been at W&L for six months. My office furniture and curtains had been delivered and installed several months earlier. Everything looked great. I had visited students in the SABU house (Student Association for Black Unity) and talked with them individually and in groups. The first thing I suggested to the members of the black student organization was that they consider changing the name from SABU to MSA (the Minority Student Association). They agreed and voted on the name change during the next meeting. It passed. The next time I saw the president of the university, he congratulated me and said my suggestion to the black students about changing the organization's name was brilliant. I thanked him for the compliment, but I didn't think it was so brilliant. It just made common sense. In suggesting this to the students, I told them that white people have always felt uncomfortable when blacks talked about unifying. Plus changing the name would open their organization to a larger number of students from other ethnic groups.

The MSA members said, and I agreed, that their house needed refurbishing. They also wanted some new furniture in the common areas which consisted of the entry hallway, a room to the left of it, and a larger sitting room to the right with glass doors on the outside wall and a window in the front. A small dining area was behind the sitting room and adjacent to it on the right was the kitchen. There were four bedrooms upstairs that were rented to students—four black men at the time. I talked with Dean Jefferies about the students' requests for the house to be upgraded and outfitted with new furniture. He said he would discuss it with Tom and see what they could do.

The Minority Student Association members were good citizens. They not only contributed to causes on campus like the W&L Independent Union but also to the needs of nearby communities. For example, in the fall of 1985, the rain had flooded many of the areas near the college. Buena Vista, a small college town southeast of Lexington, had extensive damage. The MSA gave a contribution to the Southern Seminary Flood Relief Fund in Buena Vista.

By Sunday, October 18, 1986, the MSA house had been refurbished, new furniture was in place, and the trustees had granted permission for it to be named the John Chavis house. We held a dedication ceremony on that sunny afternoon. The president of the MSA presided. One of the residents of the house who was serving as student manager gave a brief history of minority students at Washington and Lee. A memorial to Mr. Chavis was presented by another MSA member and I gave closing remarks. The dedication was held in front of the house and the guests who had stood outside during the ceremony were invited indoors for refreshments.

Back then, Washington and Lee was, and I'm sure it is still, a school of student self-governance. The term had slightly different meanings to various administrators and students. One of my colleagues, an Associate Dean in Student Affairs, probably stated the responsibility best when he said, "Every student comes to this university not only with the opportunity but the obligation to practice self-governance." This is what was expected of every student and when self-governance was not practiced, the school had student committees to deal judiciously with the acts of misconduct. Among the punishable acts were lying, stealing, and cheating for which the Executive Committee (EC) held hearings and set punishments. Their hearings were highly confidential. There was the Student Judicial Committee (SJC) which handled vandalism and other acts beyond the EC's purview. There were many white fraternities on campus. Some invited black students to their parties, but approximately four did not. The Interfraternity Council was the governing body for the Greek system. There were so many student organizations with different names that I won't try to name and define all of them. Since officers' positions were nominated for the committees, for many years, black students were not elected.

Things have a way of changing with time. In the fall of 1985, a group of minority students attended an Executive Committee meeting for the purpose of asking the committee to pass a resolution to annually appoint a black student to the committee since there was no one in it to represent students of color. The request was discussed but did not pass. As the minority student population grew a little larger and different speakers and racial unity activities were held on campus, black students and other minorities began to be recognized by the general population. Thus, they were voted into positions minority group members had not had before.

My first year as associate dean, 1985, was very busy. In addition to my professional responsibilities, I was also committed to finishing the work on my Master's Degree in Sociology at the University of Nebraska at Omaha. I completed the last remaining course after arriving at W&L. The lecture part of the course was over and the professor allowed me to mail in the paper that was due.

The chairman of my graduate committee was equally accommodating. The title of my research project was "Black Students in Private White Colleges Changing Coping Strategies." My theory was that black students experiencing life in a white environment for four years would make them more likely to seek predominately white associates and organizations as adults. (My dream was to one day see blacks and whites as well as others intermingle socially and on the job in all of the United States.) I had discussed my theory and methodology with the committee chairman and received approval of the project. My method was to design questions for *black graduates* of four private predominately white colleges and a questionnaire for *currently enrolled black students* at the same private schools. The questions were to evaluate identical variables for each group and to determine the degree of change, if any, between them.

It took time to get the cooperation of the selected schools. After gathering contact information from them, I mailed out and then received student and alumni responses. Finally, I calculated the results and wrote up the findings. The outcome was not definitive because the samples were so small. When everything else was completed, I took a comprehensive exam. Fortunately, my chairperson knew a sociology professor at Washington and Lee, so he asked this acquaintance to receive and proctor my exam. Everything was completed on time and I was very pleased to return to the University of Nebraska at Omaha, four years later, just before Christmas in 1989 to participate in the mid-year commencement and receive my Master's Degree. Of course, my husband, Verable, was present and shared my joy.

Back in 1985, during the first semester of my first year at Washington and Lee, I took time to study relationships, the campus environment, and resources. Since program designs and proposals had been successful at UNMC, I decided to use the same approach at W&L. Of course, differences in institutions had to be taken into consideration. One was a large state university for training health professionals, more mature students, and the other was a small, privately endowed university, with one post-baccalaureate professional school and an undergraduate college with a large, mostly immature student body.

During the latter part of the first semester, I devised and wrote a plan I named "The McCloud Proposal, A Six Year Plan for Increasing the Recruitment, Admission, Integration, Retention, and Graduation of Ethnic Minority Students at Washington and Lee University." It was designated Draft #1. I sent a copy to every administrator and faculty member. After receiving responses, the McCloud Proposal would be revised and renamed the Washington and Lee Minority Student Recruitment and Retention Plan. Draft # 1 had seven major objectives and methodologies for accomplishing each. The objectives and some of their methods were as follows:

"Creating and maintaining a pool of eligible ethnic minority students . . ." This objective required working with high school students in the state. The administration determined this would not be practical for several reasons, but mainly because of costs and the uncertainty of producing results for W&L.

I. "Provide large and diverse minority applicant pools . . . [for] undergraduate and law school admissions . . ." The Law School and College admissions offices were to devise plans for accomplishing this.

II. "Promote the rapid adjustment to campus life . . ." This objective involved establishing an annual pre-orientation program for undergraduate minority students the first year; for minority and international students the second year; for minority, international, and selected white students the third year.

The addition of new groups each year was mainly due to the increase in the type of student groups with whom I worked. The pre-orientation program had been approved by Dean Lawrence Jefferies and was conducted from 1986 to 1992. Dean Jefferies and several professors complimented the program. Participants expressed appreciation for having had the experience.

III. "To promote a positive image of ethnic minorities on campus and furthermore to encourage cultural understanding as a means of enhancing the general student population's chances for greater personal and professional fulfillment in their future lives."

This objective required working on integrating the student population and demonstrating that the Minority Student Affairs Office could serve all students. Accordingly, I began conducting activities of value to the general student population, such as pre-med advising, medical school interview workshops, study skills sessions, and student advising on personal concerns. Minority and white students were encouraged to sponsor functions that had a general appeal to all students. Sometimes, this was with faculty assistance. These functions included a get-together for pre-enrollment program participants in September and a reception in January for students, faculty, and people from the community. Finally, encouraging students, regardless of race or ethnicity to eat with new and different groups in the dining hall at various times.

IV. "To retain a large percentage of the ethnic minority and non-traditional students . . ." To be accomplished by the Associate Dean for Minorities holding individual study skills sessions. Maintaining a list of all health, personnel, and academic counseling services on campus. Referring students to any of these services when there was a perceived need.

V. "To assist students in gaining the skills necessary for personal development." To have speakers conduct sessions on topics related to personal enhancement and self-esteem. To conduct skills training sessions with individuals, for example, on participating in an interview.

VI. "Encourage and formalize alumni support for minority students." Sponsor a weekend when alumni and currently enrolled minority students have various opportunities to participate in forums, socialize, and generally spend time together.

Nearly everyone who had received a copy of the proposal responded. The statements showed that it had been read carefully and with deep thought. Perhaps, the following quote from a respondent provides the best summary of the sentiments expressed:

"You have done an impressive job of planning and research. Your need for institutional support is critical up and down the ladder. The university will be strengthened in direct relation to its support."

Chapter 31

The most important project during the 1985-1986 academic year at Washington and Lee was enrolling women for the first time and making the necessary adjustments for their presence on campus. In anticipation of the women's arrival, a Coeducation Steering Committee had been appointed by the president the previous year and was charged with defining physical changes that needed to be made on campus, rules, and regulations that should be formulated or revised, and discovering ways of ensuring a comfortable environment for women and men. Dione Rhinehart, the professor of art and the first female faculty member hired some years earlier, was the chairwoman of the committee. The president of the university asked her to write a letter inviting me to "serve the University" by accepting an appointment to the Coeducation Steering Committee for the academic year. I was pleased to do so.

As I mentioned earlier, student governance was very important on campus. Therefore, there were student governing committees for nearly all aspects of student life. Inasmuch as W&L had traditionally been an all-male college, the committees and their officers had been elected by friends and acquaintances. Thus, black men had been left out of leadership positions and now the same thing was happening with women. In view of this, the Coeducation Steering Committee suggested that an ad hoc woman member be appointed by the Student Executive Committee (EC) to the SCC (Student Conduct Committee). This suggestion was taken to the EC. During the meeting when it was discussed, two representatives from the Coeducation Committee attended. They reported that after a two-and-a-half-hour debate, the EC voted seven to six to appoint an ad hoc woman member to the SC. (Reference: Coeducational Steering Committee minutes, December 10, 1985.)

Minutes from later meetings showed the appointment was never made by the EC. The Coed Committee members speculated that the men were stalling due to their belief that the women were getting better treatment than they were. For example, it was reported that some male students were complaining that the female dorms had lounges and theirs didn't.

Associate Dean of Students Joan Montel reported on the Women's Forum she had organized. The topics planned for discussion were leadership, social life, recreation and athletics, health and counseling, Greek affairs, academic and career advising, minority issues, social and community service, housing, and spiritual growth. The Coeducation Steering Committee met about every two weeks. Sometimes, topics Dean Montel listed became subjects that the Coeducation Steering Committee also addressed. Other members introduced points for discussions, such as Fancy Dress, the annual spring ball, campus politics, and health care personnel. At the end of the academic year, the chairperson, Dione Rhinehart, ended her report to the president by stating:

"One philosophical stance we recommended last year was that the university should plan for what it can plan for but should also plan to be responsive to needs and problems as they arise. We believe that the wisdom of this attitude has been demonstrated in the happy transition we have experienced this year. We recommend that this be a continuing policy."

Coeducation Steering Committee Minutes, May 27, 1986

The Coeducation Steering Committee had drafted a brochure on sexual harassment. It was waiting for the President to approve the wording of the university's statement. This was the beginning of a movement to have sexual harassment policies and procedures established on campus. One of the first issues related to this was naming an appeals person for the Washington and Lee sexual harassment policy. In a memorandum to the university president on August 28, 1986, Associate Dean Dione Rhinehart recommended me to be appointed the appeals officer for sexual harassment cases. She had conferred with the Dean of Students about this and he agreed. The president concurred and sent me a letter formalizing the appointment.

My training for this duty came from the affirmative action activities in which I had participated at UNMC and by attending two different workshops during my employment at W&L. One was a three-day program at the Community Mediation Center in Harrisonburg, Virginia, and the second, a two-day conference sponsored by Tulane University on "Resolving Commercial Disputes Without Trial."

In 1987, after several meetings and much planning, the policies and procedures for sexual harassment reporting and resolution were put into effect. There were three main steps involved in attempting to resolve a complaint. First, when someone thought he or she had been harassed in some way, that person would come in to talk with me about the incident. We had literature that defined the types of behavior that were considered harassment. I would listen while the student described what had happened. We would then discuss the course of actions that could be taken. 1) Filing a written formal complaint with me—the mediator; 2) My consulting with the accused; 3) The complainant and accused meeting together with me to determine if they could reach an agreement on what if anything should be done to solve their problem; 4) If a satisfactory conclusion was not reached in step 3, the complaint and the mediator's report would be forwarded to the Confidential Review Committee (CRC) for a formal investigation and decision; 5) If either of the parties was dissatisfied with the CRC's decision and wanted to take the matter further, she or he could contact the University Board of Appeals and/or the University President.

As shown in the following campus newspaper headlines, students had varying feelings about the new sexual harassment procedures: (1) January 19, 1989, "*EC Mulls CRC Rules, Sub-Committee Discuss with [Chairman] Concerns with Recently Released Confidential Review Committee Procedures,*" January 26— same year—"*Sexual Harassment is a Reality at W&L,*" and February 2, 1989, under Letters to the Editor, "*Sexual Harassment is [an] Affront to the Honor Code.*"

During a time of adverse attitudes among male students on campus, I received the first complaint. I shall never forget, after interviewing the complainant, the accused, some witnesses, and determining the situation warranted referral to the CRC, I sent my summary report to the two parties and the CRC Committee Chairman. The male who had been accused came to my office after getting the report. He banged on the door, threw it open, and walked in before I could respond. Then he began to scold and threaten me in a very loud angry voice. I spoke calmly, invited him to sit down so we could discuss his concerns. He reluctantly did as I asked. I responded to his opinions and, once again, explained the steps of the procedure and the reasons for them. He argued some and asked questions but finally accepted referral to the CRC. This was an unusual situation. After that, most of the complaints were resolved during the first step with only me and the two people involved.

A few years and some cases later, the CRC was somewhat restructured and its name was changed to the Student/Faculty Hearing Board (SFHB). The

Vice President of the University who was in charge of faculty affairs asked me to include faculty to faculty complaints as part of my responsibilities. I had only one complaint of that type and it was the accusation by a male of verbal harassment perpetrated by a female. The three of us worked together in solving their problem.

Chapter 32

Before continuing with descriptions of my duties at W&L, I need to comment on my health. I had experienced a lot of discomfort but none of my conditions had interfered with me doing my job. Having various responsibilities to think about even when I was at home, my angry moods were not as abhorrent as they had been. On the other hand, I tried to push aside feelings of sadness when they occurred. I was still taking the muscle relaxer the doctor in Omaha, Nebraska had prescribed for the torticollis, the involuntary head jerks. My mood swings, the irritating condition over which I had little to no control, were continuing to be a problem, and the medicine I was taking for it had little effect.

When the time came for me to have my prescriptions refilled, I went to a psychologist in Roanoke an acquaintance recommended. The doctor was a tall, slender, white male and, even with moderately gray hair, he seemed to be quite young. He took the time to question me about all the symptoms I had been experiencing and for how long. He listened thoughtfully. When I had finished describing my health history, he explained what he thought to be the diagnosis. He agreed with the doctor in Omaha on the torticollis diagnosis and said not much could be done about it at the time except taking muscle relaxers. (It was 1988. Years later, a neurologist gave me botox shots in the neck about every four months to control the head jerks.) The psychologist was able to help with my mood swings. He said it sounded to him like I was having manic-depressive episodes. He explained the symptoms, which matched many of mine. I told him that no one had ever mentioned that condition to me. He talked more about it and said a new medicine was available that some were finding to be very helpful. He asked if any of my doctors had mentioned Prozac. I said, "No, they had not." He told me to discontinue the medicine the other doctor had given me for the moods and to start taking Prozac. He gave me a prescription. He told me to call him if I experienced any of the side effects he had described. But if there were no problems, I should return in two weeks.

I left the doctor's office feeling confident. At last, I knew there was a possibility that body chemistry was involved in my untoward feelings and behavior. I had waited so many years to learn what was really wrong with me. Mental illness was looked upon with shame as well as disbelief. I hoped the new medicine would help. Verable had retired from his position at Mutual of Omaha and was living in Lexington with me. I decided not to try to explain to him what the doctor had said. I didn't think he would believe me anyway. He was like my older brother, Jim; neither believed someone could be mentally sick unless they acted very demented and unaware. That makes for a difficult situation when you need so much for loved ones to believe and try to help you.

I was one of the lucky patients. Prozac did work for me and continued to do so throughout the years, plus my growing older and the public's increased knowledge about some medical problems have helped, also.

Chapter 33

Back on campus—in addition to supervising minority student affairs and being University Mediator at Washington and Lee, I was given the responsibility of foreign student affairs. The first thing I had to do was assist students from foreign universities with whom W&L had exchange agreements in getting their visas. Afterward, we prepared packages and sent them information about the college and the three-day program to which they were invited. The International Affairs program was assigned to me by Dean Jefferies. He had approved our starting the pre-orientation program for black students the previous fall. The new international students fit into the existing program very well. Since they were new to the country as well as the college, we solicited faculty members whose families were willing to serve as hosts to an international student during the week of pre-orientation. We received very favorable comments from the host families. They felt they had benefited from the experience as much as their student guests.

A few faculty members, not the host families, were concerned that having only black and international students in the pre-orientation program would make each group feel stigmatized—the black students might think we were classifying them as "foreigners" and the international students that we were considering them "blacks." The program participants never seemed to think that. However, for the program the next year, I asked the admissions office to please identify and send me the contact information for white students whose applications showed them to be from rural areas, to be the first college attendee in their family, who seemed to be coming from a background of poverty, or any other factors that might cause them to benefit from arriving on campus early. The admissions office did so and I sent separate letters of invitation to them that explained the reasons we used for student selection. This was a very delicate matter because I didn't want anyone to feel insulted. I listed all of the possible reasons and said they could have been selected for anyone. Only one white parent wrote me with further inquiries after her child received the invitation. I responded to her in a way that soothed her feelings. Most of the students were just happy to have the chance to be on campus before others arrived.

The pre-orientation program turned out to be three days of fun for all of us. The selected students arrived on the Wednesday before regular orientation for all students, which was to begin the following Monday. We had a "Let's Get Acquainted" session as our first activity. There were ethnic minority students from various parts of the United States, exchange students from Oxford, Kansai Gaidai and Rikkyo in Japan, and Chung Chi in Hong Kong. There were approximately 25 students in all.

Group discussions were held throughout the day on topics such as the difference between high school and college, using the computer, study skills, and other college-related points of interest. The students had meals in the regular dining hall. We gave them a tour of the campus and of downtown Lexington. Saturday, the final day of the program, we took them to Roanoke, for sightseeing and shopping.

Unfortunately, Dean Jefferies who hired me and had been such a strong supporter of our Minority Student Affairs programs, retired in 1990 after 21 years of being Dean of Students. He was also a Washington and Lee alumni. He returned to teaching full-time on campus.

Henry Brut, a short, slender, white man with an EdD, was hired to replace Dean Jefferies. He was not as easy to work with as the former Dean had been. After complaining for two years about the pre-orientation program for minority students, he ordered me not to plan one for the fall of 1993. In a letter to me, he said "philosophical" and "pragmatic" reasons were why he objected to the program. I thought it was for other more unsavory reasons. He was in agreement with our continuing the program for *international* students.

A white male student who had not been a participant in the pre-orientation program, but was familiar with it through others, approached me one day to ask if he could help with the next one. He was disappointed to learn the program was not being continued in its usual form. He wrote a "My View" article for the campus newspaper, *The Ring-tum Phi,* expressing his thoughts about the situation. The title of the article was "Cancellation Hurts Minorities" and he proceeded to explain why he thought this was true. Among other things, he said many friendships had resulted from participation in the program. I wrote him a note thanking him for his keen observations and expressions in the article.

I thought it important for the office of Minority to be viewed as an office to serve any student on campus. The best way for me to get the message across was to offer services that could be of benefit to white as well as black students. Thus, I let the science department know that I was interested in assisting any of the pre-med students in preparing personal statements for their applications and/or helping them prepare for their medical school interviews. Professors passed the offer to the students and I had an excellent response. The pre-med students made individual appointments and after explaining the process, the two of us would have a practice interview. Many told me later how helpful they had found the exercise to be.

In a similar manner, I advertised my willingness to assist students with study skills. This was something new for W&L because the general assumption was that the students accepted were very capable and didn't need any extra help. Fortunately, I had been a college student and I knew that a certain amount of discipline and learning skills were necessary for maximum success. So, I designed a course for teaching them to read for meaning, to schedule their time effectively, to use memorization techniques, and to understand the value of repeating previous materials as they learned the new. I kept a record of each student who came in for study skills and the amount of time spent. One semester, I had intensive, individual study skills sessions with 13 students who returned for an average of two additional sessions each. All those students made significant academic progress and were very grateful.

Each spring, the staff of the student newspaper, Ring-tum Phi, held a program during which they presented awards to faculty and staff members whom they evaluated to have been of outstanding service to the Washington and Lee Community. I was very surprised to be a recipient one year. My reward was due to students' complimentary statements about the study skills program.

Every year, usually in March, the Washington and Lee students held the Fancy Dress Ball. It was a formal occasion planned by a board of students elected for that purpose. The gymnasium was decorated around a specific theme each year. A band was hired for the main ball on Friday night and other activities, such as concerts, were planned for the Thursday night before the ball. In 1988, the Fancy Dress Board expected 4,000 attendees consisting of students, alumni, and invited guests. Black students would not be among them.

The black students spearheaded by the Minority Student Association voted to boycott the ball because of the theme, *Reconciliation Ball of 1865*.

The MSA based its decision to boycott on their belief that the theme "North-South Reconciliation After the Civil War" would recall a time when there was the oppression of blacks." (News-Gazette, Lexington, VA, March 2, 1988.) The president of the MSA and the Fancy Dress Board chairman met together with me to discuss the situation. As a mediator, my role was to guide the two students in solving the problem. The MSA president explained the negative feelings black students had as they thought about the oppression and treatment black people experienced at that time. The chairman of the board expressed understanding but said decorations and everything had been purchased for the ball theme and the board could not redo everything because of expense and the lack of time.

I said, "Both of you have made good points and I appreciate the calm manner in which you two are addressing this issue. But can either of you think of what if anything can be done to reach a compromise?"

The chairman explained, "Decorations for the ball will depict American scenes in both the North and South around 1865 and will include buggies, park benches, a gazebo, and lighted trees." When neither the MSA president nor I said anything, he continued, "The board agreed not to display the Confederate flag at the ball, not to encourage people to come to the ball in blue or gray Civil War uniforms, and not to depict a southern plantation in the decorations."

The MSA president said, "I'm afraid we still can't lift the boycott because the Fancy Dress Board last year used a theme, 'Africa: The Dark Continent,' which we thought showed a lack of sensitivity by them. We let that be known but things are no different this year."

I asked the board chairman, "Is there anything else you would like to add?"

He replied, "No ma'am."

I said, "It doesn't look like we can come to an agreement on this matter. I do thank both of you for meeting with me and the civil manner in which you have conducted yourselves." To the Fancy Dress Chairperson, I added, "Thank your board for me for their willingness to make some concessions in our trying to resolve this problem. Maybe it will help in the future if there is a black member on the board or if there can be some communications with the MSA about the Fancy Dress Theme before things are purchased for the ball. I turned to the MSA president and said, "Thanks for your cooperation, too. Please let the MSA members know what concessions the board was willing to make and why you declined their offer. I understand your feelings. If the MSA wants to ask the administration for permission to have its own party at the Chavis House on that night, I am willing to assist you in talking to the Dean and President.

I stood and the other two followed. We shook hands. I thanked them again and they left. There were no more complaints from either group. The MSA did get permission to have a party at the Chavis House while Fancy Dress was being held in the gym.

In a continuing effort to encourage the integration of the students, our office started publishing a bi-annual newsletter called "Una Vox," a Latin phrase meaning "one voice." While other newspapers on campus did an excellent job of reporting news, we wanted to focus primarily on news and activities that reflected cultural and ethnic diversity at Washington and Lee. Each year, I advertised for a student with a journalism background to be the editor of the multi-cultural newsletter. That person was paid by our office and worked with the journalism department to produce an interesting and informative publication. Once published, a copy was sent to everyone on campus and some to supporters in the community.

I thought it would be a good idea to try to bring the university and the black community closer together. Plus, our office could use extra help.

Therefore, in the spring of 1987, we formed the Chavis House Board of Supervisors. The group consisted of three African Americans from the community, three faculty members from the university, and six members of the MSA who served as a sub-committee for planning MSA affairs. I was included but suggested that the board elect its own chairperson. They elected one of the men from the community.

The purpose of the board was to be advisors and supporters of the MSA. There were 43 black students enrolled that year. Through frequent meetings, the Board members would determine what they could do to assist with future activities. Their first big project was the Parents Weekend in the fall of that year. This was an annual function for the parents of all students on campus. Our goal was to encourage more of the African Americans' parents to attend and we planned activities of interest to them. Prior to the weekend, board members wrote to the parents offering them transportation in town and help in getting places to stay over the weekend if necessary. The MSA members sent letters inviting their parents to a special dinner on Friday night of that week, featuring one of the successful black Washington and Lee graduates as speaker. The meal was sponsored by the Minority Affairs Office. On Saturday after the football game, the MSA held a reception in the Chavis House and it was catered by the board. The wonderful help the community gave was repeated on other occasions.

Chapter 34

The Washington and Lee Law School did not have a person designated specifically to work with their minority students. One of the law professors did have a pre-orientation program for black students at the beginning of the school year. He invited me to the first session he had after I began working there. When the sexual harassment policy for the university went into effect, the dean and associate dean of law thought I should have regular office hours in the Law School at least one day a week for the minority students as well as for students who wanted to discuss harassment complaints. I elected to be there on Tuesday of each week. Administrators of the Law School worked with me directly in making these plans. I'm sure they realized I would discuss these arrangements with the Dean of Students—Jefferies. Everything was approved and the plan was helpful to me and the students.

On March 17-19, 1989, the first Minority Student /Alumni Conference was held on the W&L Campus. The conference started on that Friday evening with a welcome reception in the Alumni House. The next day, Saturday, consisted of "An Open Discussion Between Alumni and Students," student-led campus tours, a buffet luncheon, a panel discussion on "A University Update" by the admissions staff, and a general discussion on "Where Do We Go From Here?" In other words, how could the college administration and the alumni work together in assuring minority student success? There followed discussions about future meetings and activities. The weekend, which had been co-sponsored by the Alumni and Minority Student Affairs Offices, was considered a success and the start of another program to support minority students.

In the fall of 1989, two men from the State University of New York in Binghamtom (SUNY Binghamton) came to my undergraduate office inquiring about minority students who might be interested in going to graduate school at Binghamton. They introduced themselves as Frank Connor and Clarance Williams. We talked about what they were offering, which included a scholarship for applicants who met the requirements. Unfortunately, we had only seven minority seniors expecting to graduate in May. None was interested in going to graduate school right after finishing W&L.

I mentioned that I had completed all requirements and would receive my Masters in sociology from the University of Nebraska at Omaha in December. I said I wish I were in the position to take advantage of the offer. They congratulated me on my upcoming commencement.

Mr. Connors, the black man asked, "Have you considered going on to work on your doctorate?"

I said, "No, not really. With my job here, a husband, and two college age daughters, I did well to finish the MA."

Mr. Williams, who was white, chimed in and said, "With the graduate credits you have from your Masters, you would only have to take one additional year of course work and then write some papers to complete your Ph.D. It wouldn't take you more than one year's leave from your job for the courses, then you could write your two area papers and dissertation at home, returning to Binghamton when you needed more research materials. The library would allow you to check out books to bring home."

I had always wanted to get my Ph.D., but there never seemed to be the time or money. Here they were offering me a scholarship. I said, "You make it sound very appealing but there are so many things to work out for me to be able to take a year off. I'd have to give it lots of thought and check on the possibilities."

Mr. Connors said, "Why don't you look into it? You seem ideal for the type of student we're trying to recruit. We would love to have you at Binghamton. I'm going to give you my card. Stay in touch and let me know if I can help in any way."

I thanked both of them and promised to let them know if I decided to apply. Since it was the fall, there was more than enough time to get an application completed to enter in the fall of 1990. I talked first with my husband Verable about it. As always, he wanted me to do what I wanted to do, whatever I preferred. He thought it was a wonderful opportunity if I were willing to give it a try. My main concern was getting permission from the president to take a year off. (It was Dean Jefferies last year before taking a year's sabbatical and then returning to teaching full time.) Of course, I needed his approval to take the year for studying. As I expected, getting permission from him was not a problem. He thought it was possible for us to make arrangements for me to be away a year. He was very happy for me. I told him I would ask the president for his approval.

I was really nervous about approaching him. So before talking to the president, I decided to try the idea out on two other deans whom I considered supporters. I went to the first one and asked if he would speak to the president on my behalf for his permission to take a year off to work on my Ph.D. To my surprise, he said "no," that he didn't think I should go. The second person I asked was higher up the chain of command, the vice president, and the dean of the faculty. He gave me the same answer, "no," I shouldn't be granted permission to take leave, and that if I thought my getting a PhD in Sociology would allow me to return to W&L and teach, I was wrong. I should have said, "Gee, I hadn't thought about that, but it is a good idea." Unfortunately, I was too hurt to think of being flippant. I thanked him for his time and walked away. It was hard in those instances to know if their responses were due to my being black or female. At that time, W&L had only one undergraduate black professor. If teaching there had been my desire, it should have been seen as a plus for the school.

I made an appointment and went to talk with the president. He was always soft-spoken and pleasant but if he didn't like something, his soft voice would let you know that, also. Fortunately, he was very much in favor of my taking a year off for studying. He said they would be willing to give me 50% of my salary and when he learned I had a daughter in one of the Virginia Colleges, he said he would make arrangements for W&L to pay her tuition for the year. He said they usually do that for employee's children up to a certain age. He explained why he was willing to assist me in going back to work on a PhD. He said, "Education is so helpful even as people age. When you are no longer able to do anything else, with education, you can always write, conduct studies, and perhaps do experiments." To be treated with respect, like a fellow human being by him, meant so much to me. I thanked him when I stood to leave and told him that Dean Jefferies and I would work on plans to have my duties covered while I was away.

Primary duties in the office at that time were all aspects of minority student affairs; responsibility for communications with the foreign universities, monitoring their exchange students' application processes and getting them settled on our campus, serving as university mediator, and conducting various student workshops and administrators training sessions on sexual harassment and affirmative action. By getting the cooperation of different colleagues on campus, we only had to hire one additional person. She was the wife of a third-year law student. She had a Master's Degree and was hired to be the temporary director of the office.

My academic year at Binghamton was different and rewarding. Most of my time was spent reading, participating in class discussions, and writing papers for homework. I took three or four courses (can't remember which) each of the two semesters and signed up to participate in a group research project. I lived in a dormitory apartment with three other women. They were younger than I but we got along very well. In fact, we teased each other about being a small United Nations because of our different races: I am black; the person in the room next door to me was Asian. Across the hall, a Hispanic occupied one room and a Caucasian from Massachusetts the other. The other three went out some nights but I stayed in to study or went to the library or office. The sociology department assigned me a desk so that I could share an office with another doctorial female.

All of us in the apartment went home for Christmas break. I was pleased to find things going well in my W&L office and at home. Our daughters joined us for the holidays. So, we had an old fashion celebration with lots of decorations, gifts, and the usual turkey dinner.

Upon returning to Binghamton, I studied hard and got my assignments in on time so that I could concentrate on doing one of my area papers at the end of the year. The two areas I chose were "studies in stratification" and "studies in education." I should have known to choose smaller sections of each of the topics rather than considering the whole of each field. I had done well in the classes and only had the papers to finish. The one on stratification was about half-finished when I returned home at the end of the academic year. My plan was to complete it during the winter and submit it, then start on the second one, education. The university and my advisor were still available to me.

I was back at W&L on the first of August 1991. Colleagues who had done some of my special tasks, like mediation, as well as my temporary office manager, had done good jobs which made it easy for me to return to the routine tasks. There was not a pre-orientation program for minority students because the new Dean of Students, Henry Bruto, had disapproved of it before I left. It is interesting to note that during the years when there was a pre-orientation program for American minority students each year, their retention rate increased from seven in 1985-86 (my first year on campus) to 45 in 1989-90. Yet the new Dean of Students wanted it discontinued for minority students, so I had no other choice but to follow his orders. As I said before, he did want the orientation program for international students continued. So, we had the first International Visitors Orientation Program for foreign students who came in that fall. Each year, we had an increasing number of foreign nationals and some coming in from various countries.

Chapter 35

The first exchange students from the Soviet Union had attended during the 1988-89 academic year before my taking time off. They were three of the 56 Soviet undergraduates coming for a year of study under the auspices of the American Consortium for East-West Cultural and Academic Exchange at Middlebury College. The 56 were divided into smaller groups and sent from Middlebury to different colleges in the U.S. Their arrival marked the first time Soviet undergrads were permitted to study in the United States without officials in residence with them. I was excited to be part of that historic event. My records show that the largest number of international students, 16, entered W&L in the fall of 1996. They were from Bulgaria, Spain, Great Britain, Asia, Israel, Korea, the Netherlands, Ethiopia, the Caribbean, and Canada. They seemed to have settled in well.

On November 21, 1991, the Ring-tum Phi ran a special edition announcing the IFC (interfraternity council) had endorsed the Alpha Phi Alpha (an African American Fraternity), the first to be colonized on the Washington and Lee Campus. This was something the black students had met and debated with members of the IFC for a few years. The vote was 11-4 in favor of the colonization. I was very proud of the young men who had pursued this objective so diligently. Getting that first approval was the most difficult. Having other black fraternities added in the future should not be as problematic.

The university administration hired a new Law School Dean, Anthony Mackel. There had been two other Law School Deans whom I had worked with prior to his arrival. As I mentioned earlier, the Dean and Associate Dean of Law had invited me to have office hours in the law school one day per week to be available to the minority students and any others who needed special counseling. The Associate Dean sent me a memorandum after I returned from

Binghamton, inviting me to resume regular office hours in their Lewis Hall in the fall. I told Dean Bruto about the arrangement I had with the Law School. He approved the continuation of the plan.

I don't know exactly when Dean MacKel started as the new Law Dean. I think the first I heard from him was during the summer of 1993. The Dean of the law school and Dean of the undergraduate college each gave a member of their faculty a three- or four-year rotation serving as Associate Dean. When he arrived, MacKel replaced the male associate dean with a female faculty member. We knew each other. It was summer and I was at home on vacation, working on the second one of my area papers. She called me and said the dean asked her to tell me that the Law School would not need me to have office hours on their campus anymore. She said, "I'm sorry." I was surprised and wondered why but I said "okay" that I would make an appointment and discuss it with him when my vacation was over. Dean Bruto, my supervisor, called me that afternoon to give me the same message. I said the Associate Dean of the Law School has told me. I started to ask him if he knew why but decided to let it go.

However, I did write a letter to Dean MacKel, the new Law School dean. I told him that I had received his message about my not having office hours in the Law School in the fall. I asked him why the change; did he not want me to work with the law students? I also told him that the original plan was discussed with me by the previous dean and his associate. I could not understand why he, Dean MacKel, had thought it necessary to bypass me and go to my supervisor to discuss the matter. I told him that usually on campus, when someone wanted to engage my services or discharge me, as he had elected to do, they would come to me directly and I would have appreciated him doing the same. Furthermore, I said when someone wants me to do something that I feel the Dean of Students needs to approve, I will go to him about it myself.

I think I had heard that MacKel had come to W&L from a law agency, although he may have worked at a law school before. I don't know if that was true or not. If he had been working in an agency, he was probably accustomed to disregarding lower-ranking women. After all, that was in the early nineties. He responded to my letter, explained the chains of command as he saw them, and apologized if he had offended me. But he never said why he had cancelled my having an office in the Law School. In the fall, the law students went to my undergraduate office if they needed assistance.

By 1995, my scholarship from Binghamton came to an end. I still had more to do on my second area paper and the dissertation to write. But family began to need more of my attention. My oldest daughter became sick and had to miss several months out of college. My husband was beginning to experience PTSD symptoms from having been in Vietnam.

When we were having dinner one evening, he stopped chewing his food and exclaimed, "Did you hear that?"

I said, "Did I hear what?"

He listened a few seconds longer. Then he said, "It sounded like a machine gun."

I said, "No, dear, I didn't hear anything. Maybe you imagined it." That was the beginning of his problems.

Anyway, life was getting a little too hectic for me so I withdrew from Binghamton knowing I couldn't finish all the research and writing I still had to do. I felt sad about withdrawing but I worked at keeping myself from feeling like a failure. After all, my family needed me more than I need a PhD at that stage of life.

Chapter 36

My work at W&L continued. During a staff meeting in the fall of the academic year 1996-1997, the Dean of Students, Harry Bruto, announced as an objective for the year, "strengthening the Washington and Lee Community through the implementation of a diversity initiative." He appointed me to head this project. I selected three other staff members and three students to work with me in determining major goals, objectives, and initial activities. The three staff members were the outing club manager, the career development coordinator, and one of the counseling psychologists.

Early during our meetings, we deliberated about a title for the project. Finally, the psychologist suggested **P**rograming for the **R**espect of **I**ndividuals and **D**iversity in **E**ducation—**PRIDE**. The idea was adopted. The committee devoted our meetings during the fall and winter months to determining the basic dynamics of the organization. These included developing major goals, supporting objectives, and determining how members would be recruited and selected.

We wanted interested and capable members. Accordingly, the seven charter members sent letters to all faculty and administrators, explaining the focus of **PRIDE** and asking them to nominate students to apply for membership. Approximately, two hundred nominations were received. All nominees were sent a letter of invitation to apply. From the 46 applications that were received, 27 new members were selected following interviews.

The seven charter members held an overnight retreat, including training sessions at one of the off-campus properties. We also had a reception in the college lounge during the spring to introduce **PRIDE** to the campus. Planning meetings, which included all members, were continued in the fall of 1997. As a result, two activities to which the campus was invited were presented: first the showing of the movie "Skin Deep" and in the spring, a workshop on diversity conducted by a leader from the National Conference of Christians and Jews.

In the fall of the academic year 1998-99, **PRIDE** had an upsurge, as members active in other organizations on campus were elected by their groups to represent them in the diversity initiative. By the middle of the fall term, the **PRIDE** membership had increased to a multiracial group of 60. Diversity programs for the campus were planned by our dedicated members for each semester.

The Black Law Students Association sponsored a panel discussion on October 23, 1996, "Million Man March, One Year Later." The association had invited me to be a panelist along with three professional men. We were to talk about the male march that had taken place in Washington, D.C. the previous year. Being the only woman, I had been asked to address the topic from the female perspective. Mainly, did I think it was unfair for black women not to have been included in the Million Man March? Did our not being included show a lack of respect or put us at a disadvantage in some way? I did not think any of these suggestions were true and explained why I thought they were wrong. Whatever benefits resulted from the march for men would positively impact black women also.

In 1997, the W&L Black Students Association wanted to attend the Mideast Regional Convention of the National Black Students Association in Baltimore, Maryland. As it was so often the case with student organizations, they didn't have money to finance the trip. So, they talked with me about it and the Minority Affairs Office gave them what they needed. The theme of the convention was "Breaking the Chains That Bind Us . . . Preparing for the 21st Century." When the students returned, they brought me the gift of a tall wine glass embossed with all the convention information. I loved all the students with whom I had the pleasure of helping and I think they thought a lot of me.

Community organizations and others are always pleased to have the involvement of educators. My colleague and, by then my good friend, Associate Dean of Students Joan Montel, nominated me to participate in the eighth session of the American Council on Education/ Virginia Identification Program (VIP). Joan had attended the program previously. Each session was for the purpose of bringing together emerging women with *established* men and women leaders in higher education in Virginia. I attended a two-day session during which we discussed critical issues affecting higher education. It was a very enlightening meeting and an honor to have been invited.

I served in more egalitarian positions as a member of the Rockbridge Area Housing Corporation for four years and as an appointee for two terms to the Virginia Advisory Committee of the United States Civil Rights Commission.

Around 1997, the administration decided to open an International Affairs Office and hired a person to take over the responsibilities I had for incoming foreign students and professors, plus the duties of the faculty member who had been in charge of the Washington and Lee participants going to foreign countries in exchange. Therefore, I no longer had responsibility for the international program.

In 1998, I received a request from the Marquis editorial board asking me to submit my resume for inclusion in the 1999-2000, 21st edition of Who's Who of American Women. I wasn't familiar with the publication, so I talked with my previous supervisor, Dean Jefferies, who had then returned to the classroom full time. I told him about the request and asked if it was something to which I should respond. He said there were several Who's Who Publications but the only one he had ever replied to was Marquis. He thought that one to be respectable. I sent in my resume and was included in that edition. In 1999, Marquis contacted me again, this time to make inquiries for my inclusion in the Millennium Edition (2000) of Who's Who in America. Here again, I submitted what was requested and my information was included in the 54th Edition

As the saying goes, my plate was still full in my position as Associate Dean of Students at Washington and Lee University, but I decided to retire at the end of the 1998-1999 academic year. My husband had been retired for more than six years. He was being treated for his PTSD at the Veterans Administration and was doing well. Our older daughter who had lost some time out of college because of an illness some years earlier was well and going to Brown Institute in Minnesota to study broadcasting. Our younger daughter was married but would finish her bachelor's and master's degrees later. Both stayed in touch with us.

I wanted to have more time to spend with my husband. While he thought Lexington where we lived would be a good place to retire, I wanted to be in a better climate. After reading one of his military magazines which had an article on ideal locations, we decided on Tucson, Arizona.

During my last two weeks on campus, there were several farewell activities for me. Dean Bruto and his wife gave a party at their home for the staff, me, and my husband. The MSA Organization had a cookout during which they gave me a certificate of appreciation. The **PRIDE** members held a reception on the back lawn. They gave me a nice-framed picture showing a scene from "The Underground Railroad." One of the members said, "We went to Washington, D. C. to get this." I had to choke back tears as I tried to thank them.

I took the four weeks in June as vacation using the time I had accrued for that year. We contacted a moving company, arranged for a packing date, and put the house on the market. On the last day of June 1999, we left Lexington for our newly built home in Saddlebrook, a housing development about 16 miles from Tucson, Arizona. I was 62 years old and my husband, Verable, was 68. We enjoyed 18 happy years of retirement together in the sunshine state.

About three years after I retired, in 2002 to be exact, the **PRIDE** members invited my husband and me back to Washington and Lee for a ceremony during which they gave out the first two plaques for the "Anece F. McCloud Excellence in Diversity Award." It has been given annually to a student and a professor who showed exemplary service in support of diversity. I felt somewhat embarrassed but highly honored. My final acknowledgment of service to education came in 2017. It was an acrylic, spear-shaped plaque with a black background from the Who's Who Marquis biographers. It is inscribed in white: "MARQUIS WHO'S WHO, ANECE F. MCCLOUD *has been selected* as a MARQUIS WHO'S WHO LIFETIME ACHIEVEMENT *inductee representing outstanding professional dedication and career longevity."*

The anticipation of awards was not the reason for the services I had given. Rather, I worked to prove to myself that I was and still am a worthy human being. As Confucius implied in his quote, I had been seeking what was in myself that was worthy of being shared with others. Did I become a "superior" person as he indicated? I don't know. My lifetime experiences have taught me to respect and be kind to people of all races, complexions, and social statuses. I have found that helping others tends to lift my spirits. Most of all, I love myself. These qualities plus many others I had developed along the way have made me satisfied with who I am and grateful for the person I have become.

The End

Acknowledgments

My first words of appreciation must go to my late husband, Verable L. McCloud, who provided the opportunity for me to live in locations that opened the doors of opportunity for me. Secondly, I thank our daughters, Aja and Carla, the first ones to witness my dream of writing my memoir and who encouraged me to pursue telling my story. They have continued to be my inspiration through times of uncertainty and frustration. Thanks to my graduate school professor, Mark Rousseau, PhD with whom I have remained in touch for his friendship and guidance. He read several chapters of the book and evaluated it to be well worth continuing and completing. I thank a very good friend and former colleague, Anne Schroer Lamont, PhD who suggested the subtitle for the book and is a loyal supporter, even from a distance. Thanks to the wonderful people who are friends and co-residents here at the Fountains of LaCholla for their kindness and help, especially Frain Marian who did the first proofreading of the manuscript, and Peggy Rapp who insisted that I add photographs to the book. She has also tolerated my reports on my work nearly every day at luncheon. Like a lot of people my age, I often had trouble with some necessary functions on the computer. The person who always saved me was Ricky Garrett, the Fountains' technology concierge. Thank you is not sufficient for all his assistance—always with a pleasant smile and understanding. Finally, my sincere thanks to the professional, knowledgeable, and pleasant people at Rushmore Press for their interest in and help with my first experience in publishing.